EXPERIENCE WORKETH HOPE

BEING

SOME THOUGHTS FOR A TROUBLED DAY

PRINTED IN GREAT BRITAIN BY
MORRISON AND GIBB LIMITED
FOR
T. & T. CLARK EDINBURGH

EXPERIENCE WORKETH HOPE

BEING
SOME THOUGHTS FOR A TROUBLED DAY

BY

ARTHUR JOHN GOSSIP, D.D. (EDIN.)

"We exult even in our troubles, knowing
that trouble worketh endurance, and endurance
experience, and experience hope—and this hope
never disappoints."—ROM. v. 4.

EDINBURGH: T. & T. CLARK, 38 GEORGE STREET
1944

TO

MY WIFE

NOW A LONG TIME IN THE FATHER'S HOUSE

" Till a' the seas gang dry, my dear,
And the rocks melt wi' the sun ;
And I will love thee still, my dear,
While the sands o' life shall run."
BURNS.

" In that age they will neither marry nor be given
in marriage, but will be as the angels. We are
destined to a better state—destined to rise to a
spiritual consortship. So we, who shall be with God,
shall be together : since we shall all be with the one
God, though there be many mansions in the house of
the same Father ; and, in eternal life, God will still
less separate them whom He has joined together,
than, in this lesser life, He allows them to be
separated."—TERTULLIAN.

CONTENTS

Parts of I. and of XIII. have appeared in *The Expository Times*, and the whole of VIII. in *The Speaker's Bible*. They are reproduced here through the kindness of the Publishers and the Editors.

"Even though others may form the first line, and your lot may have placed you now among the veterans of the third, do your duty there with your voice, encouragement, example, and spirit. Even though a man's hands be cut off, he may find means to help his side in a battle, if he stands his ground, and cheers on his comrades. Do something of that sort."—SENECA.

"What else can I do, a lame old man, than sing hymns to God? If I were a nightingale, I would play the part of a nightingale. But I am a rational creature; and I ought to praise God. This is my work. I do it; nor will I desert this post so long as I am allowed to keep it. And I exhort you to join in the same song."—EPICTETUS.

"Scientific knowledge is indispensable, but it is, as the schoolmen said, 'evening knowledge' *cognitio vespertina*, cold and grey and shadowy: religious knowledge is 'morning knowledge' *cognitio matutina*, where all is seen in the growing light of a new day. So we come back to the God of our fathers, whose name Jehovah was held to mean 'I am that I am,' but according to other scholars, means 'I will be what I will be'—the God of evolution."

J. ARTHUR THOMSON.

CHAPTER I

THE PRIVILEGES OF A CHRISTIAN

" Unto you it is given on behalf of Christ not only to believe on Him, but even to suffer for His sake."—PHIL. i. 29.

HAD you and I stumbled into that little Christian meeting-place at Philippi, we should have found ourselves in a small and unimpressive-looking company—some slaves healing their hurt self-respect in a gracious atmosphere where they were no longer chattels and things, but men and brothers, often even leaders, to whom others looked with confidence : some ordinary folk, notably generous with what they possessed, as Paul gratefully acknowledges, but not likely to have very much ; for here too, no doubt, the usual rule held good, and not many wise, not many noble, not many mighty were called—a little group of simple undistinguished men and women facing a bleak and lonesome and perilous life—cut off, many of them, from their own families by their new faith ; ostracised and left out, in their own home town, from its life, its interests, its religion ; constantly having to fall out of step with their neighbours round about them, and irritating and exasperating them by what these others set down as their stubborn prejudices, and their obstinate and stupid ways—a daft, impossible lot, with whom there is no living, so they would sum them up : and they would say it angrily ; for in those days men were cruel, and human life was very cheap. So, with grim things always gravely near, these people faced their dangerous days.

And yet, as that little room rises before his memory, Paul gasps, almost audibly, at thought of the fullness and the riches and the splendour of the life that has been heaped on them. " Unto you it is given on behalf of Christ, not only to believe on Him, but even to suffer for His sake ! "

Everywhere throughout the Scriptures men are dazed and staggered by the enormous liberality of God, and that towards every one.

You and I don't think much about it, take it for granted, mass together a whole multitude of things, every item of which is a wonder and a wistfulness to those who do not happen to possess it. But we impatiently brush it all aside, as the mere small dust of the balances, what does not count, as the barest minimum, less than which would

1

be an outrage at God's hands. And yet one of the very oldest Christian writers in a letter to his friend Diognetus, speaking of these many benefits which we accept so callously, cries out—" Who could have expected any of these things! And yet they are all ours, simply because God willed to give them to us!" And that is strictly true. Take flowers, as an illustration. Conceivably, plants might have propagated themselves in a dozen dull uninteresting ways. And all this witchery of loveliness that so delights us is an extra, spilled upon us out of God's full and overflowing hands. We have it, simply because God willed to give it to us. So with a thousand things, with every thing, indeed, that we possess that matters. Plato, in one place, draws a distinction between God and man. We men, he says, are churlish creatures. To us, part of the joy of possession is to have what others do not have, and the sense of superiority that gives us over them. But, says Plato, there is none of that dog-in-the-manger feeling about God. To Him the joy of possession is to be able to share. And so He keeps creating new souls, new worlds, new universes, that He may spend Himself for them yet more, and more, and more.

Aye, says Jesus Christ, and He rains His benefits even upon the most undeserving, seeming to pay no heed at all to that. Look at that crofter yonder! He is an openly irreligious man. Yet the sunshine does not skip his fields! Or at this other bustled creature. In all his hot, perspiring, crowded days he can find never a second nor a thought to spare for God. Yet the rain falls as healingly upon his land as on his pious neighbour's.

> " Earth gets its price for what earth gives us.
> The beggar is taxed for a corner to die in.
> The priest has his fee, who comes to shrive us.
> We barter for the graves we lie in.
> In the devil's book all things are sold ;
> Each ounce of dross costs its ounce of gold.
> For a cap and bells, our lives we pay ;
> Bubbles we buy, with a whole soul's tasking.
> It is only heaven that is given away ;
> It is only God can be had—for the asking !
> No price is set on the lavish summer,
> June can be had by the poorest comer."

Or, as an astounded Psalmist puts it, gazing in bewilderment at this marvellous heritage that comes to us as our natural birthright, " Blessed be God, who daily loadeth us with benefits."

And if that is the note of the Old Testament, far more is it that of the New. There, the central word is always grace ; which, as an old translator liked to put it, means what is given gratis, for the taking, for the carrying away. And what amazing things are offered to us on these easy terms ! God's most, God's best, God's all ! Who could have expected any of these things ? And yet they are all ours, simply because God willed to give them to us.

And so Paul says nothing at all about the glorious inheritance that falls to us by nature through God's grace, but fastens on two further gifts that come to us only by, and through, and in, our Lord and Saviour Jesus Christ. Unto you it is given—to believe this wonderful gospel, to be allowed to suffer for Him. And what are we to make of these ?

Well, I suppose that, when we take time to think about it, we all agree that that first boon is a marvellous thing that makes a mighty difference. To believe in Jesus Christ, and in the things for which He stands ; to have these underneath our feet, a strong foundation upon which to rest, and at our back to lean against, and as a gracious atmosphere surrounding us—that makes all life another and a better thing.

When we take time to think of it ! But how seldom we do ! Balzac declares that, towards God, ours is the gracelessness of children who can never repay, because we owe too much. And that is true. But is not this, too, no less true, and much less seemly—that towards God ours is the gracelessness of children who have grown so accustomed to God's steady, dependable, unvarying kindness that we never notice it, accept it as a matter of course, and think no more about it. " Yes," said Rainy of the gospel, " we do believe it in a way, but we are no longer startled by it in our own minds." Children grow up in their parents' house, and everything is done for them ! The father toils, while they themselves are at their games, that they may lack no real necessity ; the mother works on for them, hours after they are fast asleep. Yet the children are not particularly grateful. They never think of it at all ! It is the way of things that children have parents to look after them ; and they leave it at that.

So, the mystery of God's faithful and persistent love can dull into the merest platitude, that leaves one's mind entirely unarrested. " Of course," said Heine, " God will forgive us. That is His job : what God is for." And, even the Cross on Calvary can become such a familiar object in our mental landscape that the eye, unarrested, slips over it, and never notices that it is there.

And yet if it be true, if there be any chance that it is true, surely this gospel of ours is, by far, the most astounding thing that we can ever hear. Isn't it an extraordinary thing, for instance, that—as we Scots say in our vivid word—God is not scunnered at you and me—sickened of us, filled with a shuddering loathing at the thought of us ! For He well might be. And, indeed, how is it that He, in His holiness, can be anything else ? For think how we have treated Him ; how we have failed Him, forgotten Him, impudently disobeyed Him—how we have irritably twitched our shoulder from underneath His hand, crying peevishly, " Let me alone : it is my life, and I need it all for my own purposes and plans " : how we have spat our futile rebellions up towards His feet !

And, after all that, He still loves us, believes in us, trusts us, is still sure that out of our uncouthness He can fashion a Christlike thing !

Ah ! it is not for nothing that, in our prayers of thanksgiving, we rise up and up, until we reach the climax. But first of all, most of all, all in all, thanks be to Thee for Jesus Christ ! For He is, far and away, the biggest thing that life can ever give us. Think how it would have been with you if you had never known all He has shared with you. Or if they could disprove it, and filch it all away again !

The Fatherhood of God would go. For it was Christ who taught us that. I know that some before His day had glimpsed it—the writer of the 103rd Psalm, for instance, my own favourite Psalm—

> " As far as east is distant from the west."

And some of us, with lads out yonder, know how far that is ! Well, make a gospel of it, man !

> " As far as east is distant from
> the west, so far hath He
> From us removed, in His love,
> all our iniquity.
> Such pity as a father hath
> unto his children dear."

The man who wrote that knew something of the Fatherhood of God. But it was Christ who brought it home to us men in the street. And, suppose it wasn't true, or that you didn't know about it ! Suppose there were no Mercy Seat, no throne of grace, nothing to draw upon, no Father's heart to guide and help and bring us through—nothing at all but our own blundering souls, and easily tired spirits, how were it with us then ?

Richter once had a dreadful vision of Christ returning to earth, with the tears raining down His cheeks, to tell us : " I was wrong ! I was wrong ! I thought there was a Father. But I have searched through the Eternities, and can find never a trace of Him. Poor little helpless orphaned souls, you must make shift to manage for yourselves as best you can ! " And even stout old Carlyle's spirit shook within him at the horror and sheer terror of that thought.

It makes a mighty difference to hold the Christian faith.

Or, the forgiveness of sins would go. For it was Christ who made us sure of that. Again, I know that some wise souls had seen it long before He spoke—that other psalmist, for example. " If Thou shouldest mark iniquity, O Lord, who should stand ? But there is forgiveness with Thee." But it was Christ who made us ordinary people sure of it. And suppose it wasn't true : suppose that, once we had sinned a sin, we were tied to it for ever—to the guilt of it, and to the habit of it ! Browning, in a most uncharacteristic passage, declares that, in a sense, that is what really happens. We are set here, he says, to climb higher and higher, up to the very feet of God. That is our aim, our duty, our glorious destiny, if we will take it. But every time we sin a sin, or fall before a temptation, we slip back and down. We can pick ourselves up, and keep on climbing. But we can never recover the lost ground, must be, to all eternity, lower, by every sin we sinned, than we could and should and would have stood, had we climbed on uninterruptedly. That is hell, says Browning ; what it means, and is. But I have seen James Denney, that man of iron self-control, with his face tortured over that. No ! he cried, No ! The most and best that Christ can do for me is not to leave me a maimed and dwarfed and stunted thing to all eternity ! And the Scriptures are upon his side. Forty years ago, Rainy, the man of all the men whom I have known who lived closest to God, gave us a marvellous address at a Communion service in the church where I then served. And suddenly, pulling himself up, he asked, Do you believe all this ? Do you believe these promises ? Do you believe a day is coming when, not somebody, but " you will stand before the throne of God, and the angels will whisper together, and say, ' How like Christ he is ' ! "

That is the hope that my faith sets before you ! Match it for me, elsewhere, if you can !

Or, to take but one other facet of this many-sided faith, it was Jesus Christ who made us sure of our own immortality. I am aware that no people have ever been discovered—so far as I know—who have not some conception of another life. But, often, it is not a dream, but a nightmare. In India, for example, they have their doctrine of transmigration. And what is that? We say that the wages of sin is death. They hold that the wages of sin is life: for every sin we sin another and another and another life in endless sequence! Till, shut into this prison-house of life, with its sorrows and its perils and its grim possibilities—a prison-house in whose strong walls their groping hands can find no smallest egress, through which they might squeeze, and so escape, their hearts are near to screaming! And in the Old Testament, for long enough, they had a bleak and wintry prospect on the other side of death, with good and evil herded together into a dark, dumb, desolate world, eerily silent, thick in dust that choked the footsteps, and towards which God never looked, in which He took no manner of concern or interest. And in Europe, it was, at the best, a thin and watery hope. Does not one of the greatest spirits of those days set down to a friend how he was musing upon immortality, and the thing had grown half possible, " and then your letter came, and it all vanished into nebulosity and nothingness again, like the cobwebs it is." And it was Christ, as even Gibbon, hostile witness though he be, frankly admits, who showed us our tremendous heritage of an eternity with God.

No doubt belief in immortality is, in essence, not a primary, but a secondary religious truth. I hope, at least, that even if I thought that there were no beyond, and the grave ended everything, I would still choose Christ, for the glory of His service even here and even now. But how impressive is the mass of testimony that keeps crowding in from poets like Tennyson and Browning and Wordsworth, and scholars like Renan, and philosophers like Kant and Pringle Pattison, and men of literature like MacNeile Dixon, all passionate in their belief that the mass of us tired wayfarers are kept going only by the far-off twinkling of the lights of home; only because as

> "We travel the dusty road till the light of day grows dim,
> The sunset shows us spires away on the world's rim";

that, without faith in immortality, there is small sense in life.

And surely we must see the tremendous difference it makes. Here were we, petty ephemerids, dancing out our seventy brief years. And suddenly it came home to us that we are august creatures who will last as long as God Himself! Our dear ones died: and so an end of them. No, say the Scriptures confidently, they are not dead, but alive, more really and more richly than before, in that wonderful world where there are no more pains and failing powers ; but where they are all young and well and strong again, and serve Him day and night, and never need to rest at all. I love that glorious scripture, "Blessed be God, who hath abolished death, and brought life and immortality to light through the Gospel." What a saying to be dropped in the mere by-going !

Oh, you Philippians, how rich you are ! The great ones of the world roll past, and splash you with the mud flung from their chariot wheels. Yet what have they ? These brittle seventy swift years. And then, what then ? But you have an eternity of Christ-likeness before you, and of unflawed service of Almighty God.

It was a foremost classical scholar who burst out, You Christians haven't even begun to realize the difference that your faith makes to you ; or you have grown dully and bovinely accustomed to it, and no longer realize its wonder. I, said he, love the great Greek authors (and well he might !). But "to turn from the greatest of them to the New Testament, is to pass from the austerity of a mountain-top to the security of home."

It makes a mighty difference to believe in Christ. It is a marvellous heritage He gives us.

And yet you notice that Paul brushes all that aside as the mere small dust of the balances, and lays the main stress upon a gift yet greater : unto you it is given, not only to believe the glorious Christian faith, but to be allowed to suffer for the Master.

And what does he mean by that ? These Philippians were once, not people in a book, but real living folk with hearts as sensitive and woundable as yours or mine are now. And some of them were finding life was difficult ; that Christ was costing more than they had esti- mated ; beginning—some of them—it may be, to look back, hesi- tatingly, across their shoulder. And Paul does not condole with them ; he congratulates them : does not pity, but envies them ! And that is the valiant and audacious line he always takes about those untoward things in life that are apt to set men, even Christian men, grumbling and fretting. And what does he mean ?

Well, perhaps it is easier in these days of strain to follow him. Some of us, who are older, are conscious that, on occasion, querulous moods blow into and across our minds, though, please God, we don't grant them harbourage. Twice in a lifetime, we muse, we have seen the whole world sway, and give, and rumble into ruins—twice in one narrow little lifetime. It is too much—too great a strain on faith and courage, too heavy a demand on human nature.

And yet would you really like to be out of it all, living in some dull, uneventful time, when life drowses on lazily, from day to day, and hardly moves in its green-grown, scummy pools ? Is there no thrill in being called by God to play the high part that He asks of us ? As Churchill put it grandly, in the darkest hour of all thus far, " Unto you it has been given so to bear yourselves that, even though the British Empire lasts another thousand years, men will look back at you, and say that was its greatest hour ? " That thrills ; that steadies ; that makes a man out of a weakling ! Yet there is better far, even than that ! It is a mighty honour to be given a place in the eleventh chapter to the Hebrews, that far-shining roll of the men and women, down the ages who, when everything was collapsing, and all that matters, sagging and tottering sickeningly, was going down, held it up—each in his own day—with their bare little human hands, until it righted, and steadied, and the danger passed. And in that glorious record—mark you—there are, not only mighty spirits like Moses and Abraham, but very questionable folk like Rahab ; and others so unimportant in themselves that their very names have been forgotten, and they had to be put in anonymously. Yet they, too, saved all that has value to the soul of man in their own generation. And to-day " This at least is certain," says Miss Dorothy Thompson, the American publicist, " that it is the plain, ordinary, unknown men and women of Britain, whose names will be forgotten even before the grave closes over them, who have saved the freedom of the world for the next thousand years." And you would like to be out of it ? Not you !

But it hurts ! Of course it hurts, hurts terribly. We are all in this thing—you and I. But don't you remember how Simon of Cyrene—our Cyrene now !—hastening into the city about his own affairs, was held up by that sad little procession ? And how Christ, after the horror of the scourging, could carry His cross no farther ; and the soldiers were not going to bear it for Him ; looked about for a likely victim, and saw Simon. There's a man who will do, they said. " Hie you ! Come here and carry this cross ! " And when he, no doubt, indignantly protested, " Less of that," they said, " or you will be upon a cross before you are much older ! " And, with a face on fire, and a heart bursting with indignation, the good man had to stagger through the crowded streets, like a criminal on his way to execution. It hurt. It hurt abominably. But the glory of it after-wards! "Simon of Cyrene," so the record stands, "who carried the Master's cross," who made things somewhat easier for Him in His agony, who helped Him in His evil hour. And, now, you have the chance of that!

Does that help you at all? Then don't let them rob you of that inspiration. To me, at least, it is an axiom that He, who remembers even a cup of cold water, given for His sake, takes it very lovingly, that you have not held back even your nearest and your dearest. To me, at least, it is an axiom, that if—well—if my lads don't come back, don't bleat to me about a wasted life. Why wasted? Shortened here, that I can understand. But wasted? Has not the final authority laid it down, " Greater love hath no man than this that a man lay down his life for his friends?" And if your lad has done that greatest with it, then, in God's name, how can his life be wasted? To me, at least, it is an axiom, that if the blow does fall, no one will so sym-pathize as that wonderful Father who, in a far fuller way, gave His Son to save the world.

> "Can I see another's woe
> And not be in sorrow too?
> Can I see another's grief
> And not seek for kind relief?
>   No! No! never can it be,
>   Never, never can it be.
> Think not thou canst sigh a sigh,
> And thy Maker is not by.
> Think not thou canst weep a tear
> And thy Maker is not near.
> O! He gives to us His joy
> That our grief He may destroy.
> Till our grief is past and gone,
> He doth sit by us, and moan."

And, since it is God and you together, you *can* face it, and can see it through—with honour.

O, you Philippians! how rich you are! For unto you it is given, not only to believe the marvellous Christian faith, but—to be allowed, to be allowed, to be allowed—to suffer for Him.

CHAPTER II

A MESSAGE FOR TENSE DAYS

" In quietness and confidence will be your strength."—ISA. xxx. 15.

IN itself that is a plain and even platitudinous fact, a law and axiom of life which many voices in all kinds of spheres keep pressing upon us urgently. Doctors, for example, are emphatic that many crippling ailments have their roots in anxiety and fearfulness and worry ; that, if only the patient could escape from these glooms and shadows, and keep his mind in the sunshine, his body also would be saved from much that makes this life we find so glorious, for him only a long wearisomeness and a burden grievous to be borne.

And spiritual experts have always maintained that carewornness and fretting sour the mind, jangle and jar the soul, create noxious mental germs which work incalculable damage in a personality and life. Buddha, in his day, pondering over the problem why so few of us ever really grow up into a mature way of living, sets down what his experience had taught him are the main reasons. And high up in the list he ranks " worry and flurry." These hot, distracted, anxious, desperate folk, he said, are not giving themselves a chance. What they need to bring them through this perilous life with honour is some coolness in their spirit, and some calm in their mind. And, in his message He sought to give them that. And the Lord Christ seems to have reached the same solution of the same enigma. In a kindly parable He lays it down that the reason why in many cases the spiritual life comes to little or nothing, why He Himself makes so slight an impression on masses of folk, is not that they are actively bad people, but simply that they are so bustled and harassed by this and that, by an endless procession of innumerable things, trifling enough in themselves, and yet to which they must attend ; or else by fears that keep nagging at them, and anxieties that won't let them rest, till, in their crowded, distraught days, there seems to be no room left for Christ. Perhaps the business is growing and making ever-increasing claims upon one, which now absorb the leisure that used to be devoted to other interests—the Church, for instance, and its services ; or one is getting older, and the daily task that must be put through grows increasingly exhausting, and one tumbles into bed dog tired, and forgets prayer; or the family is at the stage when there are always calls on one for something for them; when, what with getting them off in a morning in time for school—for the schoolmaster must be attended to, whatever comes of God—and one thing and another the whole day through, the unseen becomes dim indeed, and the eternal crowded into a corner where it is easily overlooked and forgotten. And what they need, said Christ, is to realize that they are not dependent solely on their own planning and efforts, but have something at their back, which they can safely lean against, and know it will not give; to grasp that, even where there are grim things to be faced, life is not meaningless, " a tale told by an idiot, full of sound and fury, signifying nothing "; in short, to attain and use that faith which gives quietness to the heart, and steadiness to the unfrightened eyes, and a bigness of nature to one's whole being.

All which sounds excellent in theory; only, how does one gain it? At any, and at every time, life is for very many a hazardous adventure with constant calls upon their courage; an insecure and uneasy existence in which, quite literally, they never know what a day or an hour may bring forth. Once, when I was addressing a meeting in a mining town, a note was handed to the chairman, who glanced at it and over the gathering, and, pointing, passed it down. One can still feel the sudden ominous, tense stillness, the unanimous agony of suspense, the holding of the breath, the stopping of the heart of the whole gathering as that terrifying message made its way nearer and nearer to one's own seat, and—past it; and so on and on to the woman to whom it was directed who, with a face grown white, took it, with every eye fastened upon her, and opened it; read it, and smiled; and instantly everyone relaxed. They had assumed, instinctively, that someone in the pit had been injured, or was dead. For always, always, they live with that terror brooding over them. And, everywhere, how many there are from whom want is never distant, a step or two at most; and who, run how they may, with heaving chest and panting breath and a cruel stitch in the side, can never get so far away from it but that they can still feel its cold breath on their very necks. An accident, some weeks of illness, and then—what then? It is not difficult to live on faith,—and a fixed stipend. But to make shift on faith alone, and little else—that is a different proposition. And how many have to face that year by year!

And so, many dismiss Christ's teaching on these matters with

2

impatience. All very well, perhaps, for the simpler kind of life He had about Him in that cosy little corner of a primitive world, that knew nothing of our intricate problems, our complicated social system, our ferocious cut-throat competition—each man for himself, and the devil welcome to the hindmost—or of the endless noise and whirring of machinery, and the rush and pace and danger of it all. But in our day it just can't be ; won't work. Were I, says many an one, to try to live out in the business world the principles He lays upon us, there would inevitably be a bankrupt stock for sale within six months. And how, answers another, can I be expected to keep cool in this hot, dusty life of mine ; or calm with ugly possibilities always surrounding me, and pressing in upon me ?

But was the world Christ knew so very different from ours ; or, in essentials, really different at all ? Open Josephus and study his description of the Galilee Christ saw and loved, and to which He spoke face to face, and you find nearly all of what we choose to call our modern problems. There was a shocking over-population with its attendant ills. And, indeed, did it never strike you how, in a moment, and out of nowhere, a crowd gathers in the Gospels ? And a crowd with such masses of suffering among it—diseases that betoken ghastly housing, and a low standard of living, and the like. The taxes then were terrible, more drastic even than ours are to-day. And there were unemployment, and many claimants for a job, men standing all the day long idle in the market-place—all which sounds quite familiar. Or, here is a vivid description of our times. " The world has had too much of war and waste, the sheer destruction of human life, the loss of home and gear and all that makes life livable. Very generally it has lost heart and hope, it has ceased to believe in anything but blank endurance, but acceptance of whatever the selfishness of rulers and adventurers, and the malice of irrational fortune may bring upon them." Very vivid, is it not, and tragically true. Only, it is Glover's description, not of our day at all, but of the world into which Christianity was born, and in which it was cradled and grew up. So that excuse we confidently offer does not serve us much. And, indeed, the Sermon on the Mount, for instance, makes it plain that Christ was well aware that the people He kept urging not to worry were living perilously near the edge of things ; were bothering and struggling, not for luxuries and extras, but for the bare necessities of life, for food with which to feed their families, and to find clothes to put upon their backs. Are we not told that, so acutely did He feel the economic difficulties of the times, that, with His life in His hand, determining the best use to which He could put it for His fellow-men, He seriously considered embarking on a daring crusade of social reform. The thought, at one time, haunted Him, kept following Him about, even into the wilderness, and breaking in upon Him ; though, later, when He had decided on a spiritual mission, He was quite sure that it had been one of the deadliest and subtlest of temptations ; that it was, not God's voice, but the devil that had summoned Him to make stones into bread, to give Himself to the easing of the economic pressure on the tired and desperate men and women round about Him, rather than to the saving and upbuilding of their souls.

And, to-day, many appear to be quite sure that He chose wrongly ; agree wholeheartedly with the Grand Inquisitor in Dostoievsky's marvellous pages, where he jeers at Christ, come back, and working the old gracious miracles of healing ; and, knowing that He was Christ, fiercely bids Him be gone, like the poor futile unwanted bungler He had proved Himself to be by making, and by obstinately standing to, His fatal twofold initial mistake.

You offered to give men their freedom. Yet they, you poor fool, have no wish to be free. They are afraid of life, and dare not face it alone. Instinctively their hands feel for a wiser, older, stronger hand to hold and guide and steady them. And the Church gives it to them. And with a contented little sigh, they stop thinking, and obey ; and, at a step, are out of all the howling winds—a child within the security of home. And you would force them out into the hurricanes again, to stand unsteadily on their own feet ! Who wants your dangerous freedom ?

And even more impossible is your other error. You would not give them bread. Yet it is bread they need, and bread for which they clamour, and bread that they must have. Your spiritual gifts— who wants them ? Bread is a solid thing : it tastes ; has substance and reality. But what you bring is thin, ethereal, nebulous. Off ! cease to bother us who know men, as you do not do !

Is one mistaken in imagining one hears echoes at least of that in many a pulpit message in these days, and in the pronouncements of Church dignitaries not a few ? " I am old fashioned enough to think," says Dr. Christie of Winnipeg, " that a minister should be at least as much concerned about the unconverted as he is about the unemployed." And so am I.

Well ! well ! you break in ; there may be some smattering of

sense in what you say in ordinary times. But in these days, when
the orderly and stable world we know has swayed before our eyes,
and toppled, and gone over—sheer into the abyss ; when " chaos has
come again " ; when the boys, and the girls too this time, are away,
and facing who can tell what—perhaps at this very moment ; when
the home that meant everything to me is desolate, like a last year's
nest, built with such loving patient cunning skill of beak and claw
and an indomitable little heart, and now it lies empty, sodden, rotting.
And you tell me not to fret, or to be anxious ! And my mother's
heart resents it, crying hotly, " And how can I keep from worrying,
and fretting, and lying awake at nights ? How ? how ? how ? "

A German will tell you. Religion, says Goethe, exists—is there—
to enable us to bear the inevitable which often seems unbearable.
Not a full definition, yet profoundly true. Oh ! I know that Karl
Marx breaks in, flouting and scoffing, twisting the saying round to suit
his purposes and views. Exactly so, says he. Religion is an opiate to
keep drugged people quiet, who should not be quiet, but be up and on
their feet, their angry hearts on fire, protesting and denouncing and
destroying ; aye, pulling down with their bare hands what ought not
to be borne one moment longer. But this accursed Christianity dopes
them, and keeps them passive, resigned, bovinely placid ; squeezes
manhood and courage out of them, and leaves them tamed and cowed
—the meek things that allow their wrongs last on, and on, and on !

But a spate of stormy eloquence, out of a hot, indignant heart,
does not change facts. And history is there to show that nothing,
not even patriotism, has so shining a record of sheer audacity of
daring, of unreckoning gallantry, of daft unbreakable courage, as
religion has to show.

And in these grim days that are gathering and drawing near, we
had better tighten our grip on it, for we shall need it, if we are to come
through with honour. Strange, says Jeremy Taylor, that one day the
bells will toll for somebody's burial. And they will ask, " For whom ? "
And they will say, " For you—or me." Before the end comes, ah !
how many homes are to be emptied, and hearts broken, and lads
struck down ? And what if, among all the rest, ours too must go ?
What if the telegraph boy coming up the street is asked " For whom ? "
and one day says, " For you."

Believe me, to see this thing through with gallantry we shall need
" to gather our faith together and our strength make stronger " ; to
bear this unbearable we shall require all our religion.

And they say that, as a generation, we have lost it, as no previous generation ever did ! If that be so, then we have left ourselves fatally exposed. " For the first time a generation has arisen that has no religion, and that feels the need of none." So Joad, with confidence. Though, indeed, it must be wonderful to be as sure of anything as he is about everything ! And Lippmann, a much more balanced spirit, with his fingers on the pulse of the age, pronounces this diagnosis over us. " The irreligion of the modern world is radical to a degree for which there is, I think, no counterpart." Or again, " It is possible to drift along, not too discontentedly, somewhat nervously, somewhat anxiously, somewhat confusedly, hoping for the best, and believing in nothing very much. But it is not possible to be wholly at peace. And it is not possible to be wholly alive. These are the gifts of a vital religion. Our forefathers had such a religion." We have not.

If that be so, then we had better make haste to get hold of it again. For there is going to be much to bear. Kipling once, exulting in the valour of the Irish and the Scottish soldier, thought that he saw this difference between them. The Irish lad, without an instant's hesitation, will throw away his life with a reckless laugh. The Scottish boy, briefly commending his soul to the God of his fathers, pulls down his bonnet on his brow, and dourly faces what is to come. And it is he, so Kipling judged, that sticks it out the little longer, and that dares the little farther, that last five all important minutes, that may prove decisive.

How does religion help ? Why is Christ the gallantest figure in human history ? It is because He was so sure of God ; so certain that He is here, alive ; that, if we call, He answers ; that, even if we forget Him, He remembers and aids us ; that we are never alone, but always the Father is with us. How can I bear it ? your heart cries. You can't. The thing is, as you see, too much for you, in your own strength. But then you are not asked to face it in your own strength. In the most lonely of experiences there are always two. And, with God there beside you, and since you can draw upon all His infinite resources, even if it does come, the unbearable can be borne.

And we can trust God even in the dark. Certainly Christ did. But can you ? Aldous Huxley, in an interesting passage, warns us that it is easy for us with Nature's prettinesses round about us, with our friendly little hills and smoothly swelling uplands and trim and cosy fields, to believe that God is beneficent and kindly. But did we live in the Tropics, with their earthquakes and howling tempests and dark, mysterious, frightening forests, where fears lurk behind every tree, and terrors leap out of nowhere, and clutch with cold hands at the heart, we, like the inhabitants yonder, might easily be devil worshippers. So, while our life ran on softly and happily, and lay out in the open sunshine, it was easy to believe that God was kind and good. But now that the old accustomed peace and security are gone, and terrors have surged in on us; with possibilities even more awesome reaching out towards us from a little farther back, do we still hold our faith undaunted and unshaken ? Are we still sure that God is Love, and too dependable for us to dream of doubting Him ? Now that we need it, have we, in very deed, the quietness and confidence, the peace of mind and the serenity of spirit, that will enable us to see this through ?

MacMurray, the philosopher, has a deep and telling passage in which he declares that most of us are fear-haunted. In the main, men are brave enough about it, hide it away, fling themselves into life with a noisy and overdone exuberance, which, to wise eyes, tells its own tale. We slap each other jovially on the back, we call each other, almost at first sight, by our Christian names, to give the sense of comradeship, and conceal from ourselves our essential daunting solitariness. But, none the less, the things we fear keep glaring in at us, sending a shivering through our hearts. And, wisely, men turn to religion for security and safety. But, unhappily, he says, there are religions, and religions. And some of them are will-o'-the-wisps, deceitful wandering fires that lead us, not along the proved and beaten track, but into bogs and quagmires. If your religion, so he confidently lays it down, tells you that there is no need for you to fear the things of which you are afraid, because they will never happen to you, God will see to that for you, then your religion is a lie ! Into innumerable homes sorrow and loss are going to force their way, as indeed they do, the whole world over every day.

But if your religion promises that, if and when they come, you will find nothing in them to cause you to be afraid, hold to it, for it will make a man of you, and bring you through whatever you may have to face, death or life, principalities or powers, things present, with their long suspense, or things to come, perhaps with their terrible realities, or all of them together, with a brave heart and quiet eyes. What we need is a religion which will not, indeed, remove the things of which we are afraid, for that cannot be done, but will conquer in us our fear of them. And where, asks MacMurray, can that all-important thing

be found ? " I know of no force in the world that can kill the fear of
fear in us except Christianity." Hold you to it, then, if you are wise !
But see to it that it is the genuine type.

The war had scarcely started when a frightened woman was
screaming at us in a railway carriage, that she would never pray again,
that prayer was useless, that, if there be a God at all, which she much
doubted, He was not Love, only a cold Indifference, or a horrible
Cruelty. For she had prayed and prayed that there might be no war ;
and it was here. Her pseudo-religion had told her that the thing of
which she was afraid would never come ; and, since it had come, the
religion went to pieces. No doubt her difficulty is a very real one.
For as to that whole matter of prayer, there are two sides to the
Master's teaching on it that look flatly contradictory ; and it is not
an easy matter to weave them into a consistent whole. For, on the
one side, with an audacity that dares to use astounding metaphors
which in any other would seem shocking blasphemy ; comparing God,
in some sense, to an unjust judge who has to be badgered into justice,
and to a churlish neighbour who, snug in bed grunts sleepy objections,
and yawning protests, and peevish complaints.—Oh, go away ! The
children have just fallen asleep at last. And we can't have them
wakened up again at this time of night ; and yet he has to rise and
give—Christ bids us cry and strive and batter on the door with an
obstinate dogged persistency that won't take a refusal, and will not
cease, nor budge one foot, until the answer comes. You don't receive,
because you don't ask. Ask, man, seek, knock, keep knocking !

And, on the other hand, there is the prayer of resignation which
Heiler claims, with only some exaggeration, to be a discovery of Jesus
Christ, in which the soul stops asking, and accepts God's will, now
patently revealed to it ; and this not sullenly and of compulsion, but
eagerly, and even gladly, like Paul when he besought the Lord thrice,
and then stopped ; or like Christ Himself in the garden. But when
and for how long to use the one type, and when to cease from it,
and betake oneself to the other is, for me, one of the most real and
difficult problems of the spiritual life, which I have never solved.
And little wonder, when a great saint like Herrmann frankly confesses
that " no advice, however careful, can direct us how to balance the
two exactly in any individual instance." The thing appears to be an
instinct one acquires, a feeling in the finger-tips into which, some
quickly and some very slowly, we gradually grow. Meantime the
solution of the problem and dilemma usually offered us is the phrase

" for Christ's sake." There is your test. We have the right to come to God our Father, and turn out our foolish little human minds to Him boldly and confidently and unafraid, and yet with seemly diffidence, and a humility that is willing to be corrected and refused by One how vastly wiser than our hearts, and who knows all things. But what we can claim " for Christ's sake," as a benefit for Him and for His cause, that we can urge with passion and assurance and a faith that won't turn back till this has been achieved. True, and a most serviceable guide. Only, so foolish are we and ignorant, that we know not what to pray for as we ought, even " for Christ's sake" ; and there too often deceive ourselves, and ask amiss. But, you say, surely there can be no shadow of dubiety that that woman had the right to pray " for Christ's sake " that this desperate world should not again be torn and agonized and crucified by war ; and, picturing the countless dead and maimed, the ruined homes, the agonies, the horrors upon horrors of bombed cities and stricken fields, keep crying it with a faith that had, and could have, no doubts about God's will !

I do not know. I am not sure. And for this reason. Had I been in Jerusalem during those hours in which Christ was betrayed, and tried, and re-tried, and condemned, and mocked, and led to Calvary, I would have prayed—ah ! how I would have prayed, and with what passionate insistence—that God would burst in, must burst in before it was too late, " for Christ's sake," and for His kingdom's sake, and for the sake of the poor, desperate, unsaved world, but always, always for Christ's sake, that He be not shamed, and His glorious enterprise fizzle out in mockery. Yet, had that confident prayer of mine—offered, mark you, " for Christ's sake "—been heard and granted, where would that same poor, desperate world have been to-day ?

Then it was necessary, as God saw things, that His Son should die, though I would never have recognized that; would have judged it to mean utter, absolute, irreparable ruin. And to-day, as God sees things, may not all this, in some mysterious way, be necessary too ?

But, you cry out with angry, passionate conviction, God has, God can have, nothing to do with it. All this is not His wish ; but the outcome of human sin abhorrent to Him ; or the inrush of evil things from the abyss that, breaking through His guard and watch around us, have marred and thwarted His real plans. I know that belief in the healing, strengthening, heartening doctrine of Divine Providence—that God is over all, and overruling all, and working through all, even the grimmest and the most forbidding happenings

and events, towards divine aims and ends, what Ernest Scott calls
" the distinguishing mark of the Christian morality, the knowledge that
the world, with all its dangers and accidents, is overruled by God,"
has become very dim these days, is held to be absurdly out of date,
with sorry consequences. "For," as Lippmann says, "in the old order
the compulsions were often painful, but there was sense in the pain
that was inflicted by the will of an all-knowing God. When a man
believed that the unfolding of events was a manifestation of the will
of God, he could say, ' Thy will be done.' But when he believes that
events are determined by the votes of a majority, the orders of his
bosses, the opinions of his neighbours, the decisions of quite selfish
men, he yields because he has to yield."

The New Testament sees vastly more in things than that, is never
of opinion that events are merely humanly contrived. There stands
the Cross, the blackest blot in history, and it will have it that that
Cross is there, not simply because men were blind and cruel, but,
far more fundamentally, because it was the working out of an eternal
plan of God. God willed it ; God worked towards it for long ages ;
God effected it. That, not the other, is the central fact about it.
" Him, being delivered by the determinate counsel and foreknowledge
of God, you took, and by wicked hands, crucified and slew Him."
You did it ! You must answer for it at the Judgment Seat ! Yet,
all unconsciously, through you, your blindness, your stupidity, your
wrath, your malice, a great aim, aye, the greatest of all God's aims for
His distracted earth, worked itself out.

And if so then, why not so now, in the dark things afflicting our
poor stricken world, and in the sorrows of our personal lives ?

" Clearly," so Farmer puts it, " any understanding of the ways of
God with men must rest upon some awareness of what the divine
purpose is seeking to achieve in human life. If God is seeking one
thing, and man believes He is, or ought to be, seeking something else,
there can be only estrangement, misunderstanding, and cross purposes.
It is fatally easy to measure the goodness of God by the extent to
which pain and trouble are escaped. But God's purpose is to conform
men to the image of His Son : and His Son died on the Cross. To
conform men to that image, and save them from trouble, even great
trouble, are two contradictory ends which not even the providence of
God can accomplish at one and the same time."

I know a man who had to pass through an experience even more
suddenly devastating than that which befell Ezekiel. " Son of man,

behold I take away the desire of thine eyes with a stroke. So I
preached unto the people in the morning. And in the evening my
wife died." A bleak message! Yet the prophet was at least granted
one full day's warning. But this poor soul had not even a second's.
In a twinkling she was gone. And that grim night amid the tumbled
ruins of what, ten minutes before, had been a home, he tried to give
her, not of compulsion, but as a free gift; and asked that, since he
had to bear the pain, he might not miss or lose what it was sent to
teach him.

The years slipped past, and many letters reached him, all of a kind;
one from two missionaries in the wilds of Africa. The one had lost
her husband, drowned on their honeymoon in the United States, and
with that, faith went out, until somebody sent her what that man
had written in the dark to steady his own soul. And faith revived in
her, and she went to the foreign field. The husband of the second,
too, was drowned in Africa; and her faith also went to pieces. Until
the one, who had been through it all herself, read to the other what
had brought her back. And that other, too, came home. And,
together, they wrote to the man, whom they will never see, " You
can be absolutely sure that it was not for nothing that your heart
was broken. It had to be, in order that two lost souls might be found
again."

So it was not chance-blown, did not just happen. It had meaning
in it : was a plan thought out by God. And the man is content.

" Father, what shall I say ? Save me from this hour ? But for
this cause came I unto this hour. Father, glorify Thy name."

We had better remember that, and hold to it. For, if the dark
does fall around us, it will help to bring us through.

CHAPTER III

HOW CHRIST'S MIRACLES HAPPEN

" The whole crowd were struggling to touch Him, because power went forth from Him, and healed every one."—LUKE vi. 19.

AND these things really happened in this old world of ours to ordinary people very like ourselves—hot, dusty, needy, worried, tired, when the Lord Christ came into their midst.

And He is here to-day ! We have His solemn promise, and He will stand to it, to the letter, aye and far more, doing exceedingly abundantly above all that we can ask or think, as is His way. The same wonderful Christ with all the old amazing power is here ! And we, too, ought to be experiencing the same bewildering results.

Yet do we, you and I ? One real reason why churches are not as full, these days, as they were wont to be is this—that people are asking " What is the use of it ? " And they keep asking, not finding themselves met by any large immediate unchallengable answer. " Yes, yes," so Chalmers broke in almost impatiently on the congratulations showered on him, after one of his most dazzling oratorial triumphs. " But what did it do ? " " Nothing happened. Nothing followed." That is what they keep asking us religious and church folk. What does it do, this church-going of yours ? What happens ? What follows ? They watch us going up to worship God—us, who know ourselves to be kindly and well-meaning people. Oh ! no doubt a little tempery at home at times ; and, on occasion—let us honestly confess it—cross and irritable even with God, when His will for us runs athwart our own desires, and He will not accept our pained or indignant advice—still kindly folk enough. And we put through our service, and rise up, and go our ways. And they look after us, we never realize how closely, to see if there is anything in it.

And we seem just the same as ever ; still tempery at times at home, and still hurt, now and then, with God.

And there's not much in that, they say, and drift away. So true is it, as Al Ghazzali says, " more people are able to see what is done than are able to understand what is taught. A crooked piece of iron does not cast a straight shadow."

And thus Christ is still betrayed, not by His enemies, but by His friends. " I will never," said Nietzsche, " believe in the Redeemer of the Christians, until they prove to me that they themselves have been redeemed "—an eminently reasonable claim. But can we meet it ? Don't you see, cries Paul to the Corinthians, how you are dishonouring Christ, you who are just ordinary people ? Just ordinary people ! No better, if no worse, with Christ, than others are without Him, leaving the impression upon onlookers' minds that He makes no manner of difference, and can, quite safely, be neglected.

And, indeed, we ourselves are taken aback by the urgency of their inquiries. For we have come to think of these services of ours as an end in themselves. It is the seemly thing to do, we feel. It is but right and fitting that we should pay this weekly act of homage to Almighty God ; and, that duty duly done, we rise, and pass on to the next thing to be carried through.

There are, indeed, those who insist that to make our own moral and spiritual betterment—such as the cleansing of our hearts, and the strengthening of our wills, and the putting on of the mind of Christ— the end, or even an end, of our services, is to drag the whole thing down to an intolerably low level. It is not so, they hotly maintain ; but we are there to worship God.

Well, I, for one, would require to have several things defined for me before I could set down my name to that. No doubt at all, to be allowed to worship God is a majestic, a nearly incredible privilege, an august right, which, when we try to think out what it means, staggers the mind. Wise and seemly is that Sulpician rule that bids us never rise from prayer without a wondering thanksgiving that God has borne with us in His presence at all—He being what He is, we being what we are. And never was worship more needed than to-day. Some poor souls, indeed, tell us bluntly that they never feel any inclination to commune with God ; that, coming on the new and living way that always lies open to Him, it never even occurs to them to take and follow it. Herbert Spencer, for example, remarks loftily, " to many, and apparently to most, religious worship yields a species of pleasure. To me it never did so—never found in me any echoes." And all too many these days think, at least, that they agree with him ; although the mass of them are vastly more religious than they realize ; and, in times of strain, find themselves, unconsciously, betaking themselves, with a child's confidence, to the God they had forgotten or ignored. But is it not pathetic that, in so many lives, there lie those bleak and empty spaces, where others meet God in His glory, face to face, and walk with Him day after day ?

No ! No ! it will not do to tell ourselves complacently in explanation that folk nowadays are busier than they used to be. For, except under the strain of war, we are, in fact, people of ample leisure, compared to what our fathers knew ; who, many of them, working incredible hours for an impossibly trifling wage, and tugging desperately, could barely contrive to make the ends of things just come together. A hundred years ago or so, the Paisley weavers sent a petition to Parliament asking for some relief of the intolerable strain of life, and saying in effect, Take our leisure if you must have it ; and if that, too, must go, much else which seems to us a part of that human inheritance which is, or ought to be, inalienably ours, as our natural birthright. Still, we can let that go. But you are robbing us of things even more precious ! For, when we kneel in prayer, we are so dog-tired that we fall asleep ; and when we go to church, our minds, drugged with toil, are too weary to follow the service. Take our lives ; take our rights, but leave us God ! For Him, too, you are filching from us.

We are not busier than were such driven people ! No ; but our lives are fuller of competing interests, that keep tugging at our sleeves. And, in this press of things enticing us this way and that, filling our eyes and hearts, something is apt to be forgotten, and that something is dreadfully apt to be—God. And these services of ours come like clearings in the jungle, from which we can see the eternal stars again, and feel the winds of God cool upon our hot faces. And we have need of them, have desperate need of them—even the best of us. Chalmers, that great soul, of whom Rosebery wrote, " Here was a man striving, organizing, speaking, and preaching, with the dust and fire of the world on his clothes, but carrying his shrine with him everywhere," none the less, sets down sadly in his honest diary one day, " My soul is losing acquaintance with God " ; found, with dismay, that the endless bustle of the ministry can be as noisy and as soul-destroying as the world itself, that he was being blinded to God by the smoke of the very incense he kept burning to Him upon His own altars, was losing Him among the endless calls upon him of His own service, and among the courts and pillars of His own house. And if he felt that, what possible chance have most of us, unless we take pains to recall God to our minds ; to feel for His hand, and find it closing over ours, making us sure that we are not alone, never alone, for always God is there ?

But what is worship ? What ought to result from it ? What is the point and peak and heart and centre of it ? Is it the offering we bring to God of praise and adoration, of thanksgiving and sacrifice, our praise, our sacrifice to Him ? That has its place, not legitimate only, but imperative. And yet to put that in the foreground is to make the service fundamentally man-centred and subjective, which, face to face with God, is surely almost unthinkably unseemly. Or is the ideal we should hold before us that other extreme, so ardently pressed on us these days, that, face to face with the Lord God Almighty, High and Holy, it is for us to forget ourselves, and, leaving behind our petty little human joys and needs and sins, rising above thanksgiving and petition and confession, to lose ourselves in an awed adoration of God's naked and essential being, blessing and praising Him, not even for what He has done for us, and been to us, but for what, in Himself, He is.

To me that seems, not an advance, but a pathetic throw-back to the primitive of Brahmanism. We shall not learn to know God better, nor how to worship Him more worthily, by carefully rubbing out from memory every item of the wonder of Christ's revelation of Him. What makes God God, what constitutes, and is, His glory, His " topmost, ineffablest, uttermost crown," is not even His eternity, or His almightiness, but His divine forgiveness, and the tenderness of His compassion, and His immeasurable loving-kindness. When we bless Him for these, we are offering, not a lower, but an infinitely higher praise. Miss Underhill, quoting the seraphic hymn, " Holy ! Holy ! Holy ! Lord God of Hosts, Heaven and earth are full of Thy glory," adds " That is worship ; its very essence." But not worship at its highest. The redeemed in heaven crying continually, " Unto Him that loved us and washed us from our sins in His own blood," give, say the Scriptures, an adoration which, in depth and fullness, no angel of them all can ever equal.

Yet even then we have not reached the centre. For, when we worship, we are in God's presence, and it is what He says and does to us that is the all-important thing, not what we say and do toward Him. Since He is here, and speaking to us, face to face, it is for us, in a hush of spirit, to listen for, and to, His voice, reproving, counselling, encouraging, revealing His most blessed will for us ; and, with diligence, to set about immediate obedience. This and this, upon which He has laid His hand, must go ; and this and this to which He calls, must be at once begun. And here and now I start to it. That is the heart of worship, its very core and essence. " Glorify God ! " cries Browning. Of course that is the end and aim and object. But then, " we are His glory ; and if we be glorious, is not the thing achieved ? " If we are lifted up above ourselves, are, by Christ's touch upon us, made new creatures, living our lives in a more royal way.

Whereas, if what we call our worship is only a stirring of the emotions, and then they re-settle as before ; a moving of the feelings, and then it passes ; a turning in to worship in a kind of little chapel, separate from our lives, which worship being ended, we leave it and pass back to ordinary things again, which remain quite unaffected and unaltered by it all ; if it is merely like a frowsy woman in some slum street who, leaving her disordered house, comes down the dirty stair, and turns into a cinema, and loses herself in the film, becomes the heroine, and passes with her through her joys and triumphs, and then it is over ; and, in a little, she is once again climbing the dirty stair, back to the still disordered house ; if—

> " On our souls the visions rise
> Of that fair life we never led.
> They flash a splendour past our eyes,
> We start, and they are fled.
> They pass, and leave us, with blank gaze,
> Resigned to our ignoble days";

if that is all that comes of it, then there is something wrong, far wrong, quite disastrously wrong. For where Christ is, things happen, and He is here among us now.

In the days of His flesh no one ever thought of Him as ineffective. There were people who objected to Him, actively disliked Him, hated Him indeed, feeling that it would be wiser to put this impossible and insufferable Person out of the way. But they never dreamed of saying He was ineffectual and futile. Rather they were afraid of Him. For where this Man was, nobody knew what might not happen any hour. And His friends, too, came to feel happily that, with Him beside them, everything was possible, that the most masterful temptations could be faced with steady hearts that did not quail, and even the most triumphant enemies be overthrown.

And if we rise and go our ways, just as we came, slinking obediently to heel as usual, at the first imperious whistle of our besetting sins, we are not getting from our worship anything like what there is in it for us. " They were all struggling to touch Him : for power kept passing out of Him, and He healed them every one." And that same Christ, with that same power, is here among us now.

I know what you are going to say, have heard it so often that I can foretell it. It will be one of two things—either a kind of grudging acquiescence that, perhaps, in the old days, when God was really God and counted, when Jesus Christ was here, a fact visible and tangible, and one could go to Him and state one's need to Him, and see Him listening to it, and watch Him coming into it, along with us, to help, much may, and indeed must have happened, with that marvellous Personality beside one.

But not now, in this shrewd, worldly-wise prosaic age, and with Christ only a dim memory, blown to us from the very long ago.

> " Now He is dead, far off He lies
> In the lorn Syrian town,
> And on His grave with shining eyes
> The Syrian stars look down."

And He can do no more for us—or anyone.

To the Old Testament prophets the fatal heresy, the supreme blasphemy, the most monstrous of delusions is to talk like that, as if God were a fading figure on the crumbling tapestries of ancient history, but not real or effectual any longer ; to think of Him as the Indians do of Brahma the Creator, once one of the great gods, none greater, none so great, but now remembered only in some handful of temples, thin sown through that continent of a land, which, elsewhere, thinks of Him as the grandfather God, who sits doddering by the fireside, His day's work long since over, for creation is done, and no one bothers about Him any longer—senile and past.

So common is that mood, so prone are men to be long-sighted, seeing God clearly enough in the dead past, and sure that He is certain to be in the dim and far-off future, but blind to Him, working at their very side ; brushing against Him, and yet never noticing that He is there, that each of the prophets bursts in on a depressed generation, eager, excited, with the same glad shout of the same tremendous news—God is alive, now, in our day, as wonderful as ever, ready and able to do for us now, in our need, more even than He ever did for all our fathers. And the New Testament takes up that cry and hands it on, assuring us Christ is not dead, but here, among us now, our own Contemporary, as He is all men's Contemporary. But we are slow to credit that. " God," cried Augustine, " did not create the world, and then leave it." And he said that because so many in his day were assuming that that was precisely what had happened, and had lost hope and heart. " Carlyle did believe in a God ; but He died in the days of Oliver Cromwell," thought Maurice. And many share that daunting and depressing creed ; agree that God did once upon a time speak to us through His servants the prophets, but since then He has fallen dumb, or has lost interest in us and never speaks through anybody now ; are sure that the Holy Ghost did counsel us until Nicea, but then vanished, and left us to shift for ourselves. Why, cries God to us in Isaiah, do you keep thinking of the far past and dwelling on the deeds of old ? Here in our day " is a new deed of Mine springing to light. And have you no eyes for that ? " That is a reproach and challenge God might well fling at us in our tremendous time. For never in history has He so manifestly broken in on our human affairs as in our day. Never has He achieved such wonders in the world as those which our own eyes have seen. The Psalmists are continually inciting those around them to sing new songs, inspired by the new wonders of divine grace in their own day. And who have better right or a more clamant need to sing such new songs to the Living God as we, who have experienced deliverance from perils and from enemies and from unthinkable disasters more grim than any that our fathers ever faced ? And as for Jesus Christ, how can a sane man think of Him as dead, after what we have seen ?

Admittedly, there is a hideous debit side to things, and yet I challenge anybody to deny that in the seventy years which I myself have known Christ's Kingdom has leapt out farther and swifter than in any similar period down the long Christian centuries ; or that His people have faced enemies stronger and more ferociously relentless than any that His Church has ever had to meet, and through His help have stood fast in their evil hour ; or that His spirit has achieved in our own day uplifts and progress and advance so striking in the mass, that where can they be equalled in a like length of time ? Christ is not dead, but alive and victorious. And to us too, He says, and has the right to say it, " In the world ye shall have tribulation. But be of good cheer, I have overcome the world." And we can watch Him doing it before our very eyes.

Or else you will object, I don't doubt what you say ; am not attempting to deny Christ's power, or even to limit it ; admit fully and wonderingly that, for the right kind of person, He can, it seems, do practically anything. Only I myself do not belong to that particular

3

type. And one must be reasonable even towards Christ, and not ask, even from Him, obvious impossibilities. If a lad has no glimmering of an aptitude for mathematics, and can make nothing of it, it were quite unfair to blame the teachers for his failure ; since the best of teachers must be given something upon which to work. So, I am a plain ordinary mortal, with no spiritual deeps in me, and even Christ cannot, fairly, be expected to make much of such crumbling, friable, impossible material. With the right type, admittedly, but not with me.

But look at the text. They were all struggling to touch Him, for virtue kept passing out of Him, and He healed—whom ? Not, one here and one there ; the easier cures, the less desperate among them. No. But everyone, even the most impossible. That, indeed, has always been the proud boast of Christianity. Long ago Celsus, in huge amusement, flouted and jeered, and heaped derision on derision, believing he was thereby scoffing this daft superstition out of court. Every other teacher, he observes, summons to him the clever and the worthy and the disciplined, but this crazy Christ calls to the beaten and the broken, and the whole rag-tag-and-bobtail of the down-at-the-heels, and the disreputable, and the failures. And the Church, far from wincing at the jest, openly exulted in it. Yes, said Tertullian, but He doesn't leave them beaten and broken and ragged and down-at-heels ; but, out of such sorry material you would have thrown away, the most hopeless of the lot, can make, and does make, new men and women, clean and self-disciplined and Christlike.

And so the answer to you is what Rutherford once wrote to certain depressed and doubting souls, not arguing with them, but accepting the bleak facts as they had stated them. " Yes ! you seem in a bad way. My advice is ' Take you a house next door to the Physician, for it will be very singular if you should prove to be the very first He ever turned away unhealed.' " Too singular for credence ! You can quite safely venture.

But how does it all happen—this wonderful thing ? We must give Christ a certain atmosphere of hope and faith and expectancy ; must act on the assumption that something is going to come of it. If we do, it will ; if we don't, it may not ; and, likely, won't. For without that expectancy in us, even Christ is largely thwarted, as the honest Scriptures candidly admit. Nor is there anything unusual in that. Rather, in all kinds of cure, the patient's faith is a huge help ; is, indeed, indispensable, if a physician is to have his chance. Galen, himself, that master of the healing art, frankly conceded that, if a patient believes in a remedy which, of itself, is without efficiency, it becomes endowed with beneficent power. And doctors will tell you that people die who have no need or right to die, because they won't believe in them, or in the possibility of cure. So Luther, speaking about Christ, declared, " Miracles take place, not because they are performed, but because they are believed." The healing, helping, saving power of Christ is here, a tremendously real and potent fact. Yet in the case of some of us, nothing at all is going to happen, while others, sitting next to them perhaps, are being uplifted, heartened, changed. It all depends on whether we want what He offers us, and will accept it from Him. It was a very real expert in spiritual things who said, "All my stock of Christ is a little hunger for Him." And it is Christ Himself who tells us that if we hunger and thirst for the righteousness we have not got, we also will be satisfied and blessed. All that is needed is some little appetite to be better and cleaner and more unselfish than we are. Give Christ that, and, for you too, He will do the rest.

Only we shall have to struggle. They were all struggling to touch Him. That seems a fair reading of the text. And you will have to struggle too. It is not that He is unwilling. Ah, no ! Once on a day I hoped that when I am dead and in my coffin, they would put the cold finger pointing to those wonderful words of infinite hope : " I will arise and go unto my Father, and say, Father, I have sinned. But, while he was yet a great way off, his father saw him, and had compassion, and ran." Put the dead finger pointing there, said I. But I don't say that now. No ! rather set it farther up that same marvellous page. For, after all, the prodigal came home ; and, after all, the sheep caught in the thicket bleated, and let them know its whereabouts. But the little piece of silver, with the King's image stamped upon it, dropped there in the dark, could do nothing for itself at all, till God's searching hands, feeling nearer and still nearer, lit on it at last. Put the dead finger there.

Still, you will need to struggle. Why ? Because it is our familiarity with certain things that is our peril. First, with ourselves. " Our one chance against sin," says Newman, " is that we be shocked by it." But we have grown so accustomed to ourselves, have lived so long with our besetting failings, that they no longer catch our eyes. We rarely notice them, can readily excuse them, push them aside as no great matter, and not worth worrying over.

And how can we cure that ? When Jesus asked Zacchæus for his hospitality and, at that, the city's noisy welcome died away into a shocked and incredulous hostility, those two moved on together in that sudden, tense, sullen silence until Zacchæus stopped, and, without Jesus having said one further word to him, shed his old settled life and habits as a snake casts its outworn skin. " I'm done with it," he said. " I promise you I'm done with it ! I thought that it was clever. I set out to make my fortune, and I've made it. And when they jeered at me, the jingling of my money-bags was answer enough in my own ears. But now I'm done with it. For I see clearly that if I am to be your friend, the old life just won't do." You see ? Get you closer to Jesus Christ, and all the rest will follow.

And then, there is our dangerous familiarity with the scheme of salvation, making it trite to us, and robbing it of its initial wonder, and the compulsion that it laid upon men's hearts when it was new and still seemed staggering. There is no grimmer page in modern literature than that in which D. H. Lawrence, that fierce loather of much that is the very heart of Christianity, tells us how he was alienated from the faith in which loving hearts had striven to bring him up. " From earliest years right into manhood, I had the Bible poured every day into my helpless consciousness till there came almost a saturation point." " Long before one could think, these portions of the Bible were *douched* over the mind, till they became soaked in " ; " the B'ble was verbally trodden into the consciousness, like innumerable foc.prints treading a surface hard ! This process defeats its own ends. The mind becomes stubborn, resistant, and at last repudiates the whole Bible authority, and turns with a kind of repugnance from the Bible altogether. And this is the condition of many men of my generation." And yet his mother was a loving soul so anxious that her laddie should belong to Christ ! But he, it seems, was sometime, and by some one, woefully mishandled. And yet we leave the religious education of our children in the schools to men and women who themselves may not know Christ, and who may sicken them of Him, or make the blessed Gospels a mere drudgery, and nothing more ! And is it not a fearsome fact that these services of ours are never neutral things ? that we can't leave them, as we entered them, and never do. Better perhaps, or worse, perhaps. But not the same. For, every time God's Holy Spirit moves us, and we stifle the impression or rub it off, or let it die without result, it grows less and less likely that we shall ever respond to Him : more and more likely that we shall fall into that strange self-hypnotism which makes us believe that we already are, what we are only agreeing we must some day set ourselves to be, some day always in the future, and that keeps receding with our advance, so that we never reach it : that the mere theoretical acceptance of God's claims will do in place of a hard-breathing resolute living of them out, and that an empty gush of transient feeling is to close with Jesus Christ. The oftener that we are so stirred and " nothing follows, nothing happens," the less likely does it grow that anything will ever happen. For stimulated so resultlessly, the feelings atrophy ; so roused and cheated, the will no longer responds, but merely stirs uneasily, like an old dog that whimpers in its sleep, remembering what it could once do in the chase, but can't do now : each time the door closes a little—farther and still farther. And one day it will shut. When Theseus and Pirithous went down to Hades on their valiant adventure, they tired, and sat down for a little— a little that grew long. And, when at last they tried to rise, it was to find to their horror that they had grown to the rocks, and could no longer move. Believe me, you will need to struggle. In God's name rise now ! Rise now ! For to-morrow it may be too late.

Do you remember that blind man, that day like any other day, sitting at his usual begging stance outside Jericho ; and how, hearing the sluffing of many thronging feet, he asked what it all meant. And they told him that Jesus, the new Prophet from Galilee, was passing by. And how, with that, seeing his chance, which might not come ever again, he sprang up, fighting his way towards Christ, and crying to Him piteously, beseechingly, yet with a sudden mad hope in it, " Jesus, Thou Son of David, have mercy upon me ! " And how they tried to silence him and push him back. For Christ was not to be bothered by the likes of him. But he would not be silenced. " Have mercy upon me ! " " And Jesus Christ stood still." " Bring him to Me," He said. " What wilt thou I should do for thee ? " " Lord, that I may receive my sight." " Receive thy sight." And at that instant it came true.

And now that same wonderful Christ, with all the old bewildering power, is here. Struggle, man, struggle ! Don't let your conscience push you back, telling you haughtily that for you to come into Christ's presence, for you to ask for benefits from One you have so slighted, for you to imagine that there can be any chance, is a consummate impudence. Struggle, man, struggle ! Fight towards Him. Cry, you too, " Thou Son of David, have mercy upon me ! " For Jesus

Christ stands still. " Bring him to me," He says. And Christ and
you are face to face ; just Christ, just you, as if there were no others.
And look ! look ! Do you not see ? The hand that touched blind
eyes, and they saw ; and deaf ears, and they heard ; and leprous
things, and they were cleansed, is coming out, is coming out—
to very you ! " They were all struggling to touch Him ; for power
kept issuing from Him ; and He healed them, every one ! " Yes,
even you, if you will have it so.

CHAPTER IV

WHAT RELIGION DOES FOR ONE WHO REALLY TRIES IT

"I bow before Thy sacred shrine to praise Thee for Thy love so true, that far excels all ever known of Thee."—Ps. 138. (See Moffatt's whole translation.)

HERE is a man who has tested God, who has made a practical and personal experiment of this thing called religion, who has taken into his hands those marvellous Scripture promises, at which most of us gaze wistfully enough, and then lay them regretfully aside, feeling that of course such things cannot be meant, or possible, for us—takes them into his hands, and examines them, and turns them round, and—what if these be really true ? he asks, and tries them, where the pinch lay for him ; where, as he confesses, life had grown bleak and difficult ; where it looked just ridiculous to take them literally—there.

And here, so to speak, he comes bursting in on all that babble and clamour round the Mercy Seat, where most of us are arguing, and complaining, and entreating, and telling God, to His face, that His way of things just won't do ; and that, if He has any sense at all, He must see that for Himself, now that we have pointed out to Him, how much wiser, and kinder, and in all ways better, this other way that we suggest would be—into all that bursts this soul crying, " Where's God ? " for I want to thank Him, and to tell Him I had no idea, till I tried it, how real and efficient His grace is, out in the strain and stress and dust of life. Aye, and where are these stammering stutterers who said they knew Him, and could reveal Him to us ? For, in my own narrow experience, I myself have come upon far more than all of them together ever even hinted. " He far excels all that was ever known of Him."

And it is impatiently he listens through the glory of the service. Almost you can see him fidgeting : almost you can hear him saying, If only they would let me speak for Him, I could bring them more authentic news of God than that ! And it is almost scornfully he tosses down the very Scriptures, as poor affairs, compared to what he has experienced and knows. He far excels, says he, pushing the greatest of them from him, all that these people ever told us of Him.

Until, a little jealous for these mighty writings, to which we owe so much, we are inclined to turn upon him almost angrily. Not so fast, my friend ; and not so cavalierly ! These are august Scriptures, not to be dismissed so lightly. When, we might ask him, did you last read your Isaiah, that wonderful prophet, who, speaking for a people with no statable case, bids them go to God, and say, We have no case. And that, he says, will be your case, and it will storm His heart, and He will abundantly pardon. Abundantly. Coleridge assures us that we never really understand a word until we see the picture that lies fossilized and imprisoned at the heart of it. Well, do you see the picture here ? Abundantly. Go down to the sea-beach, and watch the tide come in—wave upon wave, wave upon wave, until your brain grows dizzy, and your eyes are tired. And still out of the fullness yonder, still as full as ever, wave upon wave upon wave comes crashing into whiteness at your very feet. Abundantly ! Wave upon wave upon wave of it. Such is God's mercy towards your soul, and mine.

> " Till all the seas gang dry, my dear,
>   And the rocks melt wi' the sun."

So we, in Scotland, pledge ourselves to one another ; and even call it after those who have passed on. And that is the very covenant God makes with you and me. Somewhere in that wandering waste of waters your sins and mine are cast and lost. But who is to come upon, or find them, ever again any more. Abundantly !

Or, turn the page in that same daring prophet—Esaias is very bold, says Paul, and so, indeed, he is—and you find him talking of the forgetfulness of the Omniscient ! With boldness and assurance he insists that, with his own ears, he has heard God saying, " Thy sins I will remember no more." As if you and I began our prayer of confession, and God pulled us up, and said, Sins ! sins ! were there sins ? I have forgotten about them. What a metaphor to bring home to our apathetic and lethargic minds the wonder, the wholeheartedness, the thoroughness, of what God means by forgiving !

These are tremendous Scriptures, our hearts cry out to this critic of them, to be read upon our knees ; and with minds dazed, bewildered, lost in a love that passeth understanding, and that, judged by our poor human standards, has no sense in it.

But he won't listen. Vague hints, he says, mere suggestions, nothing at all to what I have experienced. " He far excels all that was ever known of Him."

And Paul agrees with that. Now that, he says, is exactly what I feel about Jesus Christ !

Paul was a great orator, though he didn't think so himself, and even speaks contemptuously of what he feels to be his stumbling efforts—a vivid personality, with red-hot lava in his heart, that sprang gushing out ; a man whó felt intensely, and could so set down what was in his own mind, that others saw it, caught the infection of it, were swept helplessly away before that irresistible and rushing torrent. " Paul," says Erasmus, " thunders and lightens, and speaks sheer flame ". What Schiller says of Mary of Scotland is truer of him, everything becomes a weapon in his hand. Or Gilbert Murray, " he is certainly one of the great figures in Greek literature." And this august soul, immeasurably gifted in spirit and in mind, masses and flings in all his powers in his endeavour to share Christ with us, to make our dim eyes see what he sees, and help our sluggish hearts to begin to know what he has learned. He heaps up language, he strains it to the cracking point, he coins new words, he invents superlatives and super-superlatives that nobody had ever heard before, he strikes out staggering metaphors. Take one of these at random. You ask me what Christ has done for me, what difference He has made in me ? I'll tell you. This earth of ours was finished, span silently in a gross darkness, inert, forgotten, dead, till something, groping its way through the blackness, found earth's face, and stayed, and played upon it. And, with that, history had begun. For light had come. And light brought everything that mattered with it—colour and beauty and life itself. And God, who once shone out of the darkness, has in the face of Jesus Christ shone into my poor sterile heart. Look at that dead ball spinning in the darkness ; look at this earth of ours, teeming with interests. That is the difference Christ has made for me.

Yet, in the end, he throws up his hands despairingly. It won't go into language, he says, won't describe. No one can know what Christ is to a soul that really trusts Him, until one has actually tried Him for oneself. He far excels all I can ever tell you of Him. We preachers, confessed Luther, when we talk of Jesus Christ, are, at best, like infants, goo-ing and gurgling, using half words and quarter words—no more than that. Don't judge Him by our poor efforts to describe Him to you !

Now what do you say to all this ? Does it blow gustily past your ears—no doubt the seemly thing to say in a pulpit, but without any very definite, or exact, meaning ? For my part I agree with it and, in my little way, feel as these mighty spirits felt. I keep telling the men at college that they will find all their best texts, not even in Matthew or Mark, not even in Luke or John, but in a fifth gospel, written by their own experience. And when things grow difficult for me, I light the lamp of memory and turn the fluttering pages of that volume, and come on things as wonderful for me as anything in the original four. How here, and here, and here, Christ called, not somebody long ago, but me ; how here, and here, and here, He laid His hand in healing, not on somebody long ago, but me ; how here, and here, and here, He raised, not some dead soul of a past age, but mine. " He far excels all that was ever known of Him."

Indeed, I sometimes go to Jesus Christ and tell Him—for as Fénelon too had found, " you can't treat God with too much confidence "—that I don't understand, that He confuses me. For, say I, you lay down certain limiting conditions : tell me quite definitely that if, and if, and if—then certain things will follow. " Ask, and it will be given you." But I did not ask, and yet it came. It was heaped up upon my undeserving as an unsought gift. " I didn't find my friends," says Emerson, " the good God gave them to me." And was it not, when I was yet a sinner that, through God's love, Christ died for me. " Seek," so you tell us, " seek and you shall find." But I didn't seek, at least, not much. Rather it was, with me, as with Santi Deva long ago, who, sitting one day like a blind beggar on a dung heap, suddenly found the pearl of salvation lying in his palm, put there, he knew not how. " Knock," you say, " and it shall be opened." But I didn't knock ! Rather has it been with me, as Samuel Rutherford found in his experience also, that while his soul was fast asleep, Christ had a way of entering and heaping gifts beside his pillow, and so out again. Aye, but the gifts were there, when he himself awoke. You lay down certain limiting conditions ; and I, to my shame, have paid no attention to them. But, then, no more has God ! He far excels even what you told me of Him.

And Christ looks at me and smiles, and says, " And did not I tell you that too ? " Now didn't I ? And, of course, He did : the moment that one thinks it out, one must see that. You came to Me, He says, and asked Me what is God really like ? And I said, Well, take your own father's heart. That will give you some inkling, at least, of God's nature. But didn't I add, now, tell me, did I not add, But " how much more " is God than any father's heart ? Didn't I make it plain and clear that even your most audacious thoughts of Him are only words thrown out a very little way in God's direction : that He far excels all you can ever think of Him.

That is what this Psalmist long ago had found, a real man once, facing the difficulties of a life as real as yours and mine, not just a figure in a book, as he is now.

For one thing, so he more than hints, he found that people round about him had teasing and unnerving problems about prayer. Did it do anything ? Had it real outcome, and positive results ? In particular why were the answers so lame of foot, and slow in coming ? Well, sometimes they are. Knock, says Christ. But He tells us frankly it is sometimes needful to " batter " and that shamelessly " upon the door," and keep on, taking no refusal. Yes : sometimes they are. Well, says this man, I have not found it so. " The very day I pray the answer comes," with no delay about it. " The very day."

Of course, it all depends upon for what we are praying. If we are whimpering, and snivelling, and begging to be spared the discipline of life that is sent to knock some smatterings of manhood into us, the answer to that prayer may never come at all. Thank God ! Though, indeed, it is not easy to say that, with honesty. Still, it may never come at all, thank God. But if we have attained as far as Epictetus, pagan though you would call him, whose daily prayer was this : " O God, give me what Thou desirest for me, for I know that what Thou choosest for me is far better than what I could choose " ; if you are not bleating to get off, but asking to be given grace and strength to see this through with honour, " the very day " you pray that prayer, the answer always comes. I know it, says this man of like passions, and like difficulties, and like temptations as ourselves, for I have proved it time on time.

And so have many of us too. Look back at your own life, and see. Did I cross these raging torrents on these green and slippery stones ? You did, sir : but only because there was some One there to steady you. Did I climb that frowning crag of duty or of sorrow ? It is unscalable ! You did, sir ! But only because a hand leapt out, and snatched you into safety, when your feet were away !

He far excels all that was ever known of Him, we who have tried Him, being witnesses. And who else has a right to an opinion ? Not you, till you have really tried Him too.

And so he goes on to say, Folk tell me they have doubts and difficulties and uncertainties that trip them up, and hamper them.

If they will give me half an hour, and come and sit down with me in a quiet corner, I'll soon settle their difficulties for them. I'll tell them the story of my life—no carried tale, no rumour blown from other people, but first-hand and authentic evidence! I'll put them into this quandary that, either they will have to say—That man is the biggest, and the coolest, and the most consummate liar I have ever seen, or else they will need to think this whole thing out again. For, with assurance and with emphasis, I stand to this, because it all happened to me. If, he declares, they knew how God has dealt with me, they would have made a song of it; and, by now, it would be being heard on every street.

Surely that is the spirit that is needed in our day. How sick and tired one grows of the perpetual moaning and self-depreciation in the Church! And what insane psychology it is! No business firm ever advertises in the Church's doleful fashion. " Our business is not prospering, and we are not so certain of the value of our wares as we once were; but if you could turn in, it would be comforting!" We can never get the people back in numbers until we prove to them that we have something worth the sharing. And then they will come running for it of themselves. And we have. The men of the Testament burst in on us, eager, excited, unable to keep their immense discovery to themselves, compelled to share with any they can get to listen, what had proved so gloriously revolutionary, and enriching, in their own characters and lives. And we, too, have found it: and we also ought to be ringing it out. " They must sing better songs," said Nietzsche, " ere I learn belief in their Saviour. His disciples must look like the saved."

John Hutton used to tell how once, at a great gathering in York-shire, he had hardly started on his sermon, when a miner leapt to his feet, and led the congregation in the Doxology. Whereat my friend, as he put it, " sank like a punctured tyre," and took some time to get upon his way again, for we Scots preachers do not like such interruptions. At the close, the man apologized, explaining he had only been a Christian for some months. I used, so he went on, to drink, to knock the wife about, to pawn the furniture, and now it is all so gloriously different. I can't sit still, want to get up and sing about it. Asked how he fared down the pit, the man said that, of his particular lot, only he and one other professed Christianity, and the others quiz us daily. " What do they ask?" " Oh, well, yesterday they said to us, ' You don't really believe that yarn about Jesus turning the water into wine ; now, do you ? ' "   " And what did you say ? " I said   " I am an ignorant man ; I know nothing about water and wine. But I know this—that in my house Jesus Christ has turned beer into furniture ! And that is a good enough miracle for me ! "

What are you going to say to a man like that, who takes his stand squarely upon his own experience ? It happened to me. And if you reply, " But, in point of fact, and Christ or no Christ, I, for one, have but little to show," are you quite sure that you have ever really closed with Christ at all ? Certainly He expects that there will be momentous happenings in His people's lives that need Him to explain them. Barrie tells us how, in the little house at Thrums, they used to tiptoe to and fro when his mother was upon her knees, awed by the knowledge that she was praying for them. And here and there in the New Testament we blunder in on Christ, and find Him on His knees ; and, once at least, ere we can escape, cannot but overhear Him pleading our names. " Neither pray I for these alone," that is, for Peter and John and the rest, " but for those who will believe through them "—that is, for you and me. Hush ! the Lord Christ is praying for you ! And what is it He asks for us ? That we be given such a spirit of unity and brotherliness and Christlikeness that people, coming upon us, will look at us, and look again, and then from us to Jesus Christ, seeking the explanation of us there.

And if you still say, rather miserably now, that you, for one, can't think of anything like that in you—well, the past is past, and cannot be restored. But there is still the present and the future. Why not really start on it now ? There was always a daft gallantry about Jesus Christ. He loved daringly to fling down His challenge before sheer impossibilities. In the porches of Bethesda, He sought no cheap and easy reputation by healing some neurotic creature with nothing really wrong with her, except that she had had too little to do. He found His way, in all that mass of suffering, to the very worst and the most hopeless case in the whole place. And if, said He, I cannot prove My powers to this man here, then there is nothing in them. And so to-day I would not put it past Him that He is making His sure and confident way to very you, and with audacity accepting you as a real and a reasonable test for Him and for His powers ; is saying, " If I can't heal this soul where it has need of healing, where the parapets are blown to bits, and the enemy keeps stealing in on every dark night, and where the ground is all trampled with its constant overthrows, then there is nothing in my claims." But there is, there is !

He far excels all they have ever told you of Him. And you, too, can prove that true.

And so, in the last place, this soul faces the future unafraid. It is not always easy to do that with a stout heart and steady eyes. Oh ! I know that you young folk are itching for the day when you can leave the quiet waters of the home haven, and sail forth, away and away to these golden lands where your dreams dwell. And quite right too ! And a great voyage to you when it comes !

But, after a time in life, the future cannot give much more ; and it can take so much away. Like travellers crouched about a prairie fire, we huddle together. What's that moving in the darkness ? We are so helpless and exposed. At any second a wind, leaping out of nowhere, may swoop on us, and leave us, roofless and alone.

And this man is quite aware it is not easy to preserve one's calm and courage in this perilous life. I know the clouds are gathering, he admits ; I see the lightning leaping ; I can hear the thunder crashing ; I am watching a tremendous tempest blowing up. Well, let it come ! For God will undertake for me, he says. And God and I together can face anything.

" We felt," said Shackleton and his two companions, in explanation of how they endured through all their sufferings and perils at the Pole, " each of us felt that there was Someone else there more than we could see." There will always be Someone else there more than you can see. And God and you together can face that that scares you.

And so to the last verse, which, in the newer version, runs : " God will not drop the work He has begun." As if to say, God is a dreamer of great dreams and, in the end, they all come true.

Once God said, Out of this tenuous fire mist I can fashion a solid earth, fit theatre for the gallant epic of humanity. Well, it didn't look like it. And, for æons upon æons, nothing happened. And did the angels whisper together and say, For once He has failed ! If they did, they were wrong. For the earth is here, a solid fact. How ? No man knows. A dream of God come true. He did not drop the work He had begun.

Or, once God said, I could make a creature able to hold communion with Myself out of this common dust. Well, it didn't look like it. For life began in such crude forms. And it was slowly, slowly, with wide and yawning gulfs between each tardy and precarious step in the advance, that it erected itself up, and up, until there came the wonder of the human hand, and the splendour of the human face, and the mystery of the human soul. How ? No man knows. Another dream of God come true. He did not drop the work He had begun.

Aye, says this poet, and I can feel the touch of these same skilled fingers at work upon my soul. Yes, cries Paul, and don't you see what they are doing ? Don't you feel them fashioning out of that dour lump of your nature a something that will grow into a hand, Christ's eager hand ; and a face, Christ's very face ; and a heart, Christ's heart. And that dream also will come true. God will not drop the work He has begun.

When things grow difficult for me, I fall back into my last trench, out of which they have never shelled me yet. I go to Christ, and ask, Did you not say, " For I came down from heaven, not to do my own will, but the will of Him that sent Me. And this is the will of Him that sent Me, that of all that He has given Me I should lose not one." And God did give me as a gift to you. And it is a poor shepherd who loses even one of His sheep. And Christ looks at me, and asks, Have I ever failed you in the past ? And I answer, No. And do you think that I shall ever fail you in the future ? And, when He puts it to me bluntly like that, what can I say but look Him in the eyes and answer, I do not. For He came down from heaven, not to do His own will, but the will of Him that sent Him ; and this is the will of Him that sent Him, that, of all that He has given Him, He should lose not one. Not me. Not you.

CHAPTER V

SOME ASPECTS OF THE CROSS

" For the word of the Cross is to them that are perishing foolishness : but unto us who are being saved it is the power of God."—1 COR. i. 18.

THE old geographers had a notion that the Cross was set up at the centre of the earth, and that the whole world spins round and about it. And certainly no fact in human history has had anything like so huge an outcome as that grim wayside scene, which at the time seemed so entirely unimportant, and the disastrous ending of a life deliberately thrown away and wasted. Is it not hinted in the Scriptures that people, hastening along the busy road that ran beside and past the place of execution, hardly turned their heads to look ? For somebody was always being crucified, and they had a full rushed day before them, and must hurry on to deal with real and momentous things that mattered, and not stand here gaping at what was to be seen every other day. And yet how that stark ugly symbol of horror and agony has gripped and held men's minds, and haunted them, and changed them ; proving itself, far and away, the mightiest moral and spiritual force the world has ever known ; accomplishing impossibilities where everything else that even God could try had failed ! Explain it how you will, it was there, at the Cross, that there rushed in on men's bewildered minds a new, a thrilling, a tremendously exciting conception of what God is really like, and is. So new that, at first, it startled them, it staggered them, it shocked them. How could a holy God, continuing to be holy, so love us, who, even to our own prejudiced eyes, are so unlovable, so soiled, so earthy. Paul tells us candidly that he never even began to understand that. If, he says, musing over it in one place, we had been winsome and attractive folk, but us ! How could it be ? Why should it be ? And yet they knew, and had experienced, that it was true.

And, once it stormed their minds, it held and absorbed them, crowding all other interests into a very secondary place. They brooded over it ; they pondered it ; they lived for it ; they had to share it ; could not be guilty of the selfishness of keeping this amazing good news to themselves. Hence every sea called to them that they had not heard of it upon the other side : and every range of hills beckoned to them to come and spread it farther. And they just had to rise and go. For this thing filled their minds and hearts and lives.

And now! With the passing of the centuries, it has become weathered to our eyes. We have heard it so often that it has grown stale, and commonplace, and platitudinous. Hardly, these days, can you get folk, in any numbers, to listen to what has become for them " a twice told tale, heard by the dull ears of a drowsy man." It raises no excitement, no attention, never a thrill. It bores. They find it dull. Through long familiarity with it, the stab and bite and cutting edge of it are blunted. Nowadays we accept it as the merest matter of course : are not at all taken aback that God should go this length for us. It is His way, we say ; what He is like ; and think no more about it ; come on the cross, and never notice it ; for our unarrested eyes slip over what has been always there.

Were it not well to make the pilgrimage to Calvary ? It is only a little way, and but a low hill when we reach it. To take our stand, and look, and still keep looking, till the fact of it comes home to us burningly again, and the meaning of it soaks into our minds, and the compulsion of it lays its grip upon our hearts and wills !

Santa Teresa, one of the most influential women that ever existed, was, for long years, an entirely undistinguished nun, lost in the mass, putting through, day by day, her offices and her religious duties, timeously and correctly enough, but, so she estimated later, coldly, mechanically, formally, and with hardly a touch of soul in them ; till one day, precisely like any one of all the other hundreds of days, as she was entering the chapel, as she had done every few hours for a full decade, her eyes chanced to fall on the Crucifix, the same crucifix which had confronted her, appealed to her, challenged her, thousands of times. But this time, somehow, she saw it, really saw it, took in at last the meaning and the wonder of it all—that it is only by that agony and bloody sweat, by that Cross and passion, and by the un-reckonable love of God that has gone that length for us, that we can be, and have been, saved ; and, flinging herself on her knees, she dedicated herself there and then, holding back absolutely nothing, to the service of this marvellous Lord who has first so loved us ; and rising up, began a new and thrilling volume in a life, which, from that hour, kept wading deeper, and yet deeper, and still deeper into achievement for her fellows, and communion with God, and fellowship with Jesus Christ.

4

And if we, here to-day, could only see it as she saw it : if the mists and trailing fogs of time, of busyness, of tradition could be blown aside for even a moment long enough to let us really glimpse it, would not the Cross have a like power upon us too ?

Well, standing here on Calvary, and speaking in low hushed tones, must we not tell each other this, to begin—There at last, is a life lived out ; used to the full ; life at its biggest and gallantest and highest. Yes : but you see what follows. Wordsworth tells us sagaciously, that what a great man accomplishes for the world is this —he does something that was never done before ; but which, once it is done, becomes a standard for the rest of us, below which we can no longer be content. That is true, of course, of any number of commonplace things—a motor-car, for instance. Before the war, because most of your neighbours were running their cars, you wanted to have one too. Once it was there, it became a standard, below which you could not be quite satisfied, but felt that, without this which everybody nowadays possessed, you were lagging behind the times, and were being left—old-fashioned and out of date. And one thing the New Testament does for us is to take us out to Calvary, set us down before that central cross, and say—that has been done with a human life, like yours ; and, henceforth, if you have any spiritual sensitiveness in you at all, it has become the standard below which you cannot rest content, but must climb towards it, holding on with hands and feet, and the very curves of your body, with many a slip and backward fall, yet straining towards it—always. For this thing —marvellous though it be, was never intended to be unique and alone—except in degree. Christ, says the Scripture, is the First Born among many brethren, and you and I are meant to be among them.

When that man of fire, Donald Fraser, came home, finally, from his triumphant missionary exploits in Central Africa, the native office-bearers sent him a remarkable minute of thanks, in which they recounted all that he had done for them : how he had found them savages, and left them how immeasurably enriched, lifted up whole centuries above where they had stood, with schools and churches, and fellowship with Jesus Christ : and it all ended with a phrase that deserves to become classic, " we are ashamed we have not caught the infection of a like heart." To be a Christian means to have caught, and to be catching ever more and more, the infection of Christ's heart, Christ's ways, Christ's glorious unselfishness, yes, even of Christ's

Cross. Did not the Master Himself tell us bluntly that a soul is saved, not by one cross only, but by two—His, and its own. Unless, He said, you are prepared to take up your cross—and this, not merely now and then, in an occasional high moment of unusual spiritual purpose, and inspiration, and heroism, but daily, making a settled habit of so doing, and loyally following where My footsteps show the way, My Cross can effect little for you. Whatever Christ has done for us, we are not Christians at all, unless we are learning to catch and reproduce that spirit seen, in fullness, upon Calvary.

Well, what do you say to that, now that we do half see the Cross, and grasp the least of what it means ? Do you resent its claims upon you and recoil from it, angry and frightened and indignant ; crying out, But it's my life : and I must have it for my own purposes and plans and dreams ; aye, and I will ; and so saying, tighten your hold upon it jealously ?

If so, then you are going far to break Christ's heart. " If," He once said, with infinite sadness, " I had not come, they had not had sin. But now they have no cloak for their sin " ; and I, who meant to save them, yearned to save them, gave My all to save them, have landed them in a worse plight, by far, than ever. Do you not see the tragedy of it ? For Christ has brought us light, has shown us what a glorious thing a human life can be, to what heights it can rise, to what lengths it can go, to what thrilling adventures it keeps summoning us ? And you won't have it, and hotly reject it, and clap resolute hands to tight shut eyes to keep out this accursed light, which you don't want to see, and won't see, if you can. It is not, you tell yourself, that you are choosing darkness. No ! no ! only the old restful, lazy twilight ; whereas this blaze of new light hurts the eyes ; and these imperious claims upon us would make life so strenuous and so hot, and so uncomfortable. If this cross is to be the rule and standard, where do I come in ? And what place have I, any more, in my own life ? Why could He not have let us be ? We had no ill-will towards anyone, asked only to be allowed to pursue our own innocent interests, without treading upon anybody's toes. " Sometimes," wrote Didon, " I am afraid that you are not heroic. It is not enough to be merely good.: you must be brave even to heroism." Well ! well ! you say, some are given ten talents spiritually and can ride forth on these gallant adventures ; but for my part, I am not built for such heroics, and will be well content if I can put in a decent quiet and ordered life that does nobody any harm.

But what the Cross claims from us is not merely blamelessness. Christ has, it seems, really no interest in that at all. Yes, yes, He says, almost impatiently, no doubt you were not an actual plague spot infecting and polluting those about you. But what did you do upon the positive side ; how did you tell for Righteousness ; and how is the world around you any better for your passing through ? What rushes in on us at Calvary, as we stand there, facing the Cross, is a new conception of what goodness means : that it is not a careful avoidance of evil, a not-doing this, and a not-being that, but an affection, a passion, an enthusiasm that gives and spends and can't keep back, in short, the very spirit of the Cross ; and nothing less than that, says Christ, will do. Nothing whatever is alleged against Dives, and his business dealings, and his home life, and his character. So far as we are told, he was a worthy and clean-living man. Only, he never looked across the boundaries of his own life, or ran out with helpfulness to those in need of it. And for that, and that alone, he is cast out. The priest and the Levite did no harm. They simply took no notice, not wishing to be mixed up in a messy affair. And for that, for all these centuries, Christ's finger, fixed and unmovable, has pointed steadily at them in utter scorn. The rich young ruler was a blameless lad. Yes, said Christ, but you are doing nothing with your life, except keeping it clean. And you are here to use it. And in the day of Judgment many who have no doubt whatever of their reception will be thunderstruck to find themselves cast out, as people with whom Christ can find nothing in common—not because they had done wrong, but because they were not actively unselfish. Bacon, recounting that strange tale of how Pythagoras claimed to be only a looker-on at life, like a spectator at the games, not himself running, or selling, or the like, but merely watching, adds the still odder comment, " but men must know that, in this theatre of man's life it is reserved only for God and angels to be lookers-on." The angels ! who are a flame of fire, burning themselves away in eager service, yet ever lasting, on and on. And God ! whose name is Love, whose delight is mercy, whose whole being is a divine self-sacrifice. And we must learn their fashion of existence. " At Oxford," said Schechter, " they practise fastidiousness, and imagine they are being holy." That will not do. Whether we like it, or do not, the new light has come. Christ's life and death have given us a far higher standard than we ever had before. And only if our character, held up against that trying background of the Cross, can stand that test, is there a chance for us at all.

For how did Christ save the world ? Always in Scripture the Cross is not just something that happened. It is an eternal divine purpose working itself out. He was not dragged to death by violent hands outside God's ordering of things. God, Himself, gave His Son to die for our salvation. And Christ became our Saviour because willingly, eagerly, and with all His heart, He entered into that tremendous divine plan, and laid all that He had, and was, upon the altar, holding back nothing, was ready to meet any cost and to make any sacrifice, if thereby He could save this foolish, ailing, desperate world. And that, having once been done, has become the new standard ; is what goodness henceforth means. For us, to be a good man, it is not now enough, as it once was, to keep ourselves from actual wrongdoing. We, too, must put our lives into God's hands, daringly, uncompromisingly, asking only this—that in His gracious condescension He will deign to stoop to use us for His glory and our fellow's weal. Must do so. For, whether we break His heart or not, Christ won't consent to lower His standard, won't accept you upon any terms, your terms, but only on His terms. Bluntly, and in so many words, He has adopted, for you and for me, the very test of Thomas, and breaks in upon our glib professions of allegiance with the one proof that will convince Him, " Unless I see in your hands the print of the nails, I will not believe." And where in our soft, flabby hands, where in our easy comfortable lives, where in our conventional, prosaic, unadventurous souls, is there the print of the nails that alone proves to Him that we are really His ?

Ah ! but there is far more in the Cross than that, or else it would drive us to despair. Alexander Whyte declared with vehemence that, with all his princely and colossal gifts, Newman was no real preacher of the Gospel, and this " because he makes Christ look sternly at us even from the Cross." No doubt that Cross has given us a new conception of what goodness means ; no doubt new virtues have sprung into being, that seeded themselves first upon the slopes of Calvary, though the winds of God have carried them, by now, far and wide across the earth ; no doubt that mighty structure so familiar to us now, so little known before Christ's day, that we call charity, the caring for others, the bearing of our brothers' burdens has come into being because Christ died, and, dying, taught us how to live more generously than we had known even to try to do before.

But, if that were all, how terrible a place were Calvary, with a demand on us far more tremendous than that heard upon Sinai itself, though there men's hearts melted with awe and fear. Iago, in the play, speaking of Cassio, a man vastly nobler than himself, grumbled, " He hath a daily beauty in his life that makes me ugly." And is that all that Christ can do for us ? We knew we were poor, ineffective creatures spiritually ; knew that—too often—our wills won't will what they ought to will, nor our fickle hearts choose steadily what we want them to choose ; that, at the best, our best is a poor second best, and frequently much lower even than that ; knew it was muddied and bedraggled figures who have blundered into many a bog and peat-hag, who were stumbling our tired and precarious way home. And then we come on Jesus Christ. And it is far, far worse than we had ever realized ! For that has been done with a human life, like mine ! And this is what I am ! " He hath a daily beauty in His life that makes me ugly." They call Him the Light of the World. But He has only made my darkness visible.

But there is far more in the Cross than that, not merely a new and higher standard, but the power to lift us up to it, and to enable us to live it out. And that is what we need. For the most part we know perfectly well what we ought to do and be. But we can do nothing about it, can't make a start, keep hanging about, futilely enough, waiting for something to turn up to shove us into action. But it never comes.

No one ever stressed duty, and its imperious claims upon us, and the unconditional obedience it demands, and the ennoblement to be found only in its service, as did Kant. Yet that great man was utterly unable to restrain himself from eating sweet and sticky cakes, for which he had a liking, but which made him sick—kept eating them, and being sick. All his high talk about the categorical imperative brought him no help whatever in his childish struggle with his childish weakness, quite failed to give the power to master it—which thing is a half ludicrous and half pathetic illustration of the monstrous fact that august creatures made in the image of Almighty God, and endowed with the mysterious potency of the human will, which has achieved such stupendous and, as was believed for long enough, impossible triumphs, go down tamely and supinely before some illicit craving or unworthy habit, whining that they don't want to do it, but that it is irresistible ; and permit such puny things to lord it over them, for years and years, perhaps for their whole life—know what they ought to do, and yet can't do it.

Time after time the tides of God come in, and reach us, where we lie stranded upon our unlovely mud flats, and cover them with a myriad-twinkling glory of shimmering waters, and lap persistently against us and about us, coaxing, plucking, urging, enticing us out to the cleanness and adventure of the open seas. And we do feel the pull of it, quiver and throb and lift to it ; are all but off, do move. And then the tides recede again, and leave us, high and dry as ever, far up the arid wastes of silt and sand.

Is not that the real tragedy of the times—that, though we did try, and that desperately hard, both nationally and internationally, to bring in the new earth where righteousness could dwell, this charred and blasted world, blown half to ruins, and shocked by the re-emergence into light of day, of dreadful evils, which we had assumed were dead, is all that there is to show for it ?

And this because we thought that we could manage for ourselves, had no need of the Saviour ; required only to gather around a table and confer—for we are all brothers under the skin, and reasonable beings—and everything would run on happily to the end of time. That hope is out : that dream is dead. We have paid down the fee, and it has been a heavy one. But have we learned the lesson—that, as Lippmann says, our times have proved that Christ was right, and that, even with the best of intentions in his heart, " the natural man can only muddle himself into muddle." " All my life," says Seneca, " I have been seeking to climb out of the pit of my besetting sins. And I can't do it : and I never will, unless a hand is let down to me to draw me up." The hand, thank God, is there. And if we have been forced back upon Jesus Christ the Saviour, as the one hope for us who have discovered that we cannot save ourselves—all things are possible. If ! If ! But have we ?

In any case, we might have known that, of ourselves, we could not manage it. All the evidence of all the centuries comes crowding in, with a unanimous testimony as to that. Have you ever tried to help someone caught fast in the toils of a disgraceful failing ? It is a pathetic, a heart-breaking business. The man wants to be free, tries to be free, is free ! And it is over, and the victory won. But no ! For this reason, for that reason, for no reason at all, the old urge suddenly surges up in him again, and he is down once more. It is like a man struggling with an octopus. Madly he slashes at these loathsome arms and clinging tentacles, but always yet another is thrown round him chokingly, and drags him down and under. Or it is like a man caught in a quicksand, who, poor wretch, the more he struggles, sinks the lower, and the lower, until—Good God ! he is gone !

As the old poet put it, writing with a pen dipped in his own agony of foiled endeavours :

> "I like, mislike, lament for what I could not:
> I do, undo, yet still do what I should not:
> And, at the selfsame instant, will the thing I would not."

Or Paul, protesting passionately, "it is not I that do it." I know it is my tongue that speaks the wounding words, I know it is my mind that thinks the unworthy thought. And yet it is not I, not the real I. There are two me's in me—a baser which I repudiate and disown, when I am sane: and a higher, which is the true me. Only, another horrid creature will come, and use my name, and "sit in my clothes," and this obscene thing gets mistaken for me.

Or Augustine. Who can forget the classic passage? And who has not lived it, many a time? "How often have I lashed at my will, and cried Leap now! Leap now! And as I said it, it crouched for the leap, and it all but leapt: and yet it did not leap. And the life to which I was accustomed held me more than the life for which I really yearned!"

It is there, in these desperate straits, that the Cross helps us. How? Well, in one of his prefaces, George Bernard Shaw remarks—as, indeed, many a one has done before him—that people rail against the passions. But, says he, there is nothing amiss with a passion. In fact, the one and only way in which really to conquer any passion is to introduce another and a stronger passion, a new enthusiasm, an overmastering affection that, storming and holding for itself the mind and the attention, will crowd out what used to keep them in perpetual thrall; will leave no room in them for what formerly monopolized them, nor any further interest in it at all. When the big things of real life begin to touch and interest him, a growing lad forgets his toys, and pushes them aside, is done with them. When a clean girl comes into a wastrel's life, idleness and dissipation become tasteless and insipid, perhaps even nauseating; and the lad gains a power and ability to rise above himself into a worthy life, which he just did not have before.

And so with many a help God has contrived for us. But there is nothing like the Cross of Christ for thus winning the heart and holding it, and making it forget and despise, and positively dislike, the ugly things that used to fascinate it; or that gripped it in an unrelaxing vice that would not loosen.

If you ask, how? Well, once, far up the duckboard track towards

Paschendaele—which those of you who were out yonder will agree was, by far, the most eerie and awesome part of the whole front in the last war—I came upon a laddie lying all alone and—dead. I don't know why, out of the multitude that one saw killed, he so impressed me. But he had given his life for us, given it in its spring and its first freshness. And I remember how—all alone there in that grim lonesome wilderness of endless shell holes, mile upon mile of them, like a grey tumbling sea—I pulled off my bonnet, and looking down into the dead eyes, promised him that, because he had done this for us, I would see to it that his sacrifice was not in vain. "I promise you," said I, "that I will be a better man, because you have done this. I promise it."

All which was five and twenty years ago. And, in the main, I have largely forgotten. Yet, even now, at times, it rises up with the old vividness, and stings and shames me towards worthier things.

And can you stand on Calvary, and not be much affected, or indeed even interested : look for a little, turn upon your heel and drift away —exactly as you came ? Make trial of it here and now, and test if that be possible. Look ! this is the very spot where Paul once stood—you are upon it now !—and, when he faced the Cross, as you are doing, it mastered him, haunted him, became the centre round which everything must henceforth turn. And does your heart remain quite cool, entirely unexcited, unarrested, and unchanged ?

Some of us find it difficult these days to pray the prayer which Christ has taught us. For the words " Give us this day our daily bread " stick in the throat, and will not utter, when one thinks out the cost of what we claim so lightly ; the vessels sinking yonder on the high seas, the lives that go out under these great waters, the anxious ones that wait, and watch, for those who do not come, until the dreadful truth breaks in on them, and a great emptiness rushes into their hearts : the fond young dreams that suddenly are blotted out ; and life becomes a drab thing, bleached and faded, and to be endured—does not the heart cry out No ! No ! dear God, but rather spare the seafaring men and lads, and we will do with less ! And can we accept God's unspeakable gift as no great matter, and a thing of course ?

Long years ago, George Adam Smith once told me how he had once travelled in a train with a young Romanist priest, about to set sail as a missionary, to a part of Africa where, in those days, a white man's life was reckoned, not by years, but months, and was upon his way to say good-bye to his mother for ever upon this side of the grave. And Smith reasoned with him, agreed that he must give his life to Jesus Christ whole-heartedly and without reservation. But why, he urged, throw it away? Why not rather use it for long years in His service? Why let it blaze up, and so die to darkness, like a thorn bush crackling a moment and then gone? Were it not better, for Christ's sake, to think things out again? And, even when the lad had alighted, Smith still leaned from the window, and still pled with him. And the boy smiled and lifted up the cross he wore, and looked at it, and answered only this, but with immense unshakable conviction, "He loved me, and gave Himself for me. And I, can I hold back?"

Whether he was right or whether he was wrong, I do not know. But I know this. You too Christ loved; and for you too He gave Himself. And from His Cross He cries to you, "Is it nothing to you, all ye that pass by?"

And do you pause and look Him in the eyes, and think it out, and answer, "Well, not much," and stroll away?

CHAPTER VI

ON CHRIST'S STRANGE CONFIDENCE IN US

" Ye have not chosen Me, but I have chosen you, and ordained you, that you might go and bring forth fruit ; and that your fruit might remain."—JOHN xv. 16.

THAT, surely, is the last and crowning wonder that leaves one staring with minds dazed and stunned. For it is not, you see, that you came upon Jesus Christ, and that your heart, stormed by the sheen and splendour that He has woven out of the selfsame stuff of which your bungling fingers have made only this, which, in comparison with Him, so shames you, burst from your control, and broke away, ran to Him, clung to Him, refusing to be shaken off, beseeching Him to lift you up a little way out of this drabness that you are toward all that glory which He is—all which would have been natural enough. But it was not that. He it was who came on you, turned, and looked after you, said, There is a man to whom My heart is drawn, and out of whom I know that I can fashion something of eternal value. You did not choose Me ; it is I who have chosen you. Yet that is the plain truth, and it is characteristic of Him.

Always when He was here on earth, He was oddly original in the folk that interested Him. All Jericho was a tumult of welcome. Yet Christ who had so little to encourage Him, was not much helped by that noisy enthusiasm, kept looking as He passed along the eager, crowding, shouting streets for something deeper, something better, something more, till His eyes, at long last, lit upon a face, and stayed, seeing in it what He was seeking. A daft choice of a friend, or even a disciple, a ruinous action that spoiled everything, and froze an outraged Jericho at once into a cold and settled loss of all belief in Him—the kind of thing that nobody with any common sense, or even a touch of practical wisdom, could ever have even thought of doing ! And yet that was the man in all these crowds who interested Christ, and of whom He had hope, and upon whom, with that magnificent confidence of His, He threw Himself unhesitatingly.

Queer people indeed ! Once, you remember, it was a woman of the streets, a poor, soiled, friendless, heartsick creature. And now—it is you.

The saints are all bewildered by it, and can see no sense in it. A wondering Christina Rossetti—

> "It was not that I cared for Thee,
> But Thou didst set Thy love upon
> Me, even me, Thy little one";

a confused, almost hot-cheeked Brother Lawrence, feeling uncomfortably that there must be a huge mistake somewhere, and, with painful honesty, reminding Christ of his unfaithfulnesses and unworthinesses, holding them up, he says, before Him, so that He could not fail to see them; and yet confessing that it makes no difference; that, knowing all there is to know, Christ still keeps heaping benefits upon him: a Paul, declaring that he can make nothing of Christ's really preposterous loving-kindness to a man like him, unless, indeed, it be that the Lord wished to have one test case—a final and unanswerable thing—to which He could point, all the ages down, and so triumphantly meet every possible doubt that could ever arise in anybody's mind, and counter every conceivable difficulty or objection in any and in every hesitating soul which cannot bring itself to credit that it can all be really meant for him.

And, in truth, Christ does choose singular companions. Give me twelve men, He said, the right twelve, and I will save the world. Well, He got them: Himself chose them, and an impossible looking lot they seem to be, these closest friends of His! Two of them were continually blazing up into temper. Was that why they were called our Sons of Thunder? And one of them, finding himself in sudden peril, could and did curse like a trooper, and lie shamelessly. And another was so slow to pick up even the beginnings of it all that even the patient Christ was openly startled, frankly taken aback. "Have I been so long time with you, and yet hast thou not known Me!" And certain of them were so unimpressive and ordinary that none of the four evangelists could come upon a single soul who could remember even one thing they ever said, or ever did—not one! And one of them fell clean away, and into a horror of sin that, ever since, has shocked a by no means squeamish world. And all of them seem, to us looking back at them, dull and material and unspiritual, and quite unworthy of their privileges.

And yet Christ chose them "that they might be with Him"—partly for their sakes, of course, that He might gradually train them into some understanding of it all—yet partly for His own sake too. Because He liked them, trusted them, found that it helped Him to have them beside

Him, and that, as in the Garden, He felt steadier, and less alone, when they were there.

And now He has chosen you, says to you what Paul said to the Corinthians, " A fair exchange, as the children have it ; your heart for Mine." That is what dazed the Calvinists with their talk of election. Stupid people—too stupid to realize the wonder of Christ's call—condemn them as proud and uplifted. But it was the very opposite. They are confused, bewildered, taken aback ; can find no reason whatsoever why they should be in Christ ; and nothing in themselves that can even begin, even remotely, to explain why this tremendous thing has come to them. Why should it ? And how could it, they being only what they are ? And yet they know that it is true. Christ must have stooped to call them, and to draw them, and to lay insistence on their own unwillingness. There is no other explanation possible. They did not choose Him. He chose them. But why ? They do not know ; they cannot see. And yet about the thing itself, they dare not doubt. And some of us, too, are as puzzled by it, yet as sure of it, as that. Montaigne was once musing on the great friendship of his life. Why is it, he asked, that we have been so much to one another, you and I ? And he could find no more definite, or statable answer than this—it was because I was I, and because you were you, and we fitted in to one another. And it looks, does it not, as if there must be something of that between Christ and you ? Else why has He chosen you to be with Him ?

And, in a kind of a way, one can begin at least dimly to understand it. Suppose you had been lost for years in the centre of China, with nothing round about you, month in and month out, but Chinese eyes, and Chinese faces, and Chinese ways—a great and noble people truly, but not your own folk. And suppose that, suddenly, round the corner of a crooked lane, there came a Scotsman, any kind of a Scotsman, the shabbiest figure, if you like, that ever bore that name. Would not your heart run out to him, shabby or no ; and thrill to his homely accent ? Would you not sit down on the bank with him, and cheer yourself by talk with him, finding—hugely unlike though you might be in almost everything—that you had much in common, seeing that you both hailed from the old grey motherland across the seas. And it would seem that Christ has something of that feeling when He comes on you. In the days of His flesh it was lonesome for Him, surrounded, for the most part, towards the end, by cold and critical faces that never lit up at the sight of Him, and hard, unmoved, disbelieving eyes ; by hearts that obviously resented Him, disliked Him, hated Him the length of Calvary. And it is lonesome for Him still. He knocks at a door, and they pay no manner of attention ; and at another, and they look out, and say, " It is only Christ. There is no need to hurry about Him. Plenty time yet, before we have to deal with Him and His bothersome claims upon us." And it matters to Him that, often and scandalously though you forget Him, when you do hear His hand upon the door, you run to open it, and draw Him in, and give Him the first place, and let Him see the difference it makes to you now He is here. Well, although Himself so lavish and so generous a Giver, He always was the most grateful of Receivers, much cheered by little nothings that, in our judgment, were no great affairs, and not worth all He made of them—that woman's jest, half crying, that leapt out of a desperate heart ; that barrack-square type of faith of a bluff soldier man ; that cry bursting from a soul half delirious with hideous pain—how much they meant to Christ ! And, to-day, He is grateful, the Lord Jesus Christ is grateful, the Son of God Most High is grateful, for the poor broken bits of faith and of affection you are half ashamed to bring to Him at all.

And, having chosen you, He holds to it, does not lose heart, and send you back, and try someone else more likely to succeed than you, with your innumerable failures, and the endless disappointments you have caused Him. No. Those who knew Him best have set this down as absolutely characteristic of Him—that, " having loved His own that were in the world, He loved them unto the end." I chose you, so He says, and, knowing all there is to know, the very worst, I stand to it still.

One of our poets writing to the man who had been most to him, admits that his own life had been a tame and colourless affair of little things put through, in a dull, petty way, with nothing memorable in it. And then he takes that back, and sets down, with enormous pride, two glories that can never he wrenched from him. " For I was Shakespeare's countryman. And wert not thou my friend ? " And if the Lord Christ stoops to call us as disciples, and to treat us as His friends—it is His own chosen name for the relationship that He desires between us, superseding lesser and more lowly ones—what honour can life give us that can be compared to that ?

Yet there is more and better. More ! you cry incredulously, better ! Yes, far more, and vastly better. You can never exhaust Jesus Christ. On to the endless end of an unending eternity, He will be still surprising us, still heaping further gifts upon us. So here. I have chosen you, He says, speaking to simple souls like you and me, because I know you have it in you to be of real and signal service to Me and the cause, to bring forth fruit that will not simply play its insignificant part and so pass away, but will remain, and tell for Me far down the years, long after you yourself have faded out of human memory. And that, surely, is a wonderful thing, and a right gracious saying, that thrills and excites the heart. Aristotle, drawing for us his ideal man, declares that he will give to all and sundry lavishly, but he will not accept from any one. For that would be to demean himself. But Christ is far above such pettiness. He deigns to stoop to take from our soiled hands, and to lean plans, very near His heart, against our frail loyalties ; assures us we can carry through for Him what He much needs, and eagerly desires.

At which, our hearts, like Sarah, may break into open and incredulous laughter at what is obviously impossible for us, so depressingly ordinary, and so meanly endowed. Yet, if Christ says it is so, then, be sure, it is so, unlikely though it be.

There was a day when everyone was laughing in the little groups at the street corners in the town. For a ridiculous rumour was blowing about the place that Christ had called Matthew the publican ! But that, of course, was nonsense ; must be only a wicked gibe born in some merry jester's brain. They knew their Matthew, the last man in the world to leave his money bags and fare forth on such a fool-hardy adventure. So they tittered and guffawed, and passed on the ludicrous tale. Yet next morning they looked foolish and their laughter died away, when it was noised abroad, and was substantiated—that Matthew had gone ! It had been in the man, though not one soul, except Christ, had ever suspected it. And if He looks at you, and asks it of you, it is in you too.

There was a laddie who kept pestering his mother to let him go and see and hear this prophet of whom every one was talking, now He had come into their countryside. And she put him off, no doubt, told him he was too young, and wouldn't understand, or really enjoy it. But he kept bothering her, as a boy will, until, at last, she made up some sandwiches for him—as we would say—and sent him off. And that night he came bursting in to tell her of the miracle that "I and Jesus did !" Put you into these same wonderful hands the little that you have to give Him, and there is no saying what He will not manage to do with that too.

At which you break in impatiently—fine words enough, no doubt, only they are meaningless and empty. Face facts and tell me what I, in my rushed bustle of a life of little nothings that absorb all my energies and thoughts and days, can possibly do for Jesus Christ.

Well, to begin with, you can pray. Pray! you say scornfully, pray! I knew it would all fizzle out, and come to nothing. I could pray!

Yes, you could pray and, whatever you may think about it, using it as a poor makeshift of a thing much lower than a second best, not really a best at all, on which men fall back only when they can do nothing effective, and are too fidgety to be able to do nothing at all, Christ holds that prayer is a tremendous power which achieves what, without it, was a sheer impossibility. And this amazing thing you can set into operation. And the fact that you are not so using it, and simply don't believe in it and its efficiency and efficacy, as our fathers did, and that so many nowadays agree with you, is certainly a major reason why the churches are so cold, and the promises seem tardy of fulfilment. That mighty preacher, Thomas Chalmers, was once pondering over why, in spite of all his efforts and enormous popularity, there was not more spiritual outcome to show for it all, and came to this of it—that he was trusting to his " own animal heat and activity " rather than to the Holy Ghost. And is not that a shrewd and accurate diagnosis of the Church's ailment in our day ? Never was there a ministry so bustled and rushed and perspiring as ours is now. If things stick, we devise yet another type of meeting, and when this additional wheel is spinning round with all the rest of the complex machinery, and a wind is blowing in our hot faces, we feel better, and have a comfortable sense that something is going on ; are tired and sticky, but happy engineers. But the whole point of the ministry, the reason why there is a ministry at all, is that people out in the press of life and finding that there they cannot keep in sigh of God but get continually drifted away from Him, that the little matters to which it is their duty to attend, of necessity crowd Him out of their preoccupied minds—lay hands upon a man, praying him, " Live in the secret of God's presence ; and in the hush there, which we cannot know, commune with Him face to face ; and week by week, come out and share with us the message which, in that stillness, you have had a chance of hearing. We'll pay you for it, man, if you will only do it ! " But now the ministry is every whit as busy as the rest of folk ; and, in the roar of its machinery, can hear no more than anybody else. If only we would pray ! But we, too, put our trust in our own animal heat and hard breathing activity. Macaulay's fault, said that shrewd judge, Lord Cockburn, is " that he is always over-talking, and so always under-listening." So is the ministry these days. And, as Euripides reminds us, " even Zeus cannot reveal Himself to a busy body."

And if the people, one by one, would prepare for the services, and so create the atmosphere of faith and of expectancy which even Christ required, and without which even He was largely thwarted, if they would make conscience of it, and with ardour fulfil their part in the House of God, things would happen, even where the minister is not, in himself, much help. In 1492 certain Mahayana Buddhists, officially laid down suggestions to make their worship of Kwan-yin effective and resultful. " One hour before, and after, service there should be no mixed conversation," so the Imperial preface runs. " The mind should be chiefly occupied in considering and weighing the nature of the vows entered upon. The thoughts should be so occupied without intermission. Even whilst eating and drinking such thoughts should be persevered in, nor should the impressions received be lost. But if, at time of devotion, there be no devotional thoughts, but only a confused way of going through external duties : and if, after worship, there be indifferent conversation, and babbling, and hurrying to and fro, lounging about or sleeping, just as on ordinary days : if there be such criminal acts of careless self-indulgence, what benefit or assistance can we look for from our religious exercises ? " Do you and I do anything along these lines at all ? What, for example, are you really saying when, on entering the church, you bow your head in prayer ? Sometimes, one fears, not much. Is it not often a convention to which many conform, as the thing that is done—formally and mechanically and little more ? Muhammed tells us that his prayer before the service started was, " O Lord, open the gates of Thy compassion to us, and let us enter in." And if, in that hush, before the minister appears, you were asking that God's Holy Spirit might be given to him and to you, and to your fellow-worshippers, and that the hour might be a meeting with God face to face, would it not be far likelier to prove nothing less than that ?

None the less, our churches are not factories where religion is woven, but, rather, power-houses, from which the energy is drawn

5

for living it out elsewhere. And what, out in the world, where my main life must be spent, can I do for Jesus Christ ?

Well, again to begin with, Luther never could see that, for a Christian, this distinction that we draw so deep between sacred and secular was a sound one, or had much real meaning. For a Christian dedicates everything to his Master, and does all that he does do for His glory, serving no man, and still less merely his own selfish interests, but the Lord Jesus Christ. " A shoemaker, a smith, a peasant, any one, has the office and work of his trade and yet, at the same time, are all consecrated bishops and priests." " Now I am cooking, making a bed, sweeping the house. Who has bid me do this ? My master or mistress ? Yet it may be true that I serve, not only them, but God in heaven. It is just as if I had to cook for God in heaven Himself." If we could get that back into people's minds instead of the snarling, snobbish discontent with, and contempt of, honest labour, as an intolerable drudgery to be got through, all life would be a temple, and all work be worship.

But, that apart, what can you do for Christ ? you ask. Are you a mother ? Then you can so live in the home, selflessly and cheerfully under the daily strain of things that, years after you are dead, your children will affirm with confidence, " You can say what you like about the Christian faith, but I saw it lived out in my mother, and know it is the finest thing in the whole world, and mean to gain that which she had." That is what you can do for Jesus Christ, and not one other in this crowded earth can do that for Him—only you.

Or are you a plain, shy man who could not put two sentences of prayer together before your family ? Still, you can so carry yourself before the eyes of your home folk that, later, at the other end of the world, your boy, faced by some ugly temptation, will start back as from an insult, crying out angrily, instinctively, without knowing that he is doing it, ." My God, no ! not my father's son." That is what you can do for Jesus Christ ; and nobody can do that for Him, except you. So, in degree, with all our manifold human relationships. " A character," said Dean Inge, " can't be confuted." People may not be interested enough in Christianity to listen to its case, or they may scoff it out of court, or may be stumbled by real difficulties in their path. But when they see a really Christian man, and watch the thing being lived out, there is no answering that ! " He made me a Christian," said Stanley about Livingstone, " and he never knew that he was doing it ! " The unbeliever was not preached into the faith. He saw the faith in operation ; and that did it. And we are meant to live so close to Christ our Lord that some touch of His glory, dimly reflected upon us, will make those among whom we mingle think of Him, and own that plain and ordinary folk can grow into His ways.

And we shall have plenty of opportunities to tell for Him of which we never hear and never know. I have read that, in his student days, Grenfell was not a markedly religious man ; but once he turned into a meeting at which the speaker, at the close of his address, rightly or wrongly, asked those who wished to declare for Christ to stand. And not one soul responded, except one small lad from a training ship, who rose and stood alone. And Grenfell, picturing the torrent of ridicule and badinage and worse which was bound to surge about the little man, wondered what he could do to help him, and made up his mind. It will be somewhat easier for him if there are two of us, he thought ; and he too rose and gave himself to Jesus Christ. I don't know what became of the lad from the training ship. Perhaps they laughed him out of it that very night. But I know this—that all that marvellous work in Labrador can, in a very real sense, be with justice set down to his credit. For had it not been for him, it might never have been at all. So, in ways of which we never know, we all keep getting chance on chance to tell for Jesus Christ.

And, indeed, Christ staked everything upon plain, ordinary, one-talented folk like us not failing Him. " Ye are the light of the world," He said, set here so to live that, without dreaming that you are doing it, you will show others the way home, and the fullness of life and being ; elected to work, in the main, through individuals ; sure that the thing will spread from heart to heart, and life to life. Our hopes, these days, are all upon the system. Change, purify, ennoble that, and everything else will follow, is the axiom on which we build. And, with our own eyes we have seen, in our own day, how deeply, drastically, unbelievably a people can, in twenty years, be moulded out of all likeness to itself—for evil, or for good.

Yet Christ holds to it that, immensely and even stunningly effective and resultful though it seems, that is, at most, a superficial method, and no real cure at all. And here, as elsewhere, Christ is right. And, if we refuse to believe Him, and try lesser, easier things, as in themselves enough, wherewith to solve our intricate problems, our sad experience and inevitable disillusionment will prove that to us once again.

" The activities and aims of our time," says Schweitzer, " are penetrated by a kind of obsession that if only we could succeed in perfecting or reforming the institutions of our public and social life, the progress demanded by civilization would begin of itself. But civilization can only revive when there shall come into being in a number of individuals a new tone of mind, independent of the prevalent one among the crowd, and in opposition to it—a tone of mind which will gradually win influence over the collective one, and in the end determine its character. Only an ethical movement can rescue us from barbarism, and the ethical comes into existence only in individuals."

It must begin, as Christ said long ago, in you, and you, and you, and me. Hartmann has a gripping passage on what he calls the noble, on those daring pioneers who are always running on ahead of the mass of men, seeing farther than they see, and daring farther than those others will attempt, who gradually teach the rest of men a more adventurous conception of goodness, filling the word with richer content ; and when slowly the mass have at length responded to that, and have appropriated it, run on ahead again, enticing these slow-footed folk still farther, by their own intrepidity, and the dazzling discoveries it makes. And Christ calls you to be one of those daring and audacious pioneers, to live ahead of your times, to show that something " more than others " He expects in all His folk, that touch of originality, and courage, and Christlikeness, by which the world is slowly taught, and lifted up above itself.

And you who, perhaps, whimper that your life is tame and dull and boring have been chosen by Christ Himself for that adventurous vocation.

As Brunner puts it very grandly, " Justification by grace alone means that God has accepted us as recruits in His army ; once this has taken place, we can go forth bearing on our banners the amazing device : " Fit for the service of God." " This is indeed the grace of God that God calls a man just as he is into His service : that God does not consider this particular person, just as he is, too bad for His service. The call, which reaches man in his sinfulness, places him, sinful as he is, in the service of God. For if man were to try first of all to make himself fit for this service, he would never do anything at all.

Come, just as you are, in your dirty, torn, everyday clothes." And Jesus Christ says all that hopefully, looking at you and me, and meaning it of us. It is all very wonderful, and thrilling, and tremendously exciting : and makes the simplest life gloriously worth while.

CHAPTER VII

THE EFFICIENCY OF CHRISTIANITY

" I am not ashamed of the Gospel of Christ. It is the power of God unto salvation to every one that believes."—Rom. i. 16.

THAT is a proud boast, face to face with this desperate world. And it admits, you note, no exceptions whatsoever. Any one, every one, the least likely, the most obviously out of the question, any one at all who wishes it, and will accept it, can become the possessor of a power to which all things are possible—yes, even that which you instinctively rule out as too good to be true ; yet even that is true, and true for you, if you will have it so. For the entire illimitable energies of God, a God who has achieved such incredible things, creating this immense and orderly universe out of a blank nothingness ; and from a little dust, august creatures who will last as long as God Himself ; whose thoughts are not as our thoughts, but unfathomable in their length, and breadth, and height, and depth, and sheer tremendousness, before which our human faculties, daring and adventurous though they be, sink, dazed, and stunned, and blinded by excess of light—this God has concentrated all His infinite resources of wisdom, and love, and patience, and self-sacrifice upon the saving of that needy soul, which looks trustingly towards Him : so that unless the Almighty can be foiled, and an eternal love be tired out and broken, and God prove Himself, at long last, insufficient for a task to which He has set Himself, that soul is going to be saved. It is the power of God to every one who believes.

So certain, indeed, are these men of the efficiency of Jesus Christ to save and uplift, and this after a prolonged experience that keeps making them ever surer, and after watching Him at work in innumerable cases of all possible types, that they are willing to take any one at all as a test case : to take you, for example, and that where your life has broken down, where you—daunted and discouraged—have lost heart and stopped trying, sulkily convinced that for you it is impossible ; or recognizing, with a too tardy alarm, that the penalty of thoughtless and light-hearted failings in the past have come upon you ; that, brick by brick, you have built yourself, with your own fool's hands, into the prison of a personality from which you cannot escape now. To all which they listen ; and, denying not one word of what you say, are still utterly sure that you need not continue as you are one moment longer ; that, if you give Him any chance at all, Christ can work what you need in you. Indeed, they feel that there is no risk in so holding. For they walk now, not as at the first, by pure and venturesome faith, but founding solidly upon what they have proved, and that over and over.

In the Early Church there was very little confession or petition in their services compared to the place we give these now. It was, in the main, a wondering, astounded, adoring thanksgiving. For these people had found what the whole world had been seeking : and it worked ! And, when they came to God, it was to bless, and praise, and magnify Him, for the mystery of His forgiveness, for the lengths, past reckoning by human standards, to which His love has gone for them ; and that He has found what He sought, has arrested them, and changed them out of all recognition ; that day by day and all the day, He keeps them from falling, as they always used to do, and gives them ever new and more convincing evidence that His grace is sufficient for every possible call upon it ; and that His strength, fa from being baffled, is made perfect in their weakness.

Pliny reported to the Emperor that the thing most noticeable about this new sect was that they kept singing in their little meeting-places, as other people did not do—kept singing hymns to Christ as God. And so, indeed, they did, with hearts that could not thank enough for all the difference He had made for them, and in them— for settled habits that were snapt, for temptations that had lost their grip upon them ; for alien virtues beginning, at least, to show through the unlikely soil of their characters and minds ; that though, like Lazarus, they had lain long dead in trespasses and sins, they too had heard that voice of power bidding them come forth ; and they had wakened out of their sleep of death, and had arisen into a newness of life ; and though, bound hand and foot by grave clothes, they could only shuffle helplessly, over them also Christ had said, " Loose him, and let him go " ; and they were free—with the joy of the Lord as their strength, with the peace of God that passeth understanding in their hearts, with the life that is life indeed, making the so-called life they used to know how tame, and dull, and shabby, a gift put anew every morning into their hands by Christ's— another whole full glorious day of it !

And in many a life about them they watched the same amazing

transformation, and kept gaining ever new corroboration of their own experience, saw drab and ordinary people changed, transfigured, glorified, touched by something of the sheen of heaven even here and even now. There was no limit to this thing. Given a weariness of what one is, a yearning after something bigger, and a belief that God can help and will help, and the poorest creature, a mere mush of concession, whom any one can squeeze to any shape, morally flabby, spiritually ineffective, whose loud and truculent defiances that sound so final and purposeful quickly evaporate in tame submissions and abject surrenders—that floppy, spineless thing, not worth the name of man, can regain self-respect, stand up on his own feet, become master in his own life, and use it with dignity and honour for high and worthy ends. We guarantee it, so these folk who have proved it over and over tell us with an absolute assurance—guarantee it to you. " It is no weak Christ with whom you have to do," said Paul to the Corinthians, "but a Christ of power." Our Physician, cry these men, does heal : and our Saviour does save. "I was once a wild thing on the coast of Africa," said John Newton, " but the Lord caught me, and tamed me : and now people come to see me like the lions in the Tower. Doubt if the Lord can convert the heathen ! Look at me ! "

Yet that odd person, Mr. Wells, a man of many talents but of no discernible soul, blandly remarks, " Why go on pretending about this Christianity ? At the test of war, disease, social injustice, every human distress it fails, and leaves a cheated victim." As for Jesus, " he was some fine sort of man perhaps ": but our Saviour of the Trinity is an ugly monstrosity " making vague promises for the cheating of simple souls, an ever absent help in times of trouble. Christianity is a silly story." What kind of reading of history is that ? It is not only in the New Testament that men burst in, with shining eyes and hearts on fire, bewildered by what Christ has done for them, and keeps on doing hour by hour. It is not only from the heavenly places that there blows back to us that shout of rejoicing from innumerable souls, for whom the promises have all come true, and the dream is the only reality, giving Christ thanks and praise for the grace that was sufficient, and the strength that was enough. In every age, from every land, in this present world of ours rises that ever-growing and unanimous testimony from hearts of the most diverse types, and out of circumstances the most dissimilar, that this thing works, has worked in them, is working for them now ; enabling them to hold out, and to do and to be, what, without it, would have been utterly impossible : that Christ stands to the most dazzling of His promises ; that even after all their experiences of Him, He keeps surprising them by the fullness of His sufficiency for every emergency ; that however big and audacious are the hopes which they have come to set in Him, He keeps making them look tawdry and unadventurous, keeps doing " exceedingly abundantly above all that they can ask or think." And this tremendous record of achievement in innumerable lives, thinks Mr. Wells, is " a silly story," and a sorry tale of impudent failure ! To which we can only reply, with Euripides, " When once I had seen the truth, there was no drug that I could take to unsee it, and lose again what I had seen."

Jung, a real man of science, has no doubt at all of the reality of Christianity and of its power to work out into solid and indisputable facts its most extraordinary claims. With an unparalleled audacity, it sets itself what seems an obviously impossible task ; declares that the slow, hesitating process of evolution from such crude beginnings, from mere living hungers, nothing more, up and up through gradually emerging elaborations and instincts and ennoblings until at long last there appear the beginnings of a brain, and so, with huge and yawning chasms of unthinkable time between each step of the precarious advance, on and still on, until the dignity of man is reached— that the long climb does not end there, as science seems to hold. Let a man give himself to Jesus Christ, and there develops a new creature— strangely new. For, by a step more radical and revolutionary than any of those that preceded it, the natural man attains a higher type of being, and finds himself endowed with new likes, new dislikes, new affections, new desires, new instincts, new possibilities and powers— lives life in quite a different and infinitely fuller way. That is the proud claim of this faith, says Jung, and adds : " And you can't laugh it out of court, because it has done it ! And, every day, we meet such new creatures in the street."

It is an amazing adventure to meet Jesus Christ ! Where He is, life becomes a bigger thing ; and must be lived more royally—both must, and can. " Go with mean people," says Emerson, " and you think life is mean. Then read Plutarch, and the world is a proud place, with heroes and demigods standing round us, who will not let us sleep." But, says the Scripture, live in fellowship with Christ, and you will grow into His likeness, and put on His mind, and learn to live after His way !

That is the claim thrown down to any, and to every, one on every page of the New Testament.

In view of all which, are you never taken aback that only such a muted echo of all that comes from your own experience ? Lay your character beside the promises and the unanimous testimony of the saints ; and, against that shining background, does not anything you have to show look drab and colourless, tame and unexciting ? It is not that Christ has failed you. This and this He has wrought for you, wonderful things indeed. Yet, you may sometimes feel, that even so, what you have experienced might have been summed up in much smaller words than the breath-taking promises. Arthur Balfour, the Premier, far on in his life, was looking back across the long years that he had travelled, and discovered, with amazement, that he was still, in all essential features, the same being he was as a boy at Eton—identically so. The thing, he said, alarmed him—that all the discipline of his full life, playing on him for all those decades, had effected so little, had left him, radically, what he was, and fundamentally unchanged. And you may sometimes feel that Christianity has not been so markedly efficient in your case, as witnesses innumerable find it ; that you would hardly claim to be a new creature, but at the best and most a slightly expurgated edition of your original self ; that life runs on, and leaves you—Christ or no Christ—still a discouragingly familiar figure. Or perhaps you have come to accept it as inevitable, and are no longer startled and almost shocked, that all this is what is promised, and that only that is what you are.

Watson, the poet, tells how certain captives, immured in their prison, learn from the warders' casual talk that Spring is once more making her triumphal progress through the land. But it does not excite them, hardly even interests them. For them " it is a legend empty of concern : and idle is this rumour of the rose." Spring for the happier folk outside, no doubt. But not for them. No roses will bloom on their grey imprisoning walls, no flowers break through and colour the dull paving-flags round which they pace in exercise. And have we come to this of it, that, while glorious rumours, rather authenticated records, of what Christ is doing in other lives keep blowing in on every wind, it is for us " a legend emptied of concern "? It will not happen to us, we say ; and so, with unlit, vacant faces, we keep trudging round and round on the hard paving-stones of our besetting failings, penned hopelessly within the straitening and unscalable walls of our characteristic ways ?

Why is it that the proved efficiency of Christianity has not fully worked out in your particular case, or mine ? And how can we set it

in motion in our lives, as in so many others ? " Religion," thought
Lord Morley at one point of his life, " is a belt that has slipped off
the driving-wheel of the world."   How can we get the belt on to the
driving-wheel, and gain results and outcome ?

Is it unfair to suggest that, in some of us at least, it hasn't fully
worked so far, simply because, at the pinch, at the decisive moment,
we don't want it to work, or ourselves to be lifted up above the failings
and disloyalties we find so alluring, but rather to be enabled to continue them without the ugly consequences of so doing, to have the
inexorable laws of life bent aside in our favour, so that we can squeeze
through and escape, without reaping what we have sown ; because,
as we misunderstand it, the whole point of the good news our Lord
brings is the, to us, gladsome announcement that God is happily
much more morally indifferent than our consciences had thought, and
is not going to make a fuss about our sins and such-like trivial pecca-
dilloes, but will surely let us off ; because in fact, we have not grasped
that the core and essence of the Gospel, what makes it a Gospel at all,
is its tremendous and glorious revelation of how deadly is God's hatred
of sin, so that He cannot stand having it in the same universe as Himself, and will go any length, and will pay any price, and will make any
sacrifice, to master and abolish it—is set upon so doing in our hearts,
thank God, as elsewhere.   Yet it is certain that some of us are less
anxious and careful to avoid sin now that they know the hugeness of
God's mercy, and His divine readiness to forgive, long after every
human heart must have been tired out and exasperated into anger,
than they would have been, had they continued to believe that His
wrath must, and will, flash out in swift, inevitable, ruthless retribution.

If so, that surely is the saddest fact in human history—that Christ
should die for us ; and we be worse, not better, for it !   Is there a word
even in Scripture which so haunts and shames as that cry from the
Master's breaking heart, " If I had not come, they had not had sin ;
but now they have no cloke for their sin."   There is a horror in that
that grips one chokingly.   How dreadful if our last sight of Christ
should be what miserable Judas saw, when, slipping from the upper
room, his mind made up at last, he turned to draw the door behind
him, and met Christ's eyes, how full of agony, not for Himself, or what
He knew was coming (" What thou doest, do quickly "), but for a
man He loved who could do this ; whom He had tried to save, and,
with deliberation, he had chosen darkness rather than the light and
was far worse for knowing Christ, instead of better !   How dreadful

if we, too, at last go out into the night, haunted for ever by those eyes, that we cannot forget !   Dear God, not that !

But there are others who do want this thing to work, yet it is all dreamy, and nebulous, and in the future tense ; an agreeing in theory, yet doing nothing practical. And the years run on and on, and there is still little to show.   " The harvest is past, the summer is ended, and we are not saved." In his *Lives of the Poets*, Johnson has a vivid photograph of Gray, and the fiasco of his abortive professorship at Cambridge.   " He accepted, and retained it to his death ; always designing lectures, but never reading them ; uneasy at his neglect of duty, and appeasing his uneasiness with designs of reformation, and with a resolution, which he believed himself to have made, of resigning the office, if he found himself unable to discharge it." That, surely, is a cruelly lifelike description of too many spiritual careers—always designing what is never done ; uneasy, and appeasing the uneasiness with brave plans of reformation that fizzle out, and come to nothing, are indeed never begun ; believing that they have made resolutions, which never materialize.

It is a mood and a spiritual disease which Johnson himself knew well, and had constantly to strive against. He was the Rasselas who " spent four months in resolving to waste no more time in idle resolves." And you and I have spent much more than that in the same futile fashion. If we will really go to Christ, not simply think of going : and really close with Christ, not merely agree that it must be done, and will be done, is going to be done—some day : and really stride out boldly on to His promises here and now, risking our whole weight on them ; acting on the assumption they are true, and true for us, we too would find them so.

And some of us do try. But, somehow, the accustomed sins continue to beset us, though Paul assures us that sometimes at least one is lifted clean above them, so that we are not merely conquerors, and that where we had always failed, but more than conquerors, no longer even needing to resist, but living in an ordered peace, where there had been ruin and chaos and constant defeat. Some of us know that that is literally true, have had experience of it. For years we strove, and failed : and then suddenly, in a moment almost, it had come, and we were lifted up above it all, and out of range of the temptation that had proved so devastating.

Dostoievsky was an inveterate gambler, and sank lower and lower through his vice. Though struggling desperately against it, he was helpless. The sturdiest resolutions snapped, the most sincere and passionate repentances passed, at a step, to a renewal of the weakness, and another fall. The man was heart-sick, ashamed, desperate : yet for years the disgrace went on and on. And suddenly one day it ended. He felt that it had ended, and it had. So that, although he lived above a gambling den, and had to pass its door each time that he went in or out, not once, ever again, had he the slightest inclination to a sin that had for years and years bullied him at its pleasure, and reigned over him, an irresistible conqueror—not even once !

But many know little or nothing of that ; sway all their days in a surging and uncertain battle, now forward and now back : have come to believe, with Stevenson, that the best that can be hoped for meantime is " not to succeed but—to continue to fail in good spirits." And for that they are prepared, with a dogged obstinate courage that, downed innumerable times, scrambles up to its feet again, unbroken.

> " For what if I fail of my purpose here,
>   It is but to keep the nerves at strain.
> To dry one's eyes, and laugh at a fall,
> And, baffled, get up and begin it again.
> So the chace takes up one's life. That's all."

as Browning says.

Fine, and heart-stirring ! And while, no doubt, the end is not attained, nor victory achieved, until our will wills what God wills, instinctively, and without effort, still, there must surely be something in this grim concussing of a rebel will that jibs and flings away, to choose the duty, which it does not naturally wish as yet, because it is duty, that must move Christ's admiration. Even if things with you move slowly, almost imperceptibly, don't you despair ! The Lord Christ healed one blind man with a word, another with a touch, but sent another with daubed eyes, and a surely bewildered heart at this most unexpected treatment, groping through half Jerusalem. Yet in each case the dream came true. Hold on ! Hold on ! Hold out ! For, says Paul, " God never goes back upon His gifts and call." No. Hold you on !

Still, when Stevenson asks so movingly if to be foiled and try again, over and over, and with little to encourage one, and nothing at all to show, except this dour determination that won't stop trying, futile enough although it seems to have been proved—is that enough ? the answer must be, No. To be a Christian means more than a courageous holding out. It is to have all things made possible ; to fight with principalities and powers, and beat them ; to tug at evils whose roots seem coiled about the central core of things, and find them come up in our hands. In Christianity there is the note, and the fact, of victory. And Christ expects them in our lives.

And how can we introduce this fullness of Christ others know into our characters and our experience ?

Some people once asked Christ " What shall we do that we may work the works of God ? " But He immediately pulled them up, and warned them that they must begin much further back than that, must get down to the roots and source of things ; get beyond action, and behind thought to what fashions and colours them, and fixes and determines character—must start with their beliefs. " This is the work of God that you believe on Him whom He hath sent." Five centuries before Christ, Buddha found himself in a land where people held, as they still do in India, that one's beliefs are one's private concern, and, in any case, largely irrelevant. For, then as now, an orthodox Hindu can be an atheist, an agnostic, a polytheist, may live in a thin, rarified atmosphere of philosophical monism where few lungs can breathe at all, or in an orgy of obscene and primitive rites. And Buddha laid it down that the first and fundamental step towards a true way of living is to think right. And so did Jesus Christ. But this age of ours does not agree with Him ; assumes that the beliefs on which He lays such stress are mere useless lumber cluttering up the mind, old junk like the useless stuff that gathers in unused attics breeding moths, and gathering dust, better away ; won't see they are the only wings upon which we can rise out of the mud of things ; and that without them we are helpless. Yet, surely it is self-evident.

If, for instance, we believe, really believe, in the Fatherhood of God —that in this perilous world we are not left to our own poor resources and endeavours, but that goodness and mercy follow us, and that grace and love are round about us—that we are children, with a Father who thinks of us, and cares for us, and delights to provide for us, and most certainly will not forget nor overlook us, if we really believe that, must we not be lifted above fretting and anxiety, and all kinds of perturbations that would otherwise keep gnawing at our minds.

If we believe that Christ died for our poor souls, must not that endow us with a new self-respect that would be ashamed to fail a love as deep as that, and that must fill us with an answering affection for Him ? Lord Clyde, when he came back to Glasgow, was ashamed of his humble father before his swell friends, and pretended he was a hired porter. And there are people who, in certain companies, if Christ were mentioned, would feel uncomfortable and would look the other way, and pretend not to hear. But we exult in Him, are proud of Him, with a pride that is not pride, but worship. And if things drag, and nothing seems to happen, and we are tempted to give up the struggle, muttering " this is what I am, and this is what I must be to the end," one look at Christ's Cross, shames such cowardices out of us, and whips us to our feet again, once more resolute and zealous. " Again and again," said Father Tyrrell, " I have been tempted to give up the struggle : but always the figure of that strange Man, hanging on the Cross, sends me back to my task."

And if we believe, really believe, that Christ can save our souls where they need saving, and if we act on the assumption that He can and will, for us too it will all come true. I know it, asserts Paul, for it happened to me, the most unlikely of all possible people. And are you going to shuffle off, the same down-at-the-heel and shabby creature that you came ? If so, you do it, not of necessity, but of free choice : and not because you must, but because you will not be held back. The way to better things lies open. Bertrand Russell, in a passage that grips the heart, describes the apes at the zoo, " when they are not performing gymnastic feats or cracking nuts," and " the strange, strained sadness in their eyes. One can almost imagine that they feel they ought to become men, but cannot discover the secret of how to do it. On the road of evolution they have lost their way : their cousins marched on, and they were left behind " ; and adds that " something of that same strain and anguish seems to have entered the soul of civilized man. He knows there is something better than himself almost within his grasp, yet he does not know where to seek it, or how to find it."

Seek it in Jesus Christ, says the New Testament, and it is yours. And the voices of innumerable souls who have so done, shout their encouragements to you, and their assurances that it is even so.

It is a horrible thing for a white man to go native ; to turn his back on his own people, and their hard-won civilization, and their ideals, and their clean ways, and, of deliberation, sink back into barbarism with its sluttishness, and its superstition, and its orgies of debasement.

But to live merely as a natural man when one might be a Christian ; to lose so much, and choose so little, how can one reckon up the gross stupidity and shame of that ? How can you so insult yourself ? Russell is right. There is something better than yourself almost within your grasp, far better, infinitely better ! And, if you are willing to take it, Christ will give it to you—here and now.

CHAPTER VIII

THE CRY OF DERELICTION

"And at the ninth hour Jesus cried with a loud voice, saying, Eloi, Eloi, lama sabachthani? which is, being interpreted, My God, my God, why hast thou forsaken me?"—MARK xv. 34.

THERE was gross darkness upon Calvary. God's own hand, with deliberation, drew a thick veil between us and the sufferings of our Lord. And, even yet, it is not seemly to peer and pry too closely—like anatomists about an operating table—into that appalling mystery. Better stand still in a stunned hush of spirit gazing silently till the thing storms our hearts, and makes it impossible to keep ourselves from One who went this length for us. And for the rest, there is much wisdom in that finding of à Kempis—that we shall best understand Christ's Cross, not by discussing it, either with heat or in cold logic, but by carrying our own cross after Him.

But nowhere is the darkness quite so dense as in this verse, on which, almost certainly, it is foolish to attempt to speak. For we are on the margin of something far too tremendous for our minds to grasp, or even picture. God's thoughts are not as our thoughts, but are infinitely deeper, huger, vaster. And this is the working out of the deepest and most Godlike of them all. Can we even begin to understand how, from some thin and tenuous fire mist, He formed this solid earth? Or tell how life came into being in the world? And the saving of a whole humanity—if it will have it—is something still more wonderful by far, that staggers and confuses us. Dimly we see that the cost of our salvation is a thing incalculable; and that Christ's physical sufferings—hideous though these were—(have they not given us that word "excruciating" in which we sum up agony all but past bearing) were, none the less, the least of it. Have you noticed the extraordinary reticence of Scripture about them? Art seeks to harrow us by dwelling on the wounds and blood and bodily travail. But in the Scriptures they look past all that to something infinitely more heartbreaking still, something they see but can't describe, except in startling metaphors that often puzzle more than help—"He was made sin for us"; "The Lord hath laid on him the iniquity of us all"; "Christ was accursed for us." Dark sayings

6

surely at the best, which Luther underlines so thickly that his words grow meaningless to me : " It is not absurd to say that of all sinners Christ was the greatest," and the like. But all of us must see that here on Calvary we are facing the climax of human history, in which good and evil front each other foot to foot in a last hideous clash. And what that meant for Christ we cannot even faintly realize. For we have gone down so often and so easily in tame little skirmishes that we can't imagine what the full force of the assault pressed home with all evil's terrific power in one last desperate onslaught must have been. But something of the strain and agony of it even for Christ comes home to us in this tremendous cry, heartshaking, terrifying, because spoken by His voice—" My God, my God, why hast thou forsaken me ? "

What can that mean ? Does it not seem, at least, as if, on any interpretation of it, it must be the loss of one or other of the two most precious of all things ? If God forsook Christ in His time of direst need does not the story of His loving-kindness and His grace collapse as a proved fairy tale ? And if God stood by Christ, then did He who, tempted to the uttermost, came through it gallantly, with His head up, and steady eyes, and never a doubt of God, falter and fail at the last step, dimming His splendour, going out, in spite of the long glory of the struggle, beaten and daunted, and even, as some dare to hold, with His very soul drowned and whirled away in some wild sea of black despair ?

There are those who seek to evade the dilemma by spinning artificial and mechanical theories with no warm human blood or feeling of reality in them, calmly denying Christ's assumptions, and picturing God—here at least—as, not a Father, but a Judge austerely just and carrying through some intricate implacable legal requirement, till the story of the prodigal (which we ourselves have proved to be true), and of the heart at home that could not rest for thinking of the foolish lad, and the eyes that hungrily watched the road, and the arms leaping out in a quick eager welcome round the shabby, hirpling, inexcusable thing, seem very far away. But that won't do. Here, at the testing place, one can't dismiss Christ's axioms without discrediting Him altogether.

And others speak of Christ in an oddly abstract and formal fashion. They have told themselves so often—what is true—that He is not just an Individual, but the Second Adam, and the representative of humanity, that they forget that, whatever else and more He was,

His was a heart like ours, that walked by faith, and looked to God, and leant on God, and needed God. Such explanations of the Cross don't help us much. Sully, the psychologist, tells of a mother reading Bible stories to her child, and passing over one of them on the ground that it was too difficult for her to understand, whereat the little voice broke in, "I can understand them all perfectly well, if only you wouldn't explain them to me." These people are like botanists leaving a little withering heap, and saying, "There is your flower, and that's all there is in it." But it isn't. Their summary of pistils and stamens and petals and the like may be scientifically accurate ; but what made the flower a flower is gone. That has evaded them. And these theories of what happened at the Cross make dreary reading, leave one quite unthrilled and cold. And yet the Cross itself haunts, masters, lays compulsion on us, as Christ said it would.

And still what does this mean ? Did God really in very fact forsake Christ ? "Yet I am not alone" He used to say in His valorous way, "for the Father is with me." And did that Father at last really turn away ? There are those who have no doubt He did, and find in that the heart and centre of the gospel. Mrs. Browning, for example, in her moving poem upon Cowper's grave sums it all up—

"Yea, once, Immanuel's orphaned cry His universe hath shaken—
It went up single, echoless, ' My God, I am forsaken ! '
It went up from the Holy's lips amid His lost creation,
That, of the lost, no son should use those words of desolation !"

Apparently, like the scapegoat, loaded with sins, and led into the bleakness of the wilderness, Christ the Sin Bearer passed into an awful Loneliness, cut off even from God—dared that, did that, for you and me, took on Himself the alienation from God that is ours. A staggering metaphor, bringing home awesomely the amazement of the Cross. Only what does it mean ? For is God alienated from any one ? Wronged, injured, wounded ? Yes. But alienated ? Sometimes we are from Him ; tire of Him, fling away from Him, tell Him bluntly and to His face that we are sick of Him, cry peevishly, "Let us alone," wish that there were no God to bother us ! But He can't give us up, not even the worst of us, keeps following us like a beggar, so Paul says, waits when we are too busy and breaks in again on us when we have any leisure to attend to Him, pleading with us to be reconciled to Him who has nothing but love for us in spite of all our waywardness, forsakes no one of us, do what we will, can't give us up. Surely that is the God Christ has revealed to us.

Or, again, it is true that the glory of Christ's sacrifice lies in the faith that could believe on in the absolute dark, and the obedience still obedient even when tested to the very uttermost. And are we to understand that, so to test Christ, God withdrew, and left Him there alone without the aids and helps He might have given Him, as even M'Leod Campbell supposes.

To me that just won't think. Surely never was God so near to Christ as in those awful hours. Doubt that, and our peace is gone and our faith shivers into fragments. For what assurance have we that He may not forsake us in our evil hour ? " Search and look the generations down," cried a bold voice in Ecclesiasticus, " who ever trusted in the Lord and He failed him ? " " Who ? " He rings it out challengingly. Now tell me who ? There is not one. And can we lead him to the Cross, and pointing through the darkness, answer, " There ! " and leave him dumb and silenced ? " Cast thy burden on the Lord, and he will sustain thee " promises a confident soul, speaking from long experience. And was Christ, carrying a load the like of which no other ever bore, left, though He cried to God, unanswered and unaided and alone ? To be forsaken of God, is not that hell, and worse than hell ? Was it not the fear of that, the dread that God had never a thought of, nor a flicker of interest in the souls in Hades that made the ancient saints shrink from it in an agony, and cling, however poor and suffering and broken, to this life where they could walk with God ? And did not one, deeper and wiser, cry aloud his scorn of such a foolish terror, declaring " even if I make my bed in Hades, Thou art there ! " There, too, and still the same compassionate God as ever. And was Christ left alone, as even the souls in Hell are not—Christ daring all for God, Christ loving Him, and serving Him, and giving all His all for Him as no one ever did ! The thing won't think. Christ would not, and Christ could not, have deserted any one in need, kept breaking through all limitations, finding reasons to make it possible to stretch things so as to reach out to this one too, though he stood really beyond the usual conditions. And is He not God's express image ? " Try you God for yourself," our hymns keep crying to the downcast and discouraged, and you will find what we all find, however desperate our case,

> " God never yet forsook at need
> The soul that trusted Him indeed."

And was the greatest of Believers left the one exception to this universal law ?

There is no difficulty in our Lord's vicarious suffering. That is the primary law of human life and progress. Bosanquet, indeed, flung away from Christianity because of its insistence upon it, feeling that that at least is certainly untrue ; yet did he not come back to the rejected faith just because life had taught him that, whatever else is doubtful, this vicarious suffering that had once stumbled him is one thing absolutely fixed and sure, and Christianity has seen and emphasized that as no faith has ever done. It was a witless jeer they flung into His face, " He saved others, himself he cannot save." Precisely so. For to save others one must sacrifice oneself ; and God allows it to happen, giving the greatest of His servants the chance of it as a prerogative and privilege, " Ought not Christ to have suffered ? " as He said Himself.

But that God should have held aloof, and turned away His face from Christ upon the tree, from One bringing Him that unique wholeheartedness of love and service and self-sacrifice—how could He, and why should He ? All those conceptions based on some idea that Christ in some way altered God's mood toward us, making Him kind who had before been stern, seem to me blasphemous and hopelessly unscriptural. " God was in Christ, reconciling the world unto himself," not standing sullenly apart, and needing to be reconciled.

If you force me into the dilemma, then better hold that our Lord's faith did falter than that God failed Him, or can fail any one. " Let God be true even if all men are made liars," thinks the Apostle. And with good reason. For if we cannot count on Him, if His self-sacrificing grace toward us is not a thing dependable and fixed, chaos comes back again, and life grows desperate and frightening, and there is no sure foothold anywhere, and what seemed soundest and most solid gives in our hand, and crumbles, and is gone.

But if God did not really forsake our Lord, did Christ's faith fail ; was His obedience less than perfect ; and the offering that He took back to God a little marred and shadowed after all ? Our Lord carried Himself with such consummate gallantry, shook off contemptuously temptations against which we have to heave and struggle with souls strained to the cracking point, did the big, brave, unselfish, Godlike thing so naturally and inevitably, that we come to forget that it was not inevitable, not a kind of instinct too imperious to be resisted, but a deliberate choice every time. Reynolds told his pupils that a masterpiece must seem to be done easily. And that is what astonishes us in Christ. We pant and perspire and lay plans and swear resolutions

and noisily push and fuss and bustle ; and with it all, make little of
this difficult life ; we draw in and rub out, and try again and yet
again, till we have rubbed right through the soiled and grimy paper,
and still can't get it to come anything like right. While He is so
effortless, so sure of touch, so masterly in doing just the absolutely
perfect thing that could be done ; and this in the most unexpected
situations leaping out on Him with never a second's warning. Yet,
though it looks as if it were dashed off, the masterprice was not done
easily. And faith was not always an easy thing for Jesus Christ. At
least three times we see Him, if not staggered, at least not sure what
God's will for Him is, or that this that is offered Him can really be that
will.

When the Greeks came to Him, and the shadow of the Cross somehow fell cold and forbiddingly upon Him, for a moment He fingered
various requests, wondering which He ought to make to God, felt
half inclined to ask for safety from this horror, and then cast that
from Him, leaving Himself without condition in God's hands.

And again in the garden with the terror drawn quite near, to be
fled from or else accepted, not at some vague future time but very now,
for a while He was not sure whether God could be asking for it yet,
with everything, as it seemed, still to do, and nothing so far really
accomplished. Yet He rose up at last, and went to meet it like the
Conqueror He was ; stepped calmly out of the safe shadows of the trees
into the ring of light and all the awfulness of Calvary, not dragged to
it, but offering Himself willingly.

And here upon the cross a fearsome darkness fell about His soul.
Had He had half unconsciously some hope that God would intervene
on His behalf, that the twelve legions of angels would flash down
indignantly to His aid ? He Himself would never ask for them, nor
dream of using His miraculous powers upon His own behalf, would
leave Himself to God. But could God let the Saviour die with the
world still unsaved ? Must He not burst in for His own name's sake,
and for that of a whole humanity whose only chance was slipping out ?
Had Christ waited and hoped and watched and known that it must
come ? There is no trace of any sign of that in anything He ever
said, rather the certainty that there was death to face, and the
apparent utter ruin of His hopes and plans. Yet as that death drew
near, and His strength ebbed, and the end came in sight, think of the
meaning of it all to Him. He who alone could save the world was
dying with the world unsaved, with not one soul that understood,

with His friends scattered, with the whole dream out, it seemed. O God! the unsaved world, the unsaved world! I gave Myself to Thee, wholly, ungrudgingly, holding back nothing; I left Myself to Thy disposal absolutely; I asked for nothing except this, that, cost Me what it might, I might be used of Thee for this. I am prepared to die, am dying for it, freely, gladly, choosing death for that. But has it failed? Has that last chance gone out? Was I too soon and rash in daring Calvary? I thought that it would draw all men to Me, and through Me unto Thee. Yet, listen how they jeer and mock—not one among them moved! O God! the unsaved world! Why? Why?

There are those for whom the fact that Christ passed through experiences of that kind is an essential element of His saviourhood for them. Without these honest Scriptures they would pass Him by as of no use to them. The fact is that, although we do not realize it, and esteem ourselves heroic souls, for most of us faith has been made a very easy thing. Easy! you cry. Yes, easy; even when the big strains come. Death enters, it may be with dreadful un-expectedness; and in one moment we stand roofless, with our cosy home rumbled into a ruinous heap. Yet even then and even there we have so much to help us—our certainty of the Beyond; the thrill of picturing the glory that has crowned our dear ones—all it must mean to them; the looking forward to the wonderful re-meeting by and by—innumerable heartenings. But there are those with almost none, to whom the promises seem but an empty mockery, and God heedless and unconcerned, it seems, though things are desperate for them. A mother's boy goes hideously wrong, and though she prays with all her being, clinging to God, eagerly offering her own salvation in exchange for his, there comes no answer, and the horror soaks deeper and further down into his soul; and she dies, leaving him a wreck with settled and disgusting habits, and his will melted into a pulpy smush; or he dies and goes out like that. Why, after all her faith? Or a man is accused of crime, knows he is innocent, and yet the jury find him guilty, and the judge speaks scathingly, and the long years in penal servitude drag themselves slowly past. How difficult for him to cling to any patch of faith in any moral ordering of an insane and chaotic world that has heaped on him hideous injustice! For many faith in God is a desperate all-but impossibility. And our facile belief in no way helps them. Aye, they say, if I walked with you in the sunshine then for me also it were simple to believe. But if you were here, with my lot to face, and my load to carry, and my experience to make faith look an empty thing, you also might not be so sure. And perhaps we are too facile, ought to be startled and shocked more than we are by slums, and folk condemned to mean, drab, squalid lives, and souls grown brutalized and stunted, and all the enigmas which we dully take for granted as the way of things, and never even see (unless they touch ourselves) nor try to solve. But the fact that Christ, too, had to pass through rushing waters, black and swollen, with His feet all but swept away, and under skies howling in tempest, and with never a star showing, gives them heartening and hope, and a sense of divine comradeship. He, at least, they feel, understands ; He, and God.

For as Dora Greenwell has it, " When I looked upon my agonized and dying God, and turned from that world-appealing sight, Christ crucified for us, to look upon life's perplexed and sorrowful contradictions, I was not met as in intercourse with my fellow-men by the cold platitudes that fall so lightly from the lips of those whose hearts have never known one real pang, nor whose lives one crushing blow. I was not told that all things were ordered for the best, nor assured that the overwhelming disparities of life were but apparent, but I was met from the eyes and brow of Him who was acquainted with grief by a look of solemn recognition, such as may pass between friends who have endured between them some strange and secret sorrow, and are through it united in a bond that cannot be broken."

What the Cross proves above all else is that God forsakes no man ; that He is not out of it all, indifferent to it all, as we had thought, but at the heart of all the suffering and sorrow of the world, bearing it for and with us, finding some way—heedless of what the cost to Him may be—of saving us who have brought ruin on ourselves. Sorrow and trouble come, and we can see no reason for it. Wait, we say. Our hopes and efforts end in utter failure, as it seems. And our eyes turn to Calvary instinctively. It is not so, we claim. For look, was ever failure more complete than that. Yet, it was not for nothing ; not in vain ; no failure. But, out of that faith that seemed wasted, and that trust that held on, though not understanding in the least, up that steep, stony, desperate way, look what God has accomplished for the world ! And you too He has not forsaken. There is motive, meaning, wisdom, love in that that has befallen you ; and you yourself will own it by and by. So says our ever valiant faith, facing the dark enigmas of this staggering world. And it is just this Cross that gives it its assurance.

We are often told that Mark ends in the darkness with a beaten, disappointed Christ. It is not so, of course. He, too, knows of the Risen, Glorified, Triumphant Lord. Still, it is well other evangelists have gathered sayings from His lips upon the tree we could ill spare.

In John He dies with the shout of a Conqueror. And it is good for us to bear in mind that, as it seems, what lifted the depression from His spirit, was that the poor soul hanging there beside Him, awed by something in this strange convict suffering along with him, threw himself on His grace with a dim inchoate nebulous faith, that was still faith, where faith seemed utterly impossible. And it came like a reviving cup of water to our Lord's parched lips and soul. The thing was working then ; and God was standing to His promises ; and it was not in vain, but coming true. " It is finished," He cried ; and gave back to God no broken hope, no failure, no mere gallantry of endeavour that had not succeeded, but a life lived out, and a tremendous task accomplished in the face of every hindrance. Let us remember that. Old Dr. Duncan used to say that of all living beings he most envied the angel who stood by our Lord in the loneliness of His agony in the garden. But why not rather this strange, uncouth, most unlikely comforter when things were darker still ? And yet there is no need for envy. Since you and I, yes, you and I, can be of a like service to Him still. For so close are the bonds between Him and His people, that to help them is to help Him, He says. If carrying ourselves gallantly, we encourage a weaker soul to rally, if trusting God when things are difficult for us we shame some other out of peevishness towards Him, if acting generously and unselfishly in the little nothings that make up our days we cheer some fellow-man or woman to hold on, He counts it in His marvellous condescension, as a personal favour done to Himself, and accepts it gratefully from our soiled hands and blundering hearts. We can help Jesus Christ.

While in Luke also it is plain that the storm blew itself out, the darkness lifted, and the day closed in an evening still and calm and golden. " Father, into thy hands I commend my spirit." Here am I ; do with Me what Thou wilt : My life I hand to Thee, for it is Thine, a weapon shaped and ready for Thy use as Thou mayest choose here and hereafter. Out of the blackness burns so glorious a star. And on the Cross itself it is we come upon the most amazing instance even in our Saviour's life of that courageous childlikeness of spirit which He taught and lived, of that audacious intrepidity of soul that had passed through the worst, and still believed undauntedly. So meaningless is it to chatter of Christ's loss of faith.

And, perhaps, none of us can gain something approaching faith to be called faith by any easier way than by treading at least a little of that same hard road Christ had to travel. "Those," says Canon Raven, "who learn by sympathy and mental effort can win their way to a faith as confident as a child's, and far more secure, a faith that has faced the facts, and shared the pains, and wrung from life the mystery of its laughter and tears. But the right to hold it must be paid for at its full price, and that price is, I suspect, a Cross."

CHAPTER IX

WHEN CHRIST AND YOU COME FACE TO FACE,
WHAT THEN ?

" For all creation, gazing eagerly as if with outstretched neck, is waiting and longing to see the manifestation of the sons of God."—Rom. viii. 19 (Weymouth).

WHAT are you going to do with your life ? There it lies in your hands, yours, within limits, to put to such uses as you choose. And, no doubt, many claimants for it, clamorous and insistent, are tugging at your sleeve, and thrusting themselves upon your attention. And to which among them all do your eyes keep slipping back ? " This life of ours," says Browning, " must be lived out ; and a grave thoroughly earned." What strikes you as a fitting definition of a life lived out, and to the full ? If your hopes could come true, what would you choose ? If you were given your chance, what would you do and be ? " If there were dreams to sell, what would you buy ? "

Many voices, not a doubt, are calling to you, urging you this way and that, confusingly enough. And yet, listen ! Among them all do you not hear another ; the voice of One who has made by far too big a mark on history and in innumerable characters and lives to be neglected, or pushed impatiently aside. And He too follows you, appeals to you, claims you; promises that He can make your life an infinitely fuller, more adventurous, and colourful, and exciting thing than it can be without Him ; begs you not to let yourself be tricked and cheated into throwing it away for some poor tinselled nothing that glitters for a moment and then tarnishes ; for, says He, I can give you life that is worth calling life, that has a rush and fullness in it, and that overflows.

Out among the hurry and roar of common things, that voice is, for the most part, lost to us ; drowned in the constant traffic of our days ; unheeded, and indeed unheard, among the thousand and one bits of affairs to which we must attend.

But now that in this narrow place Christ and you have come face to face, so that you can't push past Him, can't pretend that you don't see Him, must pause, must listen, must make up your mind, must either accept Him and His offers and His service, or else look Him squarely in the eyes, and answer bluntly and doggedly, " I will

85

not," what do you mean to do ? For something, one way or the other, you must do. The very effort to avoid decision is, itself, decision.

And, to help you towards a verdict, may I remind you of some simple facts—this to begin, that the Lord Christ and you have very much in common.

For one thing, like you, He believes in life, and wants you to know it at its richest and most splendid. And that is worth while underlining. For so many speak of this wonderful heritage of ours scornfully, fearfully, indignantly. Most Eastern thinkers, for example —and many in the West have agreed with them—are pathologically afraid of life. The mood is an obsession and a positive disease. To them this life of ours is not a boon or joy or glory, but a punishment, a kind of lesser hell; lesser, but very terrible; a dreadful retribution visited upon us for some sin into which we blundered in some previous existence. And, as each new sin that we sin now means a further life ahead—another, and another, and another—they think of life with horror as a grim prison in which they have been closely immured, and from which no escape is possible.

There is no touch nor trace of that in Jesus Christ. If we, His followers, have given you the impression that His religion is a dreary business, a shivering with chittering teeth in the chilly twilight of a monastic cell, out of the sunshine that God made for us, and meant us to enjoy; a ruthless squeezing of all the colours and attractiveness from life, leaving it bleached and dull and faded, believe me, we are caricaturing Him to you ; and judge of Him, not from us who in that case are certainly betraying Him, but from Himself. Look at the records ! What would you say was the first thing that struck our Lord's contemporaries in Him ? Undoubtedly, I think, a certain happy heartedness that jarred, and even shocked them. The thing became a scandal. Now John, they said, with his austerities, and his bare pinched life out yonder in the desert, is plainly a religious man. But this other with His zest for life, mingling in other people's happinesses, and carrying a kind of sunshine with Him—is He a religious man at all ? And they were hurt and sore about it ; and shouted ugly gibes and nicknames after Him along the streets. Hie winebibber ! Hie friend of publicans and sinners ! A right queer travesty of religion, this, they thought. And Christ admitted they were happy —He and His friends ; and asked these critical people what else could they be, knowing what they did know, believing what they did believe, experiencing what they day by day experienced at the hands of God ;—compared His circle to a bridal party on the wedding morning : raised happiness, of the right type, to a secure place among the virtues : announced that He had come to share His joy with people far too sunless, or too worried, and to show men how to lead a fuller, more abundant life than the lean thing they knew. It hurt Him that poor befooled folk so often make so little of their lives, and get so meagre a return from them compared to what is possible. Give it to Me, so He kept saying, and, I promise you, you will find infinitely more in it than that. Yes ; Christ, like you, believes in life ; wants you to know, and use, it to the full, and to get out of it the glory there is in it. " It is the gladness of Christianity," said Matthew Arnold, " and not its sorrow that has made its fortune ! "

And, further, He believes in you ; much more than you do in yourself ; is sure that it is not for nothing, or by chance, that you are here, but that there is a work of moment needing to be done, and you are here to do it, and can do it, if you will ; and that nobody else in all God's crowded creation can take your place or be your substitute ; denies that you are just one of a mass, and lost in it, and indistinguishable from it, or that you could fall out and never be missed. Each one of us—you there, I here, says Christ, is, in the sight of God, original, unique, and irreplacable. " My duty," says Royce, " I myself must do. Not even God can do it for me." And your work you, yourself, must do.

And you can live it out, if only you will train and develop yourself into that which God needs, and can use. For, as yet, you are not you, not the real you God wants and means you to be, but only a bundle of possibilities, out of which that can be fashioned. " Train," says Paul, " for life." And why not ? Any lad who takes his football or athletics or boat-racing seriously, so trains with ardour and wholeheartedness, cutting off many things in which others indulge as a matter of course, and exercising himself strenuously into thorough fitness and the best that there is in him, knowing well that, otherwise, when the test comes, flabby and soft and fat and breathless, he could not stand the pace. And to live nobly takes far more out of a man than the running of a race, or an hour of strenuous football, is too taxing by far for those who will not discipline themselves for it, and so keep fit.

Don't let yourself be fooled by these popular voices in our day, laying it down so confidently that all self-denial is a kind of maiming, and a hideous self-mutilation ; that all the urges of our nature have equal authority, and should be given unchecked play. If you would

pray, then pray ; but, if you wish to gratify the flesh, then do it—
else one is left in certain provinces of life stunted and ignorant and
undeveloped ; whereas all types of experience, say they, are needed
to produce a full and rounded and completed personality. So, if
temptation comes, the wise man lets it have its way with him, learning
—so we are told—from the sage beasts who are happy and at rest
because they obey the promptings of their appetites and instincts,
while we are wretched because we seek to repress them, not having
grasped that the real way to be done with the wearing strain and
nagging irritation of a temptation is to give way to it. Indeed, they
tell us that the lower voices are the more dependable, and the likelier
to prove trustworthy. " Don't follow conscience," declares Lawrence,
" conscience is often wrong ; don't follow reason, it can easily mislead ;
follow the flesh—the flesh is always right." The philosophy of the
pig-sty, hailed as a new Gospel!

Such finger-posts point straight to that well-beaten road, down
which so many confident youngsters, sure that they know far better
than their tamed and tired and obsolete and funnily impossible elders,
mistaking liberty for licence, and licence for liberty, proud that they
have burst the apron-springs by which prim and effete conventionalists
had tried to hold them, have merrily sung and whistled, feeling big
and brave and free ; and, in a little, if they have soul enough left in
them even for that, are sitting, they too, in their turn, among the
desolation of the mud and filth about the swine troughs, trying to
ease the gnawing of a hunger, that can no longer be stayed by such
nastinesses, with the half-eaten husks the pigs had mouthed and left ;
tired of it all, and weary of themselves, ashamed and sore at heart,
and very sick for home.

Why credit Aldous Huxley, let us say, when in his raw, green
ignorance of life, he truculently laid it down that " mortification of
the flesh in the religious sense of the term " results in " a spiritual
gangrene, a putrefaction, a stink " ; and not believe him when,
grown up a little bit, though still a mere spiritual adolescent, he, in a
later book, frankly confesses that he and his like spoke so, and flouted
at morality, and tried to laugh it out of court, " because it interfered
with our sexual freedom ? " (Another way of saying that they loved
the darkness rather than the light, because their deeds were evil.)
And, says he, our effort did not work, brought us no satisfaction. Trust
you, then, not the wild vapourings of his ignorance of life, but the
grave counsels of his sad experience and disillusionment.

Believe Montague when he so wisely sums the matter up. " There is a notion common among hobbledehoys that ' experience ' can be widened by a loss of self-control. Some of them will misbehave, just to 'see life.' Diddled by stale figures of speech, a lad at the university will get drunk ' just to have the experience ' or do something worse because he wants ' to know the whole of life.' And some half-sane or trashy-hearted writers of fuller age have erected this mess of vague thought into a kind of philosophy." And, with that, calmly, devastatingly, unanswerably, he brings the whole ramshackle structure rumbling down, and leaves it a mere sorry heap of ruins. The foundational mistake, he tells us in effect, is that life is regarded as an opportunity of collecting experiences, as a boy collects stamps, or eggs, or coins ; that the more you have of all kinds, and of any kind, the better ; that every addition to your collection of experiences is " an enrichment of the personality " ; that anything, and everything, you do must, of necessity, increase and not diminish that experience of yours. But, says he, in life, as in algebra, there is a minus sign no less than a plus sign ; and certain actions don't add to, but, on the contrary, subtract from, what we previously had. " They think of the clean boy who gives up his cleanness as if he had added something to his experience, and subtracted nothing. Whereas, with every loss of self-control, you make some exchange of the experience of moral autonomy for the dark, narrow experience of moral helplessness. You always come off a loser ; your treasury of experience depleted on balance ; your vision of life more blurred, your register of experience smudged, your faculty of delight perceptively enfeebled."

What this age of ours requires to take in, declares Lippmann, is that the call on us for self-denial and the assertion that without renunciation of many of the ordinary appetites no man can live fully and well, is not merely the testimony " of our maiden aunts," but that of every single expert in this line of things the whole world over ; of every single one of those who have given their lives to it in any age or country or religion whatsoever, and who stand out, the men of genius in these matters, to whom every one of sense looks up—without exception they unanimously lay it down as a first rule that the one and only road to know life at its highest, and its most exciting, begins as " the purgative way." And so Christ looks you in the eyes and says, Believe Me, you are far bigger than you realize ; cannot be satisfied so cheaply and so meanly as they would make you imagine ; are, each of you, a princely creature, built upon great lines and destined for vast ends. Give Me your life, and I will let you know how splendid it can be, and what it means really to live. But these poor nothings are of no use to you.

When Eliot, the poet, reviewed Bertrand Russell's *Conquest of Happiness*, he did so with the amused look of a grown-up, to whom a child has brought its toys, assuming they will mean as much to him as to itself ; and there the grown-up stands, holding the silly things that are of no manner of use to him. " This," says he, looking queerly at a man, apparently a grown man, who can be satisfied with only this, " this is the gospel of Mediocrity. Once we have asked the question What is the end of man ? we can't be satisfied with the answer, There is not any end ; and the only thing to do is to be a nice person and get on with your neighbours." No, agrees Jesus Christ, you are bigger than that ; can have, and ought to have, a life more adventurous by far than that ; have vastly nobler possibilities there well within your reach.

What things ? Look at this wonderful metaphor which, indeed, is no metaphor, but literal fact, and think it out. The whole creation, bound, helpless, desperate, agonized, has stumbled to its feet, and gazes down the road, up which deliverance must come, if indeed a deliverer can ever come at all. And for what is it watching ? For the appearing of the sons of God, of a race of men prepared to live their lives in a new way, no longer in our selfish, human, greedy, grabby way, but in God's way, of splendid divine unselfishness. So far, we can all follow. For the generation is agreed that the old way of things won't do, must vanish, and a new and better take its place. But we are banking upon something social, political, dramatic, sudden, which will effect the transformation while we watch it; we, ourselves, meantime remaining what we were ; in short, upon what Raleigh calls " the idiotic simplicity of the revolutionary idea." Well, we have got to work for a new system ; refusing to be fobbed off with vague promises of something some time far ahead, demanding readjustment now. But communities consist of individuals, and how are we to secure the right type of community unless some daring individuals, going ahead of the dull mass, lead the way to it ; and are, meantime, themselves prepared to work and sacrifice and spend their lives in the new way— God's way ?

And that is what the Lord Christ asks of you. Come, help Me in My saving of the world. You have it in you, and I need you so. Come ! Don't lose your life in merely pushing your own interests and ends, however blamelessly ; don't fancy that you have fulfilled, and met, all that can reasonably be expected of you by doing nothing to pollute the world, by leaving it no worse than what you found it. For you are here to help in heaving it up nearer to God's feet, in making it that new earth in which righteousness can dwell. Aye, and He has the right to claim that from us, for He did it Himself. " All that Christ asked from the world," says Lammenais, " was a cross on which to die for it." And He honours us by asking and expecting us to show some dim reflection of His own glorious spirit ; " seeks Christians with the power of sacrifice—sole origin of our salvation—who can face dangers unafraid and fatigues without fear " ; who can say, " We will die for this," and even more ; and, above all, Christians capable of saying, " We will live for this." For that last is by far the most drastic call upon us. It were not difficult, one hopes, in some high moment of excitement and decision, to lay down life itself, in one big glorious act of sacrifice ; but to keep faithful, doggedly and patiently, in all the little nothings of the long procession of one's common days, that is the harder task, and the more testing trial. Yet, He looks straight at you, and confidently asks it from you.

From me ! you say, starting back ! But it would cost, would hurt, would make life so uncomfortable ! And at that Christ turns and looks at you again, but this time in amazement. You are not thinking of giving a whole human life for nothing more or better than mere cosiness and comfort ! You're not a weakling ; one who, in peril, rushes for the boats, and slips off with the children, while real men stay to wrestle with the hurricane and keep the sinking ship afloat, and fight the roar of the devouring flames, and bring the charred and battered hulk to harbour.

And, indeed, you are comically out of date and antiquated and obsolete. " You are created for the sake of the whole, and not the whole for the sake of you." So Plato told the young men long ago. The very Nazis look at you with wonderment and an open contempt ! For even they are sure that to live for nothing higher than oneself is to lose life ; that life, to be called life, can be found only in serving something bigger than one's personal interests ; something that crowds these out of mind and heart, till one forgets about them and lives wholly, and without exception, for that other worthier thing. To them what you call freedom is not liberty, but licence, and they repudiate it hotly and with scorn. And, indeed, they are right, if only they had not bowed down in blasphemous idolatry before a

7

mere man and a poor, faulty, human state, had given that unreckoning passion of allegiance to what alone is worthy of such wholehearted devotion, to the Lord God, High and Holy, and to His Christ. For surely Kierkegaard is right, that we must relate ourselves absolutely to the absolute, but only relatively to the relative. But to be self-absorbed, self-centred, self-engrossed, is to be out of date and left behind, ready for a museum, and to be ticketed with other extinct species, like the dodo! Christianity, says Jung, has had biological results upon humanity. It has changed the animal called man, and its nature, and its ways—though when mankind escapes out of a Christian atmosphere, it quickly degenerates back to the old obscenities once natural to it, that had seemed dead. And yet it has in very deed succeeded in evolving a new creature, living in part, at least in a new way. And for you to cling to the primitive outworn habits of the past is to be old-fashioned and half savage. It is long since Aristotle told told us that only barbarians have as their ideal the wish to live as they please, and to do what they like. And the New Testament gravely sets us down before the Cross, and bids us gaze, and still gaze, and keep gazing, till the fact has soaked itself into our minds that that, not less than that, is now the standard set us, and that whatever in our lives clashes with that is sin.

But it's my life, you cry, clutching it tighter, and I need it all for my own purposes and plans and ends! Well, frankly, Christ did not expect that, and would not believe that it was even possible. I know men, so He said with confidence. Oh! they may not be much impressed by what I say; may take My gifts, and soon forget the Giver, may be slow and disappointing in many ways. But, if they see Me dying for them, I win. " I, if I be lifted up, will draw all men to Me." They are too gallant to keep out of it! And can you stand on Calvary, and look, and calmly turn upon your heel, and go your way, dismissing it as folly ? If He chooses so to throw away His life, well, that is His affair. But I am not going to put mine to such wasteful uses. Had Christ too honouring an estimate of us ? Did He pitch His appeal too high ? Does it go clean over your head ? Are you too small and paltry to feel the thrill of it, and to respond to it ? Dostoievsky once exclaimed that he was tired of being a man, with his human sympathies continually being hurt, and endless calls upon his human helpfulness ; wished that he were an insect shut securely into its own hard little shell, without a care for anything beyond it. Well, many a one has lived after that fashion. But there is another way—God's way. Come again to the Cross, you, fingering your life, and wondering what you should do with it, and make your decision there. Insect's or God's—which do you choose ? But it's my life ! Well, crawl away, you wretched earthworm. No doubt, you will have your little fatuous toys and joys and ploys and bits of pleasures. But you might have been God's fellow-labourer, with your hand touching His at the common task ! Come, He says. Help me !

Raymond Lull was, in his day, the gallantest knight in Spain, foremost in jousts and tournaments and manly exercises. Yet, sometimes, into his self-centred, idle, frivolous life there blew tidings of greater things. Christ, on occasion, now and then appeared to him in vision, and offered him His gifts. And, peevishly, and almost without listening, he pushed them aside, declared he didn't need them, didn't want them, would not have them. Until there came another day, when Christ again appeared. But this time He said nothing, only put His heavy Cross into Lull's hands, and left it there, and looked him in the eyes, and went His way. And that did it ! For, left with that horrid symbol of suffering and sacrifice, the man's heart rose to it. Here, he said, is an adventure worth the having ! That I should help Christ in His saving of the world ; and, with that, turned, and followed eagerly, through all the glory of his martyr life, on to the splendour of his martyr death. And now that same Christ makes that selfsame call on you. Come, says He, holding out His hands to you, help Me in My saving of the world. You have it in you, and I need you so. Come ! Come ! Come !

CHAPTER X

SOME BLESSED CERTAINTIES IN AN UNSTABLE WORLD

" We know."—Rom. viii. 22.
" I know."—2 Tim. i. 12.
" I know."—2 Cor. v. 1.

AT the beginning, faith is always an adventure ; and so lumpish and prosaic folk can't rise to it. For it needs something both of courage and imagination. And they, poor souls, have neither. Faith means, in each new individual that exercises it, a trusting of himself on what has not, for him at least, been proved as yet. And that is true of every one of life's departments, even the most abstract and academic. For the demand for faith is not an odd outrageous claim, peculiar to religion ; all life is built up upon faith : and every single step of progress anywhere comes to us as a gift from some intrepid spirit who dared to leap, sheer out into the dark—and landed, safe ! Are there any scientists these days more notable than Einstein and Max Planck ? Yet both have frankly conceded that faith is a first essential in the scientific pioneer ; that you can't reason yourself the whole way to a discovery ; that the masses of facts patiently accumulated by the industry and zeal of eager workers are only too apt to remain sterile and dead, unless, and until, they fall into the hands of some one with imagination enough, and faith enough, to see that this may lead to something central and important ; and so, daringly ventures out on what has not been proved as yet ; and, perhaps, nothing comes of it, and the surmise withers away before the test ; or, perhaps, a new " star swims into our ken," and another province is added to the realm of human knowledge. But to ask for proof without experiment, to demand certainty before you will take action, is futile and unscientific. For knowledge and assurance can come only through, and after, actual trial.

Indeed, in the whole world to-day, there are no men who exercise so audacious and so blind a faith as up-to-date scientists. And they themselves admit it, not with confusion of face, but pointing out that nothing else is possible. We have travelled a far journey from the truculent confidence with which their immediate predecessors asserted that they, and they alone, were dealing with hard, solid, actual facts ;

with realities obviously there, while the rest of us, especially religious people, they jeered out of court, as playing about with dreamy, tenuous stuff, vague and nebulous, with no substantiality or body in it. Whereas now, they calmly drop all that, and tell us that they can never know things as they really are ; don't need to do it ; don't particularly want to do it. The algebraic symbols x and y, and a and b, may stand for anything—potatoes, or princesses, or pigs : the mathematician doesn't care which it may be. Give him his symbols, and though he has no idea what these symbols represent, he will work out the sum. So, we can never know the things of the world around us as they really are—and, say the scientists, don't need to know. A summer sky is, of course, not blue at all, though it looks blue to us ; nor does a stick, held in the water, really bend, though our eyes tell us plainly that it does. We say a flower is red because, while it absorbs the other rays of light, it rejects red, and that rejected ray comes back to our eyes : but what the flower that so rejects it is like in itself, we cannot tell. We pick up certain signals from the things about us, as we can hear messages from a broadcasting station, but we can't tell from them what the station, or the thing, is like. Yet scientists work with these hidden and unknown materials with confidence. " Mind," says Eddington, " is the first and most direct thing in our experience : all else is remote inference." Yet, with the utmost boldness, they keep on making their remote inferences. Here, in very deed, are men who walk in their own province, not by sight, but by faith. Let us be up to date, and stop the silly chatter, now grown hopelessly obsolete, about the credulousness of religious believing.

And so, when the Lord Christ comes to a man fingering his life, and wondering what he should choose to do with it, and says, Give it to Me, and you will find that it becomes far fuller and more interesting, far more adventurous and exciting, than it can be without Me ; or to another, down and out, sick of himself, and yet unable to escape from himself, full of impotent longings that come to nothing, " But ah ! that a man might arise in me, that the man that I am might cease to be " ; yet that other never comes, and the hatefully familiar figure still slouches through his life, and promises that He can lift him clean above himself into a newness of life worth calling life ; it won't do to push it all pettishly away, as too good to be true. Romanes was a man of science who lived outside of the Christian faith, which he regarded as a wildly impossible story not worth a sane man's credence. And suddenly it came home to him that he was acting most unscientifically, and in open and flat defiance of all the accepted and fundamental canons of his own life-work.   Where there is *prima facie* evidence for a thing, a scientist is bound to test it.   He may not want it to be true : he may regard it as extremely unlikely that it can be true.   But his own likings and supposings are entirely irrelevant.   Given evidence that points in its direction and that seems to support it, and any matter must be tested before one has a right to an opinion on it. That is the first law of science.   But there are heaps of *prima facie* evidence for Christianity.   Masses of men and women, honest and honourable, having put it to the proof, assert that they have found it true, that it does what it claims, and has so done in them.   In face of which, I, as a man of science, am bound with unprejudiced mind to give this thing its chance of proving itself to me also, if it can. And in him likewise it worked out.

There is, indeed, any amount of *prima facie* evidence for Christianity.   These tremendous assertions in Scripture about Jesus Christ, what He is in Himself and what He has wrought in men, are not just wild words flung out into the air, without any very definite meaning, and not to be taken really seriously.   They are a sober attempt to put into words what these men, who have tried Him, have actually found in Christ and have experienced through Him.   And, as life proceeds, always to their bewilderment Christ keeps transcending their most audacious conceptions of Him.   Always the moulds into which they had run their thinking of Him, and their statements of what He has been to them, become hopelessly inadequate, are overflowed, and broken, and swept utterly away, as new and yet more wonderful experiences of Him force them to keep enlarging their first-hand testimony of what they have proved He is and does.   " The sea," cried Tintoretto, hurling down his brushes, " grows always greater.   Nobody can paint it."   And Paul, after valiantly trying this way and that way to help us to glimpse, at least, what he has found in Christ, admits finally, with a kind of glad despair, that in Him and His love to us there is a length and a breadth and a depth and a height that pass all knowledge : that these attempts of His to photograph it and explain it to us, which some impatiently dismiss as wild and meaningless exaggeration, are, in reality, ludicrously ineffective to enable us even to begin to see what Christ gives to a soul that trusts itself to Him.

The creeds are not a remote inference, but are built up upon experience. And from every age and every land corroboration of it all crowds in. So Tertullian boasted in his day : and it has been the same in every day. Not an hour passes but souls unnumbered join that heavenly host, and add their testimony to that of all these countless others, that their faith and hope in Christ were only the dimmest of shadows of what He has proved Himself to them to be.

And so while Paul freely admits that, at first, faith is a venture, calling for some daring, it justifies itself at an ever-increasing rate, so that in a very little those who give Christ His chance with them are walking no longer by pure faith at all, but founding solidly on actual experience.

In all human literature there are few pages more depressing than Aristotle's grim description of the degeneration he had found to be general in men, from the big-heartedness and generous-mindedness, and eager hopes, and illimitable faith of youth to the cynicism and the hopelessness and the apathy of age ; and not least from the assurance of " glad confident morning," ringing out its convictions, to the timidity and hesitancy of men daunted by their experience, and much less sure of anything and everything than once they were. Well, thank God ! that is not a portrait universally true. And it ought to be impossible for Christian folk to fail like that. Paul, for one, had no such tale to tell. In an unstable world of things for ever shifting and collapsing, not all collapsed and shifted. Some grew more sure, and steadfast, and immovably certain as the years slipped by, bringing more evidence and further proof of them day in, day out. I am persuaded, he grows fond of saying, not hesitant at all. And long before the end, about some things he has grown far past " I think," or " I hope," or even " I believe. " I know," he says ; and again " I know " ; and once again " I know " : has something solid and secure beneath his feet that is unshakable, whatever gives and vanishes away. And that means much.

But, further, there is this arresting and heartening fact that these certainties of his form themselves precisely where the shadows lie deepest and coldest upon human life, where men are apt to lose their way ; and faith, apart from Christ, is likeliest to break down.

For, first, there is the fact of pain and sorrow, often such colossal pain, such heaped-up, unbearable sorrow ; and the shivery shadow that it casts so far over the earth. Never a moment but it steals into some other home ; and it, too, suddenly grows dark and cold. To you, perhaps, it is, as yet, only a rumour blown from very far away, like the report of some Chinese disaster in some unpronounceable place, of which you never heard, and so, impatiently, you turn the paper, seeking for something vital, with some spice of interest in it. Yet, to how many, who had acted so for years, it has come, in their turn, horribly real at last ! And to you, also, one day it will come.

And then, what then ? It is daunting to note how many of the biggest men break utterly and shamefully under the strain. Shakespeare, for instance, with his mighty intellect, and those deeps in his nature, out of which he drew unfathomable things, at the chill touch of some sorrow, or grievance, or disaster, lost all self-control, all decency, all manhood, went berserk, obscene in his ungovernable rage, and, in play after play, frothed at the mouth like a mad thing, until, ashamed and humiliated, we steal away. No book in the whole world has faced the fact of sorrow, and the mystery of pain so honestly, and with such steady eyes, as the New Testament. It is not for nothing that the Christian symbol is—a Cross ; and a most wonderful fact that it was a voice from the agony of crucifixion that has made masses of men entirely sure that God is Love. It was men who had known the bleak and windswept places ; who, as Paul tells us in that vivid, breathless scrap of crowded autobiography in the Corinthians, had faced, again and again, the extremities of peril and agony and fearsomenesses of all kinds that life could heap upon them—had endured terrifying things, who remain so unbroken, with their heads up, and their hearts gallant and gay. They state the sinister facts more bluntly, writing them down in blacker ink, than anybody else, concealing nothing, minimizing nothing, explaining away nothing. They listen to the bleaters' snivelling complaints, and their angry demands that God owes us a full apology for offering us this botch of a life ; as we too have to do these days, when so many, like a circle of wolves sitting on their tails, are ululating miserably to the skies. And when at long last they are finished, these New Testament men look at them queerly ; and, there are mysteries far darker than that, they say, and problems vastly more tremendous ; and, with that, they take us to Calvary, and set us down before that Central Cross. There, they say, is the noblest Being this earth ever saw. And that is what became of Him in this world of God ; and with God over all ! Plato was right. He foresaw that, if the ideal man should ever be found on the earth, probably he would be crucified. And He was. And when, with shrinking spirits, we seek to shut out and forget this hideous thing, " Take down your hands," they tell us sternly, " and face the facts of life!" All which is summed up—is it not?—in that tremendous picture of creation, bound, enslaved, agonized, desperate. " We know that to this day the entire creation sighs and throbs with pain." Here, evidently, is no easy optimism, rather a resolute facing of the grimmest facts. Yet it all ends in sunny faith and quiet courage, built up upon experience. For we " know " something more—that " all things work together for good to them that love God " ; (Others they may sour and break); that even the most ghastly of them can, if rightly used, become a blessed instrument of sanctification and of spiritual progress, and of hammering manhood into us. There is a wise psalmist who, standing with a sore, bewildered heart, and very lonesome, amid the ruins of his life, makes the most wise resolve that he will keep quite quiet, absolutely quiet, and give utterance to none of the confusion seething tumultuously within his tortured mind. For it was God who did this. So he feels quite certainly. And God is very wise, and very loving, and does not willingly, nor needlessly, afflict and grieve the children of men. There must be meaning and love in this somehow, though meantime it seems only a dark mystery of unbearable pain. I will keep dumb. And one day I shall understand.

No doubt there are those who will not allow us such a faith, laugh raucously at it, burst in and seek to snatch it from us, and toss it away. A distinguished preacher of our day, for instance, tells us, with an immense complacency how, when a poor soul, whose little son had died of cholera, said, pulling himself together with the thought, " Ah, well ! I suppose it is the will of God," brushed that aside as an outrageous, even blasphemous, reading of it all. " Call it human ignorance, folly, or sin ; call it a careless nurse, a filthy drain, or unclean food, but not God." The calm assurance of that, and, still more, its gratuitous cruelty, staggers me.

Confessedly, the mysteries of Providence have unfathomable deeps in them that catch away the breath, and darknesses so dark that our human eyesight, peer and strain as it may, cannot as yet see through them to the light shining clearly and blessedly upon the other side. " Lead me to the other side of darkness," prays an undaunted soul in the Upanishads, and plunges into it unafraid, sure that there is another side, where the darkness is gone. But, meantime, it is here ; and we must walk, not by sight, but by faith. And, as Plutarch warns us, speaking with a seemly humility on these high matters, " let us be cautious in what we say about the deity, and decline to speak about these things, as if we thoroughly understood them, like unmusical people laying down the law on music, or civilians, ignorantly dogmatic about war, building on nothing more substantial than opinions and fancy and probabilities." Even the Scriptures do not all speak with one voice on these tremendous themes ; on the how, and the why, and the mystery of things. And yet, if the Lord Christ is to be credited, and His attitude adopted by us, certain points are clear. In spite of all the sin and confusion and misery in it, to Christ this is essentially an orderly universe, and not a haphazard affair, where anything may happen, for any reason, or no reason at all. Certainly, He is quite definite that the men killed by the fall of the Tower of Siloam were not, thereby, proved to have been monstrous sinners. That was too easy, and a quite untrue solution of life's problems. Yet, I think, it would never have occurred to Him that a child died simply because a cholera germ chanced, by pure accident, to be blown in his direction; and that was all that there is to it.

When it grew plain that the influential folk and learned people had decided against Him, and were about to bring all their authority to bear to put Him down, He did not say, faced by that disappointment and seeming disaster, " Call it human prejudice, or human conservatism, or human narrowmindedness, but not God. He did call it God. " Father, I thank Thee that Thou hast hidden these things from the wise and prudent, and hast revealed them unto babes. Even so, Father, for so it seemed good in Thy sight." Or, when the ugly shadow of the cross fell cold and shivery and forbidding across His path, faced by that horror and agony and shame, He did not say " Call it human ignorance or folly or sin, but not God." He did call it God ; and accepted it as put into His hands by God's. " The cup that My Father giveth Me, will I not drink it ? "

And when, taught by Him, the men of the New Testament gather upon Calvary, face to face with that hideous horror ; and, with awed hearts, thank God that He gave His Son even to death for us, does our authority still tell us He had nothing to do with it ? Call it human ignorance, or folly, or sin ; call it stupidity, or malice, or a lack of broad-mindedness, but not God. Apparently he does, talks of " the cross of wood brought about by non-divine intention." But the New Testament is sure that, in it, and behind it, there is certainly divine intention; sees past the very real and awful secondary causes of it all to the tremendous primary one; says that from all eternity God willed this thing, and planned it, going even that unthinkable length for a lost world.

2 05 70

" This Jesus," declares Peter, heaping up his words to make his meaning unmistakable, " betrayed in the predestined course of God's deliberate purpose." And God had nothing to do with it ! If Jesus Christ accepts the cup as given Him by His Father, was He wrong, and quite mistaken ? And, if He was not wrong, why may I not accept the sorrows of my life in a like spirit, as a call to some high service, hidden from me as yet ; and as a chance, under His hands, of fitting myself for it ? If there is meaning in it, love in it, God in it, it is so much easier to bear. And there is ; and life proves that there is.

In any case, the men of the New Testament are plainly right in their assertion that, if the harsh things of life are faced and accepted, not with the snarls and snapping teeth of a trapped brute, but with the loving, trusting spirit of a child, they do deepen and beautify a character, and do teach many central things, not easily, if at all, to be learned by any gentler and less painful method. So was it with the race. If human life had been planned, as aggrieved voices keep insisting it should have been planned; if there had been no difficulties to be faced, nor sorrows to be borne ; no pain nor disappointments ; if it had drowsed past sleepily in unbroken placidity and a perennial sunshine, what an appalling creature man must have remained— flabby, backboneless, lacking everything that gives him any worth or a trace of attractiveness—without courage, or sympathy, or hardi- hood, or patience : for all these lovely things are the children of danger and sorrow and pain. " A dull and neglected suffering," Bacon concedes, " effects little or nothing. But a wise and in- dustrious suffering draweth and contriveth use and advantage out of that that seemed adverse and contrary." Even Christ, declares the Scripture boldly, was made perfect only through suffering. And you will not attain it upon easier terms than He. " He took it lovingly," mused old Dr. Duncan, took the Cross lovingly : and that is why He saved the world. And if you take it lovingly, that bitter thing will justify itself even to you—in time. And it will give you a new chance of helpfulness towards your fellow-men. For always somebody is passing through deep waters, with his breath caught away by that fearsome rush and bitter cold. And an outsider cannot help much. But you should have a tact and an understanding ; for you have sat where they sit : and a far deeper intensity of sympathy that cries out for them, and that longs to help ; for you have passed that stony way yourself : and an experience of God's kindness to hurt things to share with them, that only hurt things know. Frazer of

Brea tells us that it had come to this of it with him that, whenever an untoward happening leapt out at him, he mused " this messenger is certainly harsh featured, but he brings me a love token from the King. What is this sent to teach me ? " Before the end is come, you too will find that all things work together for good, if people take them lovingly ; and will at last be able, amid all the benefits with which He has loaded you, to thank Him with an awed heart, almost most of all, for the sorrows life has sent you, and what He has taught you through them. :" I have prayed," says Fox, " to be baptized into a sense of all conditions, that I might be able to know the needs and feel the sorrows of all." The answer to that prayer is, often, to be had only through suffering or sorrow.

And then there is the fact of sin.

Sin ! you cry. You're not going to talk of sin—that obsolete conception, that boring topic to which nobody will listen, that insult to our proud human nature, which, having achieved such marvellous triumphs in the material world, has no intention of submitting to being told that, in the spiritual, it is a poor broken weakling, desperately in need of help, and doomed, unless it finds it. Dr. Fosdick is reported to have said that the business of the man in the pulpit is to preach on what is real and pressing to his hearers' minds. An excellent counsel, up to a point. But it is only a half truth. And half truths are, proverbially, dangerous. Surely it is a foremost part of every preacher's duty to lay stress on the big things which men are overlooking, or forgetting, or deliberately ignoring, or won't have. And are we to agree to say nothing about this horrid fact that stares at us, to huddle it out of sight, and pretend it isn't there ; and, because we ourselves resolutely refuse to look in its direction, to assume that God will also overlook it, and smuggle us all through somehow ; and so, toeing obediently the line of what they want to hear, get the people upon any terms, their terms ; whereas Christ would accept them only on His terms.

 ¯ Once, coming away from a conference with the French statesmen and generals, Lloyd George remarked to his companion, " You know, Grey, you are far too modest about your French. You were the only one of the whole lot that I could follow ! "

And some popular ministers are popular, not because they are spiritual experts, but rather because they preach an execrable Christianity, with all that is characteristic in it just not there ; but which the natural man can follow, simply because it is so like his own mind,

and leaves his comfort and his conscience undisturbed. As Peer
Gynt commented on a kindly sermon over a dead man of ugly reputation, " Well, that's what I call Christianity ! Nothing in it to make
one feel uneasy."

Sin, so they tell us, sin ! People nowadays don't know what the
word means. Far better drop it, and speak, rather, of " frustration."
But much sin is not so simple and half innocent a matter as frustration. It is a cold, set, deliberate disobedience.

If you won't credit the Christian faith, will you listen to Freud,
that popular prophet of the day, with his appalling delineation of this
human nature of ours, which we preachers must not presume to
criticize ; that hideous picture of the subconscious in your heart and
mine, where, as one puts it, " a turbulent company frets and fumes
and meditates violent irruptions into the open that would shame us ;
threatening to break in on our daylight respectability with male-
dictions, and strange atavistic lusts." Aye, and has done it ! Look
at the world around us ! And how, from under our smug modern
respectabilities there has burst out before our astonished eyes things
we had thought were dead and buried and left centuries behind us—
Jew-baiting, persecution, torture, hideous sadistic cruelties.

What a commentary on our jaunty optimism, and unruffled complacency, and impudent perversion of the Master's words, " They
that be whole need not a physician, but they that be sick." And
we are not sick : there is nothing wrong with us, if only we were
given a chance, and had our environment amended. A Saviour !
A Saviour from what ?

And what is to prevent unending repetitions of these tragedies
unless Christ lays His cool hand on our lunatic world : and, the
madness gone from us, we sit, once more sane and human, clothed,
and in our right mind, at His feet ?

And you yourself, do you know nothing of a divine discontent
that frets, and longs, and reaches out groping hands that never find
that something, other and better and altogether different from what
you are, which they keep seeking ? All that, says Paul, need last no
moment longer, can end here and now. What you need is a Saviour.
And there is a Saviour ; and He does save. And this is no mere hope,
or dream, or longing. I know. I give you first-hand evidence. I
tell you, you can safely trust to it ; know it, because it has worked
out in me. Never once has He failed me : and He never will. " He
rescued me ; He still rescues me : and I rely upon Him that He will

continue to rescue me." So he summed up his life to the Corinthians. "I know in whom I have believed, and am persuaded that He is able to keep that which I have committed unto Him against that day." It is as sure as that.

And, then, there is the fact of death. And that leaves Paul entirely undisturbed, say rather, eager and excited. "I know that, if this earthly tent of mine is taken down, I get a home from God eternal in the heavens." To which you answer crossly, you can't know. Well, literally, no. But it is almost as sure as that. And why are Christian folk so certain? Well, it looks—does it not?—as if Butler were right—that this life is a first volume that requires a second to explain and conclude it. And it seems unlikely that all that happened, when we were created, was that God, in an idle moment, set Himself a problem, as we do at chess, to see what He could make out of a character like yours, or mine; and worked it out, until He solved it, or else tired of it, and brushed the pieces from the board, to set them up for another game.

Bertrand Russell, indeed, thinks that God, tiring of the praises of the angels, which He knew He deserved, made a new race of creatures, and deliberately harassed them with pains and difficulties, to see what they would do. And Man, in his gallant fashion, converted his hardships and sorrows into a ladder, whereby he keeps climbing up above himself, thanking God as he climbs, for these divine-sent opportunities. And one day God will laugh, and say, "A good play that: some time I must repeat it:" meanwhile—enough; and will brush it aside into annihilation. A grim reading of a meaningless world, where, as A. J. Balfour puts it, shrinking from it as he does so, "Imperishable monuments and immortal deeds, death itself, and love stronger than death, will be as though they had never been. Nor will anything that *is* be better, or be worse, for all that the labour, genius, devotion, suffering of man have striven, through countless generations, to effect." But to the Christian it seems clear that the life given us even here is planned upon a scale so noble that it is evidently built, not for time only, but eternity: that our affections are not merely passing shadows.

> "For not in mockery He
> Thy gift of wondering gave,
> Nor bade thine answer be
> The blank stare of the grave.
> Thou shalt behold and know; and find again thy lost."

As Cowper ends a letter : " There is not room enough for friendship to unfold itself in full bloom in such a nook of life as this.   Therefore I am, and must, and will be, Yours for ever."

That was precisely how Christian people became sure of their own immortality.   Christ's love to them was a wonderful thing, even here and even now.   But they were sure that He had far more in His heart for them than even He can work out for, and in, them in this little nook of time ; that all eternity would not exhaust it; that for ever and for ever they would be wading deeper and still deeper into an ever new, and ever more original, an endless love.   Mr. Truslow Adams tells us that, so long as America was only partly colonized, the frontier kept calling men of spirit to rise up, and leave their little bits of things, and venture out into the wide open spaces, still to be possessed ; and that when, finally, the trek westwards reached the sea, and there was no longer a beyond that beckoned to them, the national spirit lost something of its old hardihood and eager seeking for adventure.   The Christian always has his frontier beckoning to him ; and it keeps him alert and young and daring.   Before him lies a whole eternity in which, past blundering and bungling, changed into Christ's likeness, grown up at last into what God planned that he should be, he will serve Him perfectly for ever and for ever.   And this, says Paul, is not a dream, a hope, a wildly glorious, but impossible, belief.   These are the things of which my life has made me sure.   I know, he says ; and again I know ; and, once again, I know.

CHAPTER XI

THE SPIRITUAL DANGER OF BEING UNIMPORTANT

" Give us to sit one on your right hand and one at your left hand, in your glory. Jesus said, You do not know what you are asking. Can you drink the cup I have to drink, or undergo the baptism I have to undergo ? They said to Him, ' We can.' "— MARK x. 37–39.

THIS is a distressing incident which leaves us, as often as we come on it, uncomfortable and hot-cheeked ; though the quiet forbearance of the Master in face of this preposterous proposition encourages us poor disappointing blunderers to make our way back to Him, hopefully, even after our own deplorable record, helped by this further vivid proof of what an amazed disciple long ago set down as one of His outstanding characteristics, that He is never ashamed to own us, and to call us brethren, even when He might well be ; never pointedly ignores us, though such disreputable creatures as we are must be very damaging to Him and His cause ; never keeps looking aloofly and ostentatiously the other way ; but eagerly comes out to greet the shabbiest figure, hirpling home, shamefacedly enough, lovingly, joyously, hopefully ; and at once sets to work again on this impossible bungler who has so often broken down, and so persistently contrived to find, or force, a way through all the safeguards He had cunningly set up around him. That was an apt quotation they applied to Him, " A bruised reed He will not break, and a smoking flax He will not quench." For, in very deed, He still hopes on, when hope seems out, and won't agree it has been proved to be quite useless.

It would seem that, in origin, this egregious scheme was the idea of a foolishly fond and ambitious mother. None the less, the fact remains that two out of the three men in all the world with whom the Lord Jesus Christ felt most at home, to whom He was most drawn, and on whom He leaned with the most confidence, allowed themselves, to the open rage of the other disciples, to be enticed into a grossly selfish plan, in itself, as Christ told them, only too clear a proof that they had imbibed next to nothing of His teaching, nor understood at all the objects of His lifework, or the spirit of His kingdom. So much is clear.

Yet I, for one, have difficulties with the usual blunt understanding of it all ; suggest, with deference, that it is possible, at least, that these blundering souls were not so crudely material as they seem ; that it was not the pomps and splendours that had caught and held their minds, but something much more worthy, if still foolish and mistaken ; that what they wanted was to be given the chance of such outstanding and unique service, of such a reckless burning out of themselves for Christ and for His cause, of such wholeheartedness of devotion that, by natural right, they would rank next to Christ Himself when He came in His kingdom. They were Christ's men. He could count on them. And what they coveted was to render Him such immense services that nobody could rival them. Give them a big adventure, a tremendous call upon them, and they would exult in it. But the little daily tasks, through which their loyalty was alone asked to prove itself, seemed to them tasteless and insipid. Into the doing of such tame trivialities they could not put their heart and soul and being, which hungered for far bigger claims on them, and felt that they could meet them. That is a reading, I submit, just possible.

And if it is a true interpretation of their minds, it is a vivid instance of what Christ, with His uncanny knowledge of human nature, found to be a very common, and a really serious, temptation, which assails masses of people, and before which all too many of them fall. Few folk, He tells us, are likelier to throw away their lives than those who are discouraged by a sense of their own unimportance ; and who, because, at best and most, they can do so little, as they judge, do nothing at all. Why bother ? For in any case what difference could it make ?

In the parable of the talents, those fortunate souls endowed with ten are eager and active and alert, and naturally so. For they cannot but see how really they make a difference, and how obviously they are telling on their bit of the world. And those with five, though less impressively gifted, have still much to encourage them ; and even those with two see something definite and solid for their labours. It is the commonplace man, with only one (and how many of us there are), with no distinction nor anything outstanding, with neither influence nor money, and no particular capacity of any kind, with nothing that he can bring even to Christ except a dogged, futile loyalty that does not seem to effect anything, or make one scrap of difference—it is he who is apt to hide away his poor little bit of endowment, as not worth using. Anything he might try to do, or anything he has to give, could make no odds. And so, because his individual gift must be so small and apparently so trivial, he holds it back ; although heaped

8

up together, in the mass, what the one talented could bring, and do, would amount to a mighty thing. So is Christ cheated out of His kingdom by depressed souls, stunned into apathy and inactivity by their own insignificance. If they could do something that mattered, could sit on the right hand or on the left, or anywhere within their neighbourhood, of course they would be up and doing tirelessly like the ten talented. But one! They look at it contemptuously, and hide it out of sight; make up their minds they can do nothing, and waste their life in doing it.

That is an old sore. " Say not," urges the writer of Ecclesiasticus, " what use is there of me ? " And he set down that warning because he had found so many were so feeling and so murmuring ; returns to it with added emphasis, is urgent in the matter. " Say not that I am hidden and lost even from God, and who remembers me ? Among so many people how can I be noticed ? For what is my soul in this boundless creation ? " The fact that you are here at all is, in itself, clear proof that there is some work needing to be done, and God has thought out—you, as the best fitted to accomplish it, and now looks to you with confidence to put it through for Him, to do and be for Him what only you can be and do. But that is difficult to credit. Those on the right hand and the left hand have that immense encourage-ment to thrill and inspire them. But we live on so small a scale, and potter about among such petty trivialities that, for us, it sounds incredible. If anything came of it, or was even likely so to do; ah ! then how we would spend ourselves. But here !

A youth gives his life to Jesus Christ, enters the ministry with some real passion for His service in his heart. If he were given some hum and stir about him, crowds in the pews, a flutter of interest and even of excitement round him, still more, some spiritual happenings to make him sure results were following on his efforts, he would toil all his days " diligently, faithfully, and cheerfully " as he promised at his ordination he would do. But he is set down in a sphere where, in a great staring church, the folk are thinly scattered about the yawning emptiness, and the tunes rise raggedly, and many things are amateur and makeshift, and no news ever reaches him of anybody being any better for all that he seeks to do for them ; and year in and year out they look the same ; until, concussed by the seeming resultlessness of anything and everything he tries, he loses heart, and hope, and faith, and gradually slips down from his first enthusiasm to a half cynical, and half unconscious, feeling that best, or a poor

hurried second best, what does it matter ? " Forty years of preaching,"
declared Manning, " often look like forty years of beating the air."
But the men in the great ministries, upon the right hand and the left,
are spared all that.

Or, some young person sets out for the first time to face a Sunday-
school class, or the like, thrilled and excited, for she is going to serve
Jesus Christ, and He has given us enormous promises ; and anything
may happen, any time, perhaps to-day ! But, after years of it, is
she still as alert, as eager, as wholehearted ? Often yes, and more ;
surer than ever of the value of it all ; and with reason. But some stick
to it only from a dogged loyalty, which holds on and keeps going, but
without much hope of fruit or outcome. They know, from long experience, what is awaiting them, the usual little row of fidgety hands,
and restless feet, and frankly bored faces. If they had had real skill
with children, had had five talents, had been worthy of a place even
on the left hand ! But they can give so little, and so little comes
of it. Is it worth doing ?

Or, on the greater stage of world affairs, the leaders, with the burden
of it always crushing on their hearts—may God fulfil to them His
promise, reopening each new morning like a flower, that as their days
are, so their strength shall be—have this to inspire and to sustain
them, that they know that the rest of us lean undisguisedly on them,
and look to them for heartening and guidance ; that when they make
decisions, there are large and visible results ; that when they speak,
innumerable hearts are steadied, and uplifted, and ennobled, given
new grit and courage ; that they indisputably tell upon, and influence,
and make a difference to, this needy, desperate world. But the rest
of us, sunk in the mass of ordinary people, each of us just one unit
in a whole battalion, which, in its turn, is only one of hundreds of
battalions ; or one hand in one populous factory out of the thousands
of such factories thick sown up and down the land ; or one miner,
or one fisherman out of so many at the face, or on the seas ; or one old,
useless man whose passion for freedom can express itself only in such
ludicrously subsidiary ways—anything we can do appears to make
so little difference—either way. Is it of any moment in this vast
world-wide wrestle, whether I do my very most, and very best, or
something less and easier ? Those on the right and left hand have, in
certain ways, the less call made upon their faith and courage.

But this whole business, this enervating, daunting sense of our
own unimportance, and of the seeming fatuousness of anything we

do, and everything we are, is one of the most pressing and insistent problems of the day, cruelly wounding many people's self-respect, and unsettling their peace of mind, as often, and in many lands, it has stung them into the fierceness of revolution.

Hegel tells us that the drama unrolling itself down the ages, on the stage of human history has for its theme the evolution of free men. In the beginning only one is free ; and all the rest are slaves, with no rights, and no standing, subject to that one's caprice and whim ! But, gradually, one here and one there emerge out of the mass, assert themselves and claim " this is my life, not yours ! " As time runs on, more and more climb up out of chatteldom : and in the end all will be free, and the plot will be worked out.

The individual has been " de-universalized " out of the mass, whereas in primitive peoples he has no clear sense of his own personality at all, apart from the tribe. And even now, in India, says that authority, Bishop Pickett, there are millions who are still at that stage ; who, if you ask them who they are, will each tell you, not his own personal name, but the name of the caste. " To address them in the singular is to insult them. He resents any suggestion that he is by himself, a man apart. And to act in affairs of moment on his own initiative, and not as the tribe directs, " were to outrage his sense of propriety, even his ethical sense."

In present-day civilization we are cruising upon broken waters in this matter, where two currents meet and clash. On the one hand, the de-universalizing of the individual proceeds apace. As James of Harvard put it, " Surely the individual, the person in the singular number, is the more fundamental phenomenon, and the social institution, of whatever grade, is but secondary and ministerial." At the moment, the popular view here is that the individual has huge claims upon the State. Its function is to be an earthly providence towards him, meeting his every want, from birth to burial—in sickness, unemployment, education, old age—everything. To the rage of Nietzsche, who declared hotly that we were building spineless parasites, not men who can stand up on their own feet, and face the storms ; that our ideal is the shabby one of " the green meadow happiness of the herd," of gross beasts standing in lush grass up to their bloated bellies.

But, on the other hand, many things point to a current opinion that the de-universalizing has gone much too far ; and that the individual must be pressed back into the mass again ; must learn that he lives for the State, and can know life in fullness only in its service. No one

any longer can do what he likes with his own. Largely it is not his own.
There are huge claims on income, accepted now as a mere commonplace, with only eighty persons left in Britain with £6000 a year,
after paying income and super tax ; and with those over a certain
limit laying down nineteen and sixpence in the pound, given themselves only the odd sixpence as a kind of tip ; and endless limitations
of what used to be considered natural liberties, and with restrictions
ever tightening upon us. Aye, and with multitudes hemmed into a
monotonous and colourless existence in factories or the like, where, as
they bitterly complain, they are, not men and women, but mere
hands, pieces of mechanism swung round endlessly as part of a complicated mass of intricate machinery : for seven or eight hours daily
their existence frittered away in endless repetitions of some purely
mechanical act, which bores them, sickens them, revolts them, dwarfs
their personality, numbs their minds, and deadens their very souls.
And they refuse to be content to be thus thrust back into the mass
again, to lose their individuality, claim their lives for themselves ;
are maddened, not helped, by the Christian assurance of the unique-
ness, and the irreplacability of every one. It is not true, they cry.
Look at my life ! A million others could do what I do. Or look
at me, denied my human rights, and forced down into chatteldom
again.

Well, any social system that leaves numbers with an outraged
sense of being stunted, and maimed, and cramped must be sub-
Christian, and in need of grave amendment.

Meantime, Isaiah agrees with you that you have been given the
hardest of all tasks. Have you ever been surprised that his glorious
fortieth chapter seems to peter out in anticlimax, like a river roaring
through its rocky gorges, urgent, impatient, irresistible, which yet
never finds the sea, but dies away in marsh and bog, and a mere wet
sponginess. They that wait upon the Lord, he says, shall mount up
on wings, like eagles ; and we, chained to the ground, watch them
admiringly ; and shall run and not be weary ; that seems much less
impressive ; and shall walk, and not faint ; so it all dies away to that
prosaic ending ! But to Isaiah that seems far the greatest achievement
of the three, that simple folk, with nothing to encourage them, and
seeing small outcome of anything they do, should hold on loyally
and zealously, still doing it eagerly, with all their heart and soul,
that is the sacrifice most difficult to give to God ; and a supreme proof
of His grace is that He enables multitudes of tired, discouraged people,

stunned by their own so obvious unimportance, to keep on offering it, day by day.

But there is this to be said. Many have pointed out that one of the main achievements of the Reformation was the sanctifying, yes, and the glorifying, of daily work : and the new, awed, happy sense of God's presence close beside one in it. As Heim puts it, " the workshop became a church ; all who were engaged in maintaining human life became consecrated priests in this vast Church of God. This was Luther's new contribution, the conception of a man's calling in the world as service given to God." But to-day that ennobling truth seems moribund or dead. Wages for oneself, profits for one's employers. Is that all that there is, and can be in it ? Is it impossible, as is often alleged, to serve God in a factory ? The men of the New Testament were sure it could be done even in slavery—obscene system though that is. And the Russians have no difficulty in their factories, and when engaged on tasks, every whit as monotonous and as mechanical as other folks' can be, in finding, says Berdiaeff, " a mystic joy in their submergence in the collective," in forgetting themselves altogether in working at their daily drudgery with a passion, an enthusiasm, a happiness, because they are so working not for themselves at all, but for something bigger than themselves, and in a service which glorifies the commonest, the messiest, the most dreary of tasks.

If it be possible to give all that to Russia, how can it be impossible to offer it to God and the Lord Jesus Christ ? " All true work is sacred ; in all true work, were it but true hand labour, there is something of divineness. Sweat of the brow : and up from that to sweat of the brain, sweat of the heart : up to that ' agony of bloody sweat ' which all men have called divine ! " So Carlyle, over and over. And, far older, from Ecclesiasticus again, where it acclaims as all-important the one-talent folk like you and me ; and in especial, gives the first place of all to the men with roughened hands, and what looks like a cramped existence. They are not found, it says, among the great and influential, nor are they, in themselves, impressive intellectually. " Yet, it is they who maintain the fabric of the world ; and in the handiwork of their craft is a true prayer." So mighty are the unimportant people after all !

Moreover, there is a large margin in most lives outside their daily work, of leisure, and of contacts, and of opportunity. Constantly we keep telling upon one another, and our influence spreads further than we ever know. Think again of the most unlikely people who helped Jesus Christ, as they strayed into His life—a soldier, his life mainly spent in the intolerable boredom, to most minds, of barrack squares, and drills, and endless regulations; a partisan who had lost everything and hung there, naked and dying; a heathen woman with her pagan mind—what, between them, could such people do to be of service to the Son of God? And yet, each of them helped Him immeasurably. And, as we move about our lives, we also touch upon so many others, and might leave them steadied, and cheered, and happier, because we passed by. And there are always some for whom we can do, what no one else can do; and be, what no one else can be. No: it was not for nothing that we were created; and, in our unimportance, we too have a unique part to play. It does not catch the eye, it makes no stir, often it seems there is nothing to show at all. " Thomas," said Jesus, " blessed are those who have not seen, and yet have believed." And He Himself was one of them, died with so little to encourage Him. And He asks nothing more from you than He Himself was willing to face and to give.

And so Jesus turns upon these unwise petitioners and challenges them to make sure that they are really of the type to which there can be granted, not a chief place in His strange Kingdom, but any entrance into it at all, reminding them that, in it, things are just reversed from our customs and ways. Swedenborg believed that angels got younger the older they grew. That is quite possible in that queer realm, where all our notions are upset and overturned and obsolete; where the greatest is the lowliest, and the least is the mightiest, and the king is the servant of all. Can you drink of the cup that I shall drink of? Can you forget yourself, and give your life for others? If not, there is no place for you at all. And the two looked Christ in the eyes, and said, " We can." It was said ignorantly, foolishly, boastfully. And yet, I think, Christ's smile came out. And, indeed, they kept their promise; broke, but rallied, and made a right honourable end.

And to us, too, in these tense days of waiting for the grim things only a little way ahead, Christ puts that same heart-searching question. " Can you drink of the cup that I shall drink of; and be baptized with the baptism wherewith I am baptized? " And, with your dear ones yonder, with so much of what makes life for you in jeopardy, can you too look Him in the eyes, and say " We can." Yes, said Christ gravely to His two disciples, you both can, and will. And how many of us also will have to drink that cup, these days, before the end is won ! The emptied homes, the shattered hopes, the broken hearts, pray God He may accept it as our poor human effort to do something for His desperate world ; and even to fill up the sufferings of Jesus Christ : and that our Lord may say to us, with a like honouring confidence, " You can. You will."

Have you never, when at Calvary, cried out, in bitter shame and confusion of spirit, because no one, no one, not even one, burst through the cordon round the crosses, crying, " I am Christ's ! And I cannot stand by and watch this ; would far rather die with Him," and did.

Some of us will be given our chance of that these days. If it comes, don't let us writhe and scream and struggle madly, but let us face it quietly, gallantly, Christ-likely. And all of us are equal here ; and the most unimportant can give every whit as hugely and as generously as the very greatest.

So, let us turn back, and live out our humble rôles, content, and saved from murmuring and fretting. When Dante reached the heavenly places, he came upon one soul, posted far out upon the extreme confines of Paradise, and asked her if she were never envious of those who stood beside the throne, and in God's very presence. Whereat, smiling at such an earthly question and idea, the other answered, His will is my will. In His will is my peace. And where He sets me, there, of all places in the universe, I would choose to be.

CHAPTER XII

THE DAY-DREAMS OF A CHRISTIAN MAN

"That I may know Him, and the power of His resurrection, and the fellowship of His sufferings, being made conformable unto His death, if by any means, I may attain unto the resurrection of the dead."—PHIL. iii. 10.

THAT, surely, is one of the very greatest tributes ever paid to Jesus Christ. For it is Paul who speaks. And if ever man did know the Master, it was he. Have not his thoughts of Christ proved, to the rest of us, far deeper and more satisfying than those of any other ? Have they not been adopted as the moulds into which our own thinking about Christ is run? Whenever spring comes back to the Church, and the clean winds of God blow, health-giving and invigorating, where it had been sultry and airless and dead ; whenever the old power leaps into life again before men's startled eyes ; whenever God stands to His promises, and it all comes true, it is largely because we have waded, out of the shallows of our own thinking about Christ, a little way into the deeps of Paul's experiences of Him.

And, indeed, it is a stupendous conception of our Lord to which Paul climbed. Look at some aspects of it, for a moment.

Would you know your duty in any conceivable situation ? There is no difficulty about that. On to the end of time, you have only to look at Christ, and keep looking, to absorb His spirit, and to follow in His steps. For holiness means Christ-likeness. And to be unlike Christ is sin. So says Paul with assurance. Yet in the days of His flesh there were those who hated Christ as a bad man, and a right sinister figure. He a prophet ! they said angrily. He ! consorting openly with impossible folk—the mere wreckage and scum of society ; and impudently breaking not a few of the traditions, and prating of the mercy of God, blind to His awful holiness ; thereby inducing silly, gullible souls to settle down, with easier minds, in their unworthiness ; for this flabbily good-natured God will no doubt see them through— this is a dangerous, indeed a lunatic, teacher, far better away. And they haled Him to Calvary.

But now we see, what Paul saw at the time, that Christ's immense originality in His conception of what goodness means and is, was right : that to be holy we must follow in His steps, and must put on His mind and ways.

Or, asks Paul, would you know what God is like ? Of course we would. Nothing can be so all-important as to be sure as to the nature and the character of Him with whom we have to do. All down the ages people have been wondering and hoping. Ah ! if only He were this ! And what if He be that ! And Paul breaks in on all that. If, he says confidently, you would know God really and worthily, you must think of Him in terms of Jesus Christ. That life and character you saw lived out upon the human scale, expanded to the divine scale—that is the nearest you can ever rise to thinking adequately about God. There was a day when men clapped horrified hands to affrighted ears to shut out so hideous a blasphemy. But now we see that it is true—that, if there is a God at all, He must be Christlike. Looking at how Jesus lived, we know how God must live : watching Him going about doing good, spending Himself for any one and every one, in any need—giving and giving, till there was nothing that He had not given—except Himself, and then He gave that too, we know that that dazzling Holiness of God, too blinding for our human eyes, is a white light composed of many rays, of love, and kindness, and self-sacrifice, and a divine unselfishness—the length and breadth and height and depth of which we cannot even begin to understand ; and, at the Cross, our awed hearts bow before the Lord God Almighty with a new lowliness of awe, and a new wonderment of gratitude, for He, too, has kept back nothing, but has given His all, God's all, counting no sacrifice excessive, and no pain to Him too sore, if thereby He can save our wayward souls, and heal His careless, desperate world.

" A God that could understand, that could suffer, that could sympathize, that had felt the extremity of human anguish, the agony of bereavement, had submitted even to the brutal hopeless torture of the innocent, and had become acquainted with the pangs of death. This is the extraordinary conception of Godhead to which we have at this stage risen." So Sir Oliver Lodge ! Or Streeter : " In the Old Testament we find the idea that God enters into the sufferings of His people. ' In all their afflictions He was afflicted.' The relation of God to the woes of the world is not that of a mere spectator. The New Testament goes further, and says that God *is* love. But that is not love which, in the presence of acute suffering, can stand outside and aloof. The doctrine that Christ is the image of the unseen God means that God does *not* stand outside." That, wrote Pringle Pattison, is the central doctrine of Christianity, and must be taken seriously, " in bitter earnest." This perpetual redeeming process " is the very life of God, in which, besides the effort and pain, He tastes, we must believe, the joy of victory won." All which we have learned at Calvary ; and it was, largely, the great Apostle who made us understand what our eyes see there.

Or, once again, would you, asks Paul, know life in its fullness ? Then get Christ into it. For nothing else will do. Apart from Him, even God's tireless loving-kindness towards us, and immense ingenuity in devising more and more benefits to heap upon us can, at the best, and most, fashion only a meagre and a barren thing for us, compared to what the humblest Christian knows, and has, and hopes.

Paul stretches language, heaps up metaphors, coins new words, seeking to bring something of that home to us, to force us to realize a little of the wonder of Jesus Christ, and the incalculable difference He makes.

Once, on a glorious day in summer, I sat beside a man born blind. For me there was so much, all really and indisputably there—beauty on beauty, and all mine—the gold of the sunshine, and the blue of the sky, and the white fleeciness of the clouds, and the innumerable twinklings of the sea, and the glory of the harvest, and the witchery of the flowers, and the restful green of tree and grass, and the majesty of the hills, and the changeful shadows blown along them, and how much more, all there, all mine. And, not a foot away, a man knew nothing of it all—shut into that blank and sullen darkness, could not begin to picture it, or understand it, and my heart cried out for him. If only he could see what I saw, and know what I know, and share all that I had—the full and glorious life that God has planned for us, and not that maimed and stunted thing of his. So Paul felt shudderingly, looking upon Christless folk. They, too, were blind, and in the dark, poor souls ; knew nothing of the joys and glories that he had in Christ, nor how colourful and wonderful a human life can be.

It is, indeed, a tremendous claim he makes for Christ ; and a staggering conception of Him to which he had climbed.

Yet here, far on in his discipleship, he is vexed and repentant because his knowledge and experience of Christ is so unworthy and inadequate, stretches out eager hands towards better things, feels there is far more in the Master than he has as yet even begun to realize. If I could know Him ! Oh ! if only I could learn to know Him, somewhat as He really is !

It is like the scientists these days of ours. There are two schools of them. The lesser men are cackling excitedly over their discoveries. And little wonder, after all ! For have they not transformed the whole face of the world, and made what were impossibilities easy, and put what had been always out of the question within anybody's reach ?

And yet the bigger men are not vainglorious and boastful, but awed, abashed, stunned, feeling that anything they have discovered is a mere nothing to what Nature has to give, if only we could tap it. " We imagine," said Seneca, in another hour of human pride, " we are initiated into Nature's mysteries ; we who, as yet, are but hanging around her outer courts." So now, men feel that in Nature there are such forces, such possibilities, such powers ! All really there, and dimly they can see them ; but if only we could lay our hands on them, and use them, what might there not result !

So, says Paul, I owe everything to Jesus Christ ; and what He has done for me cannot be reckoned up. And yet there is so much in Him I have not seen, and, still more, have not appropriated yet. If I could see it, grasp it, use it, share it with my fellows, how mankind would leap forward.

There, then, is a first lesson—the bigness and wonder of the Lord Jesus Christ.

Are we not faltering these days, largely because of our failure to appreciate that ; because, unconsciously, we have dwarfed and be-littled Him in our own minds, compared to what He really is ; because we have no adequate sense of the exceeding greatness either of Him-self, or of His power to usward who believe ; and so, keep coasting timidly along the shores of our wonderful faith, or even faintheartedly skulk in its inland waters, whereas there are vast oceans in it, and golden lands to be possessed—all ours, if we would only enter into them, and take them !

The younger generation, for example, know Christ as the Friend, the Comrade, the Companion, and, perhaps, the Leader, but as little more.

Certainly they do well to attach themselves to Him where, and as, they can, in honesty and with sincerity. Was it not so men acted, at the first, in the New Testament ? They came to One who was a Teacher with a message, they felt, for the times and for their souls. And then they recognized Him as a prophet. And then, could this be the Messiah, really come at last ? And, at length, some of them fell at His feet as dead, seeing in Him the express image of God's very Person. So, as Pascal says, though at first so humble and so lowly, " with prodigious magnificence " He kept looming up bigger and bigger before their awed hearts and eyes. In view of which fact, youth to-day, in so far as it has closed with Christ, seems to have started on lines sound enough, and well accredited. If only they do not halt too soon ! In the New Testament we do not hear much about Christ, the friend. He, in His condescension, deigns to call us friends, surely the loftiest of our human honours. But they, on their side, tell us of the King whose will and word are law ; and of the Judge, before whom we must stand ; and of the Saviour, and that is their supreme and favourite title for Him.

> " He did not come to judge the world,
>   He did not come to blame.
> He did not only come to seek,
>   It was to save He came.
> And, when we call Him Saviour,
>   Then we name Him by His name."

There is far more in Christ for you than you have taken from Him yet. Press on. And He will eagerly heap it on you. Till, by and by, as out of the far richer experiences of Him you will have then, you look back at what you now know, at what appears to you to-day so wonderful, it will seem to you then thin and meagre, a mere trickle from the fullness of the river of Life.

Yet who among us has the right to criticize the younger folk ? For are we not all constantly blundering into the same self-impoverishing mistake ? We come to Jesus Christ : and He does for us what He promised ; and the thing works out. To our amazement, it works out. And then we settle down. We have had our own first-hand and irrefutable experience. But, instead of opening the windows to the glory of the sunshine so evidently there, instead of being incited to a hugeness of faith by what Christ has already done for us, we can't believe that there can be anything more, or that even He can work for us anything better. That first foretaste satisfies us. And so we camp for life out on the confines of the Kingdom, never press on, to inherit what is there, and meant for us.

And Christ is disappointed. " Hitherto," He says in a kind of wonder at us, " ye have asked nothing in My Name." Oh, you have said your prayers, but not really expecting anything to come of them. Ask, He says, and you will receive, far bigger things than you have yet attained. But we can't credit that to live with Christ ought to be like following a country road, with every bend and turning in it opening up new and wider and more glorious vistas, for which even all our past experiences of Him had not prepared us.

That I might know Him, cries Paul, really know Him, as He really is.

What is it that he covets? The power of His resurrection—that first, that most urgently; that he might get that into his own life, and see it working there, as it did work for Christ.

But, you break in, he had it. The characteristic note of the New Testament that keeps throbbing out exultantly is that these men had found what all people in earnest had been seeking: and that, because of that discovery, they are able to do what they had always failed to do, to be what hitherto neither they, nor anybody else, could be; had been lifted clean above themselves into new creatures, living with ease in a new and higher way; no longer lowly caterpillars, with their clumsy and laborious and arching progress, but winged things, wantoning in God's blessed sunshine.

And Paul knows that: boldly throws down his own case, and the enormous difference Christ had made in him as final and conclusive evidence of Christ's full claims, to which there can be no answer: asserts, indeed, that the only possible reason he can find for Christ's call to him is that He wished to placard before the whole staring world a test case which must meet every doubt, and satisfy every objection.

Yet he wants more of it—far more. At Calvary God and the devil, good and evil, met in one final and decisive clash. And it was God who won. And, having so won, He did not withdraw out of this needy world. That power that proved enough for Christ, with the sins of the world laid on His soul, that brought Him through His evil hour in triumph, that raised Him from the dead when all seemed lost, lies now within my reach. If I could find it, and use it, where the strain lies for me, what could I not do: and what could thwart or daunt me? There is no sin to which I need surrender; there is no habit that I cannot break; there is no virtue I cannot attain, if my poor groping hands could find what lies quite near, if I could only come on it—the very power that brought Christ through.

But further, Paul's dream is not only of a life cleansed from the last traces of weakness and defilement, but of that cleansed life put to the best possible use. Once on a day he had had other ambitions, in themselves high and worthy: and they were coming true. A sure and honourable future, a name of note, perhaps even of fame, an influence telling upon many minds and lives. And then Christ beckoned to Him and, with that, everything else faded away like shadows, and this new and exciting and tremendous possibility was, so he felt, the one thing worth the doing, worth the being, worth the living out. He had taken his life into his hand and had concluded that none of the sun-bleached, dusty, faded things in the world's booths were worth it, felt he could do better with it than that ; and always his eyes kept straying back to Jesus Christ. He would give it to Him, use it for Him, and the big aims and ends for which Christ stands. Here am I on your side, prepared to pay the cost of allegiance, to lay down the full price of this I choose. All that I ask is—Deign to accept me ; stoop to make use of me, to take from my soiled hands. In mercy cast me not away, as a thing broken and useless. I will submit to any discipline, however sore, if by so doing, I can grow into something Thou canst use for my fellows, and for the Kingdom, and for Thy glory. That I may know the fellowship of His sufferings ; that I may live for others as He lived, and work for others as He worked, and die for others in His way.

> "Then, with a rush, the intolerable craving
> Shivers throughout me like a trumpet call ;
> Oh to save these ! to perish for their saving,
> Die for their life, be offered for them all."

Dear Lord, who bore so much for me, grant me Thy nature, that I, in my small way, may bear a little, a very little, for Thy needy world, that I may be made conformable unto Thy death ; that my life, held against the tremendous background of Thy Cross, may not clash with it, but may rather match with it : that the pattern I see there on Calvary, in big, may run on—very little now, but still the same pattern, unchanged and unbroken, through all the nothings that make up my days. Ferenczi tells us bluntly, that the ideal of the modern world is to get back to the embryo stage, and to prolong that throughout life : to be cosy and warm, supplied with everything we need without us having to do anything about it. That were real life ! And there is point in the savagery of that criticism of us. But Paul's dream is to be allowed to follow in Christ's steps, yes, even if it leads him to a kind of minor Calvary.

And so, concludes this noble soul, it is just possible, just barely possible, I might attain unto the resurrection from the dead : just barely possible that, even I, might be granted the privilege of serving God for ever and for ever—just barely possible. Did you ever try to think how you would fare if you were suddenly transported to the heavenly places ? Santi Deva, that remarkable Buddhist of the long ago, was once musing on this troubled world of ours, and came to this of it. People, he said, keep talking about something that they call the self, and make this self the centre of their being, round which everything else revolves. But, if I could push this intruder out of its pre-eminence, and instal in its place as the true centre of my life, my fellow-men, and make it all revolve round them—thinking of them, working for them, living for them, not self at all : if I did that, and you did that, and all of us so acted, would not the ills that so torment the world be largely solved and healed ? In heaven they have done that very thing. And there all life is an unselfishness ; a glad and eager service of each other and of the Lord God. And how would you, still selfish and self-centred, react to that, if you were there ? Would you not quickly weary of it, revolt from it, sicken of it, batter with frenzy on the gates, and say, " For God's sake, let me out of here ! The whole place bores me stiff ! " And, if you wished it, they would let you go—to your own place, where you would feel at home.

" That I may know Him, and the power of His resurrection, and the fellowship of His sufferings, being made conformable unto His death, if, by any means, I might attain unto the resurrection of the dead." These are the day-dreams of a really Christian man. You can discover your own standing very simply by laying yours alongside his. Do they match ? Or do they clash ?

CHAPTER XIII

ON THE IMITATION OF CHRIST : A WARNING

" I have given you an example."—JOHN xiii. 15.

FOR us Christians the teaching and example of the Lord Jesus Christ is final. Our business here is, with an ever-increasing skill, and a developing instinct growing ever more spontaneous and inerrable, to learn to adopt His mind, to grow into His ways, to reproduce His spirit, in our facing of the circumstances in which we are set, and of the unforeseen things that leap out on us ; in short, as Scripture has it, to put on Christ.

In the beginning we have not as yet come to ourselves, to what God had in mind when He created us ; are a bundle of momentous possibilities, no more, which have still to be worked out into fact ; a dream of God's heart which has yet to come true ; raw material, that must be shaped and chiselled into the man that we are meant to be, ought to be, can be. And the goal and ideal given us on which to keep our eyes is Jesus Christ. Anything and everything in you and me that will not match with Him must go, whatever it may cost, however it may hurt. And life must be lived after His generous fashion.

And thus the imitation of Christ, in thought and conduct, is a very real part of Christianity. But it must be worked out with skill and knowledge, or we will land ourselves in endless difficulties.

For one thing, Christ refused to be a legislator, to provide us with a set of rules, laying down the proper conduct in every conceivable situation, a book of the words with an elaborate index, so that, when in doubt, all we have to do is to look up the appropriate heading, such as, say, the ideal social system, or the like, and find it all set down for us in detail. And, because of that refusal, many tell us impatiently that Christ is out of date, an admirable guide, no doubt, in the region of personal religion, but with nothing to say about those social and economic questions which we find so urgent, and so clamant, and so insistently demanding a solution. For help, there, so we are told, we have to look to the Greek thinkers, and not to Christ at all.

But that is painfully naïve. For what Christ gives us is something far better, and more lasting, than mere rules, which, however cunningly

9

constructed, must inevitably have grown obsolete, when the circumstances for which they were designed gave way to others wholly different. Mercifully, what He lays on us are principles, and a spirit, which we must apply for ourselves in each situation in which we find ourselves. And the wise and Christlike application in one set of circumstances may be wholly different from the wise and Christlike application of the same principle in another. No doubt that is a dangerous thing for such bunglers and blunderers as we are. But even Christ cannot spare us that grave responsibility. So true is it, as Tröeltsch says, that " there is no absolute Christian ethic, rather a continual re-mastering of the changing material of the world's life."

What we require to bring us through with honour is to live so close to Christ that we shall develop a tact, an instinct, a feeling in our finger-tips for the right line of conduct in each of the ever-varying positions in which we are placed. But these things, and the conception of Christ from which they flow, must be founded, not on some selected facts out of the life and the teachings of our Lord which happen to appeal to us, but upon all the facts, honestly and squarely faced, and given their full value, or else our portrait of Him may be a mere caricature of Christ, in some ways over-developed, in others under-exposed. Proof texts, for instance, wrenched from their context, and not laid side by side with others, no less authentic, telling in the opposite direction, have wrought ruin and confusion beyond reckoning. " I am not come to send peace but a sword," for example, had in its original setting, nothing to do with war ; but, so I take it, is a vivid summing up and metaphor of the persecutions and the broken homes which the advent of Christ must mean in a world hostile to Him and His. Certainly it is a metaphor that means something—and that surely this—that to Christ peace is not the greatest thing in the world. If righteousness and Christianity mean broken homes and misery, well, these must come. But, in its primary setting, it had nothing to do with war. One may apply it, and extend it to cover that ; but if so, one does it at one's own risk. But then no more had that proof text upon the other side, in its original setting, anything to do with war ! " Resist not evil " was spoken to the individual, as the plain context—very startling even about individuals—makes clear. You may apply to war this saying also ; but if so, again you do it at your own risk.

And in a bigger way has not the Church too often been rent dramatically asunder by such gratuitous picking and choosing ?

" Work out your own salvation with fear and trembling." Is not that roughly Arminianism ? " For it is God that worketh in you to will and to do of His good pleasure." Is that not, even more roughly, Calvinism? But if both sides had mastered the whole passage, how much of heartache and confusion, and much else, might have been saved !

For this onesidedness that fastens greedily and exclusively upon certain aspects of the Scriptures that happen to appeal to us, and obstinately shuts its eyes to what one likes less, and could wish away, can have disastrous consequences. " The Bible deceived the Pharisees," declared Samuel Rutherford. And so it did, such Bible as they had. There was nothing amiss with the Old Testament, that glorious literature ; but they misread it, and misunderstood it, with the dire results that the lamp for their feet, and the light for their path became, for them, a will-o'-the-wisp, leading them into bogs and quagmires. The Bible, think the Romanists, is a dangerous book. And so it is. No doubt, as Möehler put it, " the Scripture is God's unerring Word ; but we ourselves, when reading it, are not exempt from error ; nay, we only become so when we have unerringly received the Word which is itself inerrable." And we can, so easily, trip and blunder ! In very truth, we must, at all times, read it humbly and reverently, crying for the guidance of the Holy Spirit, lest we abuse it by our crude misunderstanding of it, and lead ourselves astray.

As things are, often enough a man's whole conception of Christ seems to be that of one blind of an eye, who can, so to speak, see only one side of the pages as he reads, and so remains oblivious to much as certainly and evidently there, but of which he takes no account whatsoever.

This " gentle Jesus, meek and mild " idea, for example, with its corollary of a flabbily good-natured deity, its conception of the Lord God Almighty, before whose awful holiness the blessed angels veil their faces, as a kindly and benevolent, but somewhat weak, old gentleman—whence did it spring ? Certainly not from a reading of the Gospels as a whole. " It is a snivelling modern invention," says Shaw, " for which there is no warrant in the Gospels." There is, of course, a very central passage in which Christ describes Himself, deliberately, and with emphasis, as " meek and lowly in heart." And so, indeed, He was. Page after page, and episode on episode, make clear that He was kind beyond all reckoning, and gentle long after the most equably tempered of us would have blazed up into fury. And those who know Him now are quite sure that that is authentic, for the same tale runs on, day after day, in our experience of Him still. Hilaire Belloc, lonesome amid the sadly thinned and rapidly depleting circle of his friends, says movingly :

> " A lost thing could I never find,
>   Nor a broken thing mend,
>   And I fear I shall be all alone,
>   Ere I get towards the end."

And some of us, whose clumsy fingers have lost many dear things in life, can enter into that. And yet his is a needless panic. For Christ, at least, won't fail us. And He has an amazing skill in finding what was lost ; is, indeed, a good shepherd, who, ungrudgingly, gives His whole life for the sheep ; and the most wayward of them, headstrong creatures that keep spilling through every inviting gap in every hedge, get most of it. And when a foolish truant lames itself and can, at the best, only limp painfully, He moderates His pace, and will not hurry it, but gently shepherds it safe home. Gentle ! aye, we can vouch for that ! And His wonderful hands can mend things any one else would toss away as useless debris—broken lives and hearts and hopes and characters, building them up, with a strange cunning skill, into real wholes again, and things of usefulness and beauty.

All which who that knows Him at all can doubt or question ? But there are other, and no less authentic facts. For, turn the pages of the Gospels, and you come on places where the disciples fell behind, awed by a look upon His face, by something into which they dared not venture to intrude. And when, looking back, they pictured Him to themselves again, it was not always, and not only the meekly kneeling figure in the upper room they saw, though Peter, for one, never forgot that, as his Epistle shows, but, almost first, there rose before their minds those eyes that were, at times, so awesome and so terrible ; and the mouth that could, and did, speak to those whom He loved tremendous words with an edge to them no words ever had, and that smote to the heart implacably. And that too, thank God, is authentic, as authentic as the other, as we ourselves have proved, and know. He can be stern, implacable, uncompromising, and mercifully so ; or else He would have lost our souls. And that, too, has its right to a full place in a true picture of our Lord. Why are there no hymns, these days, glorifying Him for that ?

What is needed is to take as our standard the whole of Christ, not merely this and that, while leaving other facts, as really there, in shadow ; and, especially, His central principles, and, still more, the manner in which in differing situations He Himself applied and lived them out. That last was very far from uniform. Where we go wrong is thinking of Christ, as giving us a railway time-table for our journeys through life. That is precisely what He would not do, what He despised the Pharisees for attempting to do. He gave not rules but principles, which we must work out and apply under the guidance of the Holy Spirit, in differing ways in differing circumstances, as He did Himself. That, I repeat, entails a fearsome risk for bunglers such as us, an onerous responsibility. Yet even Christ cannot contrive to spare us that, and happily we have been given, to guide us how to apply the principles in varying situations, His own conduct and example.

Take, for instance, the Law of Love, that central Christian affirmation, or the Law of Forgiveness, so central, so insistent, so heavily and strikingly underlined in our Lord's teaching, that it becomes one of the most original parts of it. " If ye forgive not men their trespasses, neither will your Heavenly Father forgive you your trespasses." So that " the Unconditional Freeness of the Gospel " proves to be an idle phrase. There is a blunt condition bluntly stated, and it cannot be evaded, must be met. Yet how did Jesus Christ Himself live out these principles ? Often and often—on the Cross, as a supreme instance, but in many other places too—His love for the most hopeless and impossible, His refusal to meet hate with hate, His stubborn, persistent, obstinate forgiveness where we would flame out into anger, gives us our standard when we are ruffled, and angered, and insulted, and wronged. And He is imperious with us about it. Less than this will not do. But there are other passages in plenty where Jesus blazed into a fierceness of anger, into stinging, withering, blistering words that can't be matched in literature, and that scald even to this day. " Ye serpents," " ye generation of vipers," " ye whitewashed sepulchres," " ye children of hell." It does not sound particularly loving, nor yet as if He had forgiven them. Yet He would not desist from this tremendous vituperation, would not agree to let the Pharisees alone, and speak of other things ; pursued them with His stinging words, and died rather than cease from it. Gentle Jesus, meek and mild ! I don't suppose the Pharisees considered Him as being at all either the one or the other. Did He, then, in these places break His own laws, fall miserably below His own standards ? Montefiore feels He did, regarding the Pharisees. Kind to others, even publicans and sinners, why was He so fierce to them, worthy, if mistaken men ?

Well, what is the answer ? Are we to argue, or feel silently and uncomfortably in our own spirits that, whereas on the Cross Christ lived out His own principles up to the very uttermost, in these scenes we have indicated He fell far below Himself, lost His temper, acted un-Christlikely ; and so huddle these unfortunate slips and failures of His out of our memory ? Is it not wiser to take the whole of Christ as our standard of what Christlikeness really is ; and to assume, from His example, that, if there are places where, if we are to be loyal to Him, we must show the spirit He showed on the Cross, there are others where, if we are to reflect His mind, we must be moved to an implacable and burning anger ? Christ did not only now and then rise to the fullness of His stature, and upon other occasions act in a way that stumbles and distresses us : but, in each circumstance as it arose, He lived out the right and perfect thing to be done there and then, was just as Christlike when His eyes were blazing (" and He turned and looked on them with anger ") as when He said, " Father, forgive them for they know not what they do." Which surely means that, Law of Forgiveness, and Law of Love, and all, there are situations in which, to be Christlike, one must be burned up with an intensity of a clean anger ; when, as Hugh Mackintosh puts it, " lack of indignation at wickedness is a sign, not of a poor nature only, but of positive unlikeness to Christ. The wrath of Jesus is made incontestably plain in the Synoptic Gospels."

From all which it is but a step to the cleansing of the Temple, which, whatever else it is, shows plainly that, unless Christ Himself was, on occasion, the poorest of Christians, there come times when the Law of unlimited Forgiveness, laid on us as the usual rule of life, has to be laid aside ; when, if we have His spirit in us, we cannot, and we should not, stand passively watching wrong heaped upon wrong, but must take action. Pathetic efforts have been made to tone down, to explain away, to eviscerate, what, if it had been recorded of any other character in history would, as a matter of course, have been accepted as the scene of violence and drama that it obviously was. Yet there it stands, and we must face it ; and must take account of it, one of the facts, as surely there as Calvary itself, to find its due place in an honest portrait of the Master, and of His law of life for us. " There is that in Jesus," said Raven in *Jesus and the Gospel of Love*, " which would horrify the pacifist and humanitarian. He

is the lover of men and their Physician ; but at need, and for love's
sake, He will use the knife." I do not know if Raven has withdrawn
this ; but, in any case, the facts on which he founded it remain within
the Gospel records, staring as ever. And if Christ's anger was so
roused over an act of sacrilege, and the sins of the Pharisees, what
would He not have said and done when, as Niebuhr says, " a nation,
its fury fed by a pagan religion of tribal self-glorification, intent to
root out the Christian religion, defies all the universal standards of
justice which ages of a Christian and humanistic culture have woven
into the fabric of our civilization, threatens the Jewish race with
annihilation, and visits a maniacal fury upon these unhappy people ;
explicitly declares its intention of subjecting the other races of Europe
into slavery to the master race ; in short, is engaged in the terrible
effort to establish an empire upon the very negation of justice."
Faced by that situation, am I wrong in looking to the Temple to learn
what my Lord would have me do ? This thing, He said, must end;
and He rose up, and put them out.

Or was Christ wrong, and Pilate right ? And is it him we ought
to follow ? In both Philo and Josephus there are furious attacks on
Pilate, and his character, and his administration. But the New
Testament has not a word of comment. With a terrible restraint,
it allows the man's own actions to speak for themselves, and make
their own impression on the mind. We know the unhappy soul was
in a hideous dilemma. He found the Jews all but impossible. And,
more than once there had been bloodshed. And Rome had curtly
told him that there was to be no more of that; that at all costs
there must be peace. And now, at the worst time in the whole year,
when millions of inflammable Jews had crowded Jerusalem for the
Passover, and were camped round and about the city in a frenzy
of national fervour, this wretched trouble had arisen. Quite
evidently Pilate felt that there was nothing in the charges, and
wanted to release the Prisoner ; but, at the ominous growl of
anger, he had heard before, that course awakened, he wavered,
and drew back; for there must be no bloodshed. And bloodshed
there would be, unless this Innocent Person died an ugly death. And
there are those who hold that he did well. " Was Pilate right in
crucifying Christ ? " asked Sir James Stephen, the eminent lawyer.
" I reply, Pilate's paramount duty was to preserve the peace in Palestine, to form the best judgment he could as to the means required
for that purpose, and to act upon it when it is formed. Therefore,

if and in so far as he believed in good faith and on reasonable grounds that what he did was necessary for the preservation of the peace in Palestine, he was right." It is not for us to jeer, since, at the crisis of that tragedy, one of our statesman said, amid approving cheers, that the prevention of the martyrdom of the whole Abyssinian nation was not worth the loss of one Birmingham boy. Only, is it the mind of Jesus Christ ? Is it conceivable He would have stood and watched it happening ?

Or, take the Law of Brotherhood, that central Christian rule of life. Usually it means kindness and sympathy to all our fellow-men. But when, and if, some of our brothers persist in maltreating certain others of our brothers, and will not desist therefrom, then what does one do ? Does the Law mean that, because the wrongdoers are our brothers, we must be patient and unruffled towards them, protest perhaps, but take no violent action to check and arrest them ? Have the wronged brothers got no rights ? Have they not the first call upon the Law of Brotherhood ? Can we obey it, and allow them to be maltreated ? " But who is my neighbour ? " asked a captious mind. " I'll tell you a story, and you'll answer that yourself," said Christ, and improvised the immortal parable about the Priest, and the Levite, and the good Samaritan. " Who was neighbour to him that fell among thieves ? " " He that showed mercy," said the man. Precisely, said Christ. " You go and do likewise." The setting of the story, as Christ told it, is that the outrage was over, and the victim lying there half murdered. But suppose the various travellers had passed a little earlier, when the assault was being committed. What then ? Would the Priest and the Levite, in these circumstances, have been right to pass by on the other side ; justified not to mix themselves up in a messy business ? After the crime, the Law of Brotherhood meant kindly and unselfish treatment of the victim. But, while the assault was proceeding, how could one prove one's brotherhood to him, and how could one be a neighbour and show mercy, except by a lusty resistance to the foot-pads, and by rallying to their victim's support ? " If," says the Master of Balliol, " when we are told to ' resist not evil,' we are being told to have nothing to do with that maintenance of rules which resists evil, then we are being told something which is incompatible with loving our neighbours. That is the real point at issue between those who do, and those who do not, accept these particular verses literally." And let us always remember that nothing so hurt the Master in His disciples

as a certain wooden literalness of interpretation. Again and again,
one sees how sorely He was grieved by that.

But, in truth, many literalists have a way of abandoning their
position at a pinch, apparently finding it intolerable. Professor
Hearnshaw strings together what, in mass, amounts to an amazing
series of admissions by distinguished pacifists. As, for example, to
quote one or two. My own notable colleague, Dr. Macgregor, argues
that Christ " might even allow the use of the sword in self-defence
against bandits." But, go that length, and surely when bandits leap
upon an unsuspecting people, the Law of Brotherhood must rally
us to defend them too. " If any one attacked my wife, I should sock
him on the jaw," said Dick Sheppard ; and, again, " I should do my
very best to protect my wife. I hope I should not kill the attacker,
but I might." But if all this for his own wife, does not the Law of
Brotherhood demand a like defence of other people's wives from us ?
And Bertrand Russell. " You will not repudiate force completely :
you will not, for instance, refuse to protect a weaker individual from
a stronger one, if you happen to be present when the assault is committed." But if such an assault is practised upon half the world,
with a ferocity of insane fury, does one simply look on, or does the
Law of Brotherhood urge one to protect weaker things there too ?
And many other instances crowd in on us.

" If," said Joad, " I saw a man laying a mine on a railway line
just before an express train was due, I should have no hesitation in
shooting him, just as I should have no hesitation in shooting a mad
dog." And if the slow-won civilization of the world, the decencies
of life, the rights of man, the freedom of innumerable human beings
for whom the Lord Christ died, and the Christian faith itself are all
being deliberately blown sky high and into nothingness, does one
simply stand aside and watch ?

Or Mr. Gandhi, of whom one of his warmest admirers and disciples
declares, " indeed, it was with great difficulty that some of his friends
prevailed upon him not to offer himself as a combatant soldier, as
an example to others." " And this because," said Gandhi rather
sadly, " I see that my countrymen are not refraining from acts of
physical violence because of love for their fellows, but from cowardice ;
and peace with cowardice is much worse than a battlefield with
bravery. I would rather they died fighting than cringed with fear."
That was in the last war. And in this ? Here is what he states he
means by non-violence. " If a man fights with his sword single-

handed against a horde of dacoits I should say he is fighting non-violently. Haven't I said to our women that, if in defence of their honour, they used their nails and teeth and even a dagger, I should regard their conduct as non-violent. She acted spontaneously. Suppose a mouse fighting a cat tries to resist the cat with his sharp teeth, would you call that mouse violent ? In the same way, for the Poles to stand bravely against the German hordes, vastly superior in numbers, military equipment, and strength, was almost non-violence."

Face to face with the facts of life, their creed breaks down, their literalism just won't hold together.

How can one keep the central Christian principles and not defend the injured ?

I shall never forget hearing one of the greatest of the Chinese leaders, a consummate orator with an almost unbelievable command of English, and a devout Christian man, telling us of the appalling dilemma in which he, who believed that Jesus Christ forbade all physical resistance of evil, was placed, watching the ring of burning villages draw nearer and nearer, as the Japanese advanced on his home-town in Manchuria—tugged this way and that, poor desperate soul, by love of his country and his dear ones, and by faithfulness to his Lord ; looking in agony at his wife and children—so soon to be the playthings of bestial grossness and cruelty, yet firm in his resolve that Christ must be obeyed at any and at every cost ; that though he would not obey the Japs, and must be set against a wall and shot, he would not actively resist them for Christ's sake, till the listeners' hearts grew sick with horror even at the recounting of it all. For some reason, the advance was halted, and the blow did not fall, after all. And then, after a pause, the man's very soul cried out in torture and a new access of even sorer pain. " And now I know that I was wrong ! God does not work in a vacuum, but through us men. And I was meant to do what in me lay, to hold back the accursed thing. And I failed Christ ! And I failed Christ ! And, by my mis-reading of Him, I vilified and blasphemed His holy name ! How can I ever look Him in the eyes ? "

Some unhappy ones, indeed, like C. E. Montague in the last war, believing that all use of armed force is against the mind of Christ, and yet, impelled by their consciences to defend the threatened sanctities of life, had, with deliberation, to turn their backs upon Him in this one matter—a hideous dilemma. I myself sat one night in the trenches talking to a mystical Highland private who so felt, who believed that, for the sake of his fellow-men to whose help he had had to come, he was deliberately courting for himself an inevitable outer darkness, and that to all eternity. That same night he was killed. And, when the dawn came, I buried him in what was then the desolation of Tyne Cot. And when the burial squad had dispersed, standing there, all alone in that grim Aceldama, I put him and his problem in Christ's keeping. "Greater love," said I to Jesus Christ, "hath no man than this, that a man lay down his life for his friends." So Thou hast said. But this man, so he believes, has laid down his eternal destinies for them. And I leave it with Thee.

A terrible dilemma ! But there are some of us who, with Christ's contempt for neutrals in our mind (are we not told in one tremendous Scripture that they make Him physically sick ?) and, with His own example as to how His laws are to be kept put burningly before us, and, above all, His own solemn asseveration of what He counts the standards by which we must stand or fall, just cannot see how we can refuse, at times, to use force in His name. For if, not to feed the hungry, not to clothe the naked, not to visit those sick and in prison, seems to Him to prove we are remote from His whole mind and ways, how shall He look at us if He has in the end to say, I was persecuted and you paid no heed, I was enslaved and you looked the other way, I was broken and tortured and massacred, and you, My feet, did not hurry to My help ; and you, My hands, did not leap out in the one way that could have helped ; you, My body, failed Me. Where was your love, your brotherhood, your Christlikeness ? "In as much as ye did it not to the least of these My brethren, ye did it not to Me. Depart from Me, ye cursed."

CHAPTER XIV

THE TERROR AND HOPE OF THE TIMES

"Say not thou, What is the cause that the former days were better than these? For thou dost not consider wisely concerning this."—ECCLES. vii. 10.

ONCE, on a grey, drizzling day of depression, Emerson remarked, " Every one is criticizing and belittling the times. Yet I think that our times, like all times, are very good times, if only we knew what to do with them." And that is what I think about our times now, when another wave of disillusionment has broken over us, and left us breathless, and shivery, and dazed, dolefully watching our gorgeous cloud palaces we thought so solid and substantial melting into thin air ; and the brave new world of sanity and righteousness and brotherhood and peace which we imagined was at the very door, gone again, like the mirage which, for the moment, it has proved to be. Till many, in their hurt disappointment, are being forced back upon Froude's despairing verdict upon human history : " Good will never conquer evil. They are too equally matched." Why bother any further, teasing at the obstinate knots in things. Pick at them how you may, they won't undo.

And, certainly, grievous verdicts have been passed upon us as a generation by competent minds, who merit our attention. Earl Baldwin, for example, slips casually into one of his essays, as a mere self-evident platitude that requires no substantiating, the damning judgment that ours is the most irreligious age this earth has seen since Jesus Christ was born. And others scoff and jeer at that, as a very timid understatement. Since Christ was born ! Search and look, and you will never find a time, since man was man, when religion was so flouted, and morality more unabashedly mocked or ignored. We have a notion, maintains Aldous Huxley, that we are a humanitarian generation, and we are, thinks he, " in patches " ; but, on the whole, ours is a day of marked and terrible moral " regression." While Joad, who had told us in an early book that, " for the first time in human history, a generation has arisen that has no religion, and that feels the need of none," returns more definitely, and in detail, to the subject in one of his latest volumes, assuring us that he has found, from personal knowledge and first-hand investigation, that in the minds of practically all of the young people whom he meets from day to day, Christianity has no place whatsoever; that most of them entirely ignore it, and that a real proportion of them had always assumed and understood that it was dead, that no one bothered about it any longer.

I confess that I have always difficulty with such confident and sweeping general judgments. It is a long time since Aristotle noticed that young men are apt to throw things down with a brusque confidence, truculently affirming, "I know," where older men, grown cautious from experience, will only venture on "I think," and keep interlarding their conversations with saving words such as "perhaps" and "probably." And Montaigne, looking out on life with those cool eyes of his, observes that, for his part, he has a liking for words that blunt the edge of too confident judgments. There is a vast deal of time enclosed in that short word "never," which we fling about so lightly—there never was this, and there never was that—and even a little knowledge of history makes one chary of using it with any confidence. Take one vivid illustration of the danger. One of our abler living poets introduced into a work of his an attack on London, which city and its people seemed to him futile and aimless. "Here was a decent, godless people, their only monuments the asphalt road, and a thousand lost golf balls." But that same generation of Londoners, of cheery, humorous, carefree folk, have proved that they are very much more than erratic golfers and motoring enthusiasts; that, hidden away behind their quick quips and gay flippances, there lay, not in one solitary and heroic figure here and there, but in the mass of them, a courage that proved unbreakable, a soul that looked at death and horror contemptuously and unafraid; a gallantry that steadied a whole empire, and awoke the admiration of a thrilled world. There is always another side to things. Yet our religious leaders—not a few of them—have joined in the general dismal bleating rising so mournfully round us. The Congregationalists, for instance, have published findings culled from, and founded on, the answers to a questionnaire sent to their padres and the like, working among the men and women in the forces. And they appear to have no doubt that where in the minds of former generations there hung the face of Jesus Christ, often forgotten, easily overlooked, still there, and in a very central place; sometimes drawing the eyes; and, when seen, awakening reverence, and compelling loyalty and obedience; there is, in the minds of these young people now, nothing but a blank, and a dead vacant

wall ; that, for the vast majority of them Christ means less than
nothing, for they never think of Him at all, nor does a recollection
of Him ever blow across their consciousness. All which, with
deference, I venture to suspect is an exaggeration of facts in themselves grave enough, still an exaggeration. And for this reason—that
we heard like lugubrious stories, founded on like confident evidence,
after the last war as to the people in the forces then—all which, no
doubt, had horrid truth behind it, but none the less, had no resemblance
to what I myself saw, month by month, among the troops ; just no
resemblance whatsoever ; was, of these men at least, a libel and a
caricature. So now there is again much evidence upon both sides.
The very day after I read this daunting and disquieting report, a
chaplain in the Navy, off to the East, dropped in to say good-bye,
and told me how " exciting " he had found his chaplaincy, because
the men are " so unexpectedly religious," crowding, the ratings at least,
to services at any time on any day in their off hours ; and swamping
him with questions upon deep and central and spiritual things.
" There," said this witness, who himself had been a brilliant leader
in the life of his own university, and had studied social and economic
questions for years thereafter here and in America, " is where the
Church is making its mistake. They never ask me questions on social
problems ; always it is on such points as " Does this thing work ? "
" How do you start on it ? " " How does one close with Jesus Christ ? "

There is always another side to things than that which holds the
eyes. And in the present situation, critical though it be, there exists,
as really there, not a little to hearten us.

In any case, there is really nothing new and up to date or modern
in being discouraged and depressed. Hesiod, dim figure though he is,
looming up through the mists of history, was sure the best of life was
over, and the great days left behind, in a past that could never come
again. Demades lived in the days of Demosthenes : yet, said he,
" Athens is not the Athens our ancestors knew, but an old woman,
wearing slippers, and sipping barley water." And, excavating in
Babylonia, have they not come upon a tablet, far older than Abraham,
on which some discouraged soul, disgusted at the way things were
degenerating round him, had despondently inscribed, " Alas ! Alas !
Would I had lived in former days. For the times then were better
than the times now ! " So they were at it, even then ! So it has
always been ; so it is still. When things grow difficult, men's hearts
are apt, if not to fail them for fear, at least to grow discouraged, to

stop trying, to fling in their hand. And it is curious how silently, incomprehensibly, yet fatally, panic can spread, infecting more and more, till the line gives, and there is rout and chaos. It is not for us Christian people to allow ourselves to be swept away by it. We have a faith, which others do not share, to keep us calm ; a faith which is the most resolutely honest reading of life, of man, of God, that this world ever heard, shirking no fact, however hideous, facing the ghastliest of them, pulling them out into the full light ; not, for example, evading the Cross, or averting men's eyes from it, as a thing better forgotten and blotted from the mind, if we are to know any peace, but making it central, and insisting that we take our stand on Calvary, and do our thinking face to face with that ; yet, on the other hand, the faith that boldly, audaciously, gave hope a place among the virtues as no other religion ever did ; and itself dowers us with wonderful hopes that no discouragement can kill, and no delay can stun us into disbelieving.

Aye, and we have a God that others do not know, to steady us ; and never more real or Godlike and marvellous than in the deeds that we have seen, in our own days, with our own eyes. Remember how the prophet, irritated by a people, their heads turned back, their hearts musing regretfully and wistfully over the great days when God was God, and things really happened, leapt at them, gripped them, shook them, bade them take in that God had not grown either decrepit or obsolete, but was assuredly about to surpass even Himself in their time. So that in the coming ages men would rally themselves with the remembrance, not even of what God did in Egypt, but of the still more incredible miracles that He is doing, and about to work, for you to-day ! And is it not the simple fact that, with moving unanimity, our leaders, civil, naval, military, speak in hushed voices of how evidently God has broken in for us, when all human help was vain ; bidding us give the praise, not to themselves, but to the God who, making bare His mighty arm, Himself wrought our deliverance for us ? And is it not a certainty that, down the generations, men, in dark days, will fortify themselves by looking back at our times, as an unchallengeable proof that there is certainly a God, who does exceeding abundantly above all that we can ask or think. For look ! so they will cry, with awed and wondering hearts, look how manifestly He showed Himself, how evidently He burst in, how gloriously He stood to His huge promises, to these fortunate folk, who knew Him face to face, and met Him, in their great and God-filled times, day after day.

And it is true. Open your eyes, and look about you, and can you fail to see Him ? Once on a day, Mrs. Martin Luther came to her husband with a downcast face and in the deepest mourning, and to his anxious inquiries answered, " Have you not heard the news, terrible news ? God is dead ! " And when he told her, shocked and angry, not to blaspheme, " And if God is not dead," said she, " what right have you, His servant, you a Christian man, to be so downcast and depressed ? " " I hope, sir," one said to Haig on the darkest day of the last war, " you are not too discouraged." " Discouraged ! A Christian man has no right to be discouraged in the same world as God."

The truth is, these are great times, when, as at the beginning, and before the earth solidified, things are fluid, and run, and can take any form. And is it not a moving and an honouring thing that, out of all the generations whom He might have called, God has chosen us to help Him to build up a better world ; dares to make us His instruments, and looks toward us with confidence, as fit to do it for Him, if we will ? And are we going to repine at such a privilege ?

No doubt there is much to trouble and vex the old-fashioned in these days, people whose minds are thirled (as we Scots say) to the accustomed and familiar. For everything they love seems sliding from them, leaving them lonesome, and out of place, in a strange new world which they resent, saying, as Christ, with His large charity for slow-moving minds, knew that they would, " the old is better." But then, as Croce has it, it is not only of individuals dear to them, but about ways and institutions dear to them, that Christians must be prepared to say, " The Lord gave, and the Lord hath taken away. Blessed be the name of the Lord."

I think that that is where the Church, too often, goes wrong. It is so apt to lag half a generation behind the times ; to cling to methods, once effective, but now outworn ; to stand obstinately in paths, grass-grown now, by which God once visited His people, holding to it doggedly that, if He comes at all, it must be by this avenue, forgetful of the amazing originality of God, and that His ways are never stereotyped.

> " Expecting Him,
> My door was opened wide,
> Then I looked round,
> If any lack of service might be found.
> And saw Him at my side !
> How entered, by what secret stair,
> I know not, knowing only He was there."

Don't you remember that valiant spirit in the New Testament who, living in a day of transition (and every one in every generation must do that, for the earth never stands still, but spins dizzily upon its way), feeling the heavens were on fire, and the earth giving under him, and the hills toppling in, said only, " Well ! well ! if the earth I knew and loved is vanishing, that means that God is building up a better earth in which righteousness will dwell." Or, our Lord Himself, beside His mother's leaven tub, watching the bubbles forming and bursting, bursting and forming, and thinking how like the age that was—much wild talk that could only come to nothing, and many schemes too often harebrained and impossible, bubbles that formed, and burst. Yet He was not depressed by that. Better, He felt, that men should be reaching out with blind and groping hands for something ; something they know not what, something other, and something better than they had. Give God that, and anything is possible. But if the earth lie sluggish, apathetic, grossly content with what it is, what can even God do ? Or how, in such dull bovine days, can His kingdom come ? Or, Wordsworth, in the days of the Revolution, when many were whitefaced and terror-stricken, hearing all things rumbling to doom, " Bliss was it in those days to be alive. But to be young was very heaven ! " Or Rupert Brooke, when the war swept the old life clean away in roaring flood, " Now God be thanked who hath matched us with His hour, and wakened us from sleeping." Or Smuts, " Humanity has struck its tents, and is on the march again." Aye, and the pillar of fire still goes before ; and, if we follow, will lead us into a land, not of promise only, but of huge achievement.

But you cry, look about you ! Civilization is doomed ! is tottering before our very eyes, is down ! So frightened voices warned us ; and it has come ! What do you mean by civilization ? Do you, for instance, want things to remain, in all ways, as they were ? Long ago now, Lord Grey of Fallodon cried, in a kind of agony, that he thought that God must soon arise and smash the world to pieces, and build it up upon a saner plan. The present way of things, he explained honestly, suits me very well. But I cannot but see that it means, for ninety-nine men out of every hundred, a life that I would simply hate. " It is true they do not seem to hate it nearly as much as I would hate it. But the point is—Does God hate it ? " Do your comforts never taste salt in your mouth ? And do you never feel you have too much, while others have too little ? And would you not be prepared, not simply to have them wrenched out of your hands, but to give a portion of them freely, if these others might have more ? If that is coming, let it come.

But, you object, the Christian way of life is challenged, flouted, rejected, as it has not been for long enough—blatantly, ostentatiously, exultantly. That is too true, and to a length not easily exaggerated. These so-called Christian virtues, declared Nietzsche, have been taken at their own valuation far too long. It is time to call them to the bar of reason, and examine their claims. And having done so, he proclaimed these impudent imposters are not virtues at all, not for real men (though suitable enough for slaves—for " bovine creatures like cows and Englishmen "). Even the best of them are, on a long view, hideous mistakes. This pity of yours, for example, is spoiling the breed, keeping alive the weaklings, which a wise nature, when left alone, sees to it, with a ruthlessness to the individual that is mercy to the race, go to the wall and are eliminated. Love of the brethren, that you practise ; but love of the remote, that you forget ; and by your very kindness to the hurt and broken of your own generation create multiple problems for the generations still to be.

While as for self-denial and self-sacrifice, these, declare the disciples, outscreaming the master, to draw some attention to themselves, these are not virtues, but a kind of horrible self-mutilation, a cruel starving of claims and hungers that are natural, and wholly justifiable, and ought to be gratified, and so appeased ; an unwise abstinence, far worse than self-indulgence.

Or, " Purity of heart," says Hartmann, " is the primal Christian virtue. With this estimate Christian ethics opened up new roads, with this more than with its commandment in regard to loving one's neighbour. Not only did ancient ethics not know the nature of purity in this sense, but by the greatest representatives of philosophy it was consistently set aside." And now Bertrand Russell, belauding sexual freedom even in the sphere of marriage, rejoices that monogamic marriage has been left behind in civilized mankind, though " some faint traces of it can still sometimes be perceived " in queer old-fashioned people. But " the more civilized people become, the less capable they seem of lifelong happiness with one partner." On which showing, the crown and acme and apex of civilization must be Hollywood ! And, indeed, with the churches fairly empty, and the crowded cinemas, the ethic of the film, often sub-Christian, and sometimes frankly anti-Christian, keeps seeping, seeping, seeping into innumerable minds. When Newsom wrote his book upon this new morality, a friend was frankly puzzled. Why new ? He had never known of any other ! And the author had to add a further chapter, on the old morality, to state the forgotten things for which he stood.

Hitherto we have always possessed this advantage that, however stumbled by intellectual difficulties they might be, men, brought into Christ's presence, felt their knees bending of themselves, instinctively, naturally, irresistibly. But it is not so now. Rather they can stand on Calvary—if indeed they ever notice that there is a cross at all—and argue up to Christ. Why should I live like that ? There is no sense in it. I won't. And that, as Taylor warns us, is the central, the momentous thing. "If the finality of the Christian ideal of personal character, and the Christian rule of conduct cannot be maintained, no temporary success of the apologist can alter the fact that the Christian faith, as a religion, is under sentence of death." Jung warned us that the old ghastly evils that used to shame mankind are not dead, but are still alive in every human heart, crouching there in the shadows ; that it is only Christianity that masters them and holds them in check ; and that, if ever the dam that it has built against them bursts, if ever Christianity goes down, or is neglected, all the whole hideous disgrace and ruin will sweep again in roaring flood over an astounded world. And look ! wherever Christ has been rejected, how the old horrid cruelties—Jew-baiting, persecution, torture, all the outgrown forgotten infamies of the past, made doubly infamous and horrible by modern skill and technique—have come alive, and burst out of their ancient graves, and sprawl gross and obscene over the world, polluting God's clean sunshine.

Yes : these are desperate times.

Only there is that other side to things that one must not forget, how glorious a side ! And it is no less really there. That thrilling book, the Acts of the Apostles, is a serial that runs on and on, into innumerable volumes. But in not one of them all will you find annals more exciting and remarkable than those of our own day. It is indeed a marvellous record. As yet we stand too close to it to see it clearly, but it is there. Never in all its nineteen centuries, for instance, has Christ's cause leapt out across the earth, as it has done within my lifetime. Never ! Give me twelve ordinary men with some zeal for Me, and for the things for which I stand, and I will win the world, said Christ, daringly, at the start. And marvellous results have flowed from that little group gathered in that small upper room.

And one hundred and fifty years ago a similar knot of plain and

simple men, with not a fifty-pound note among them, met in a
back parlour in Kettering, and solemnly made up their minds that
the whole earth must be won for Christ, and set themselves to do it.
Every one laughed at them. Let Thackeray and Dickens show you how
they laughed. The churches were slow to adopt and countenance so
strange and quixotic an enterprise. The powers that be frowned on
them, and sternly opposed them. Carey had to be smuggled into
India, and even so, not into British but to Danish territory. And
the years came, and the years went, and nothing happened ; and
the whole daft scheme was obviously a complete fiasco, as had been
foretold. For two whole decades there was hardly a convert. But, in
a hundred years, there were one and a quarter million members, and
in the next twenty-five this had risen to six millions ; and since then
the pace of the influx has quickened enormously, till in the last ten
years the thing has swollen to an avalanche. " Verily, verily," said
the Master, " the works that I do ye shall do also, and greater works
than these shall ye do." Whereat we look up at Him, startled and
bewildered. Yet He has kept His word, and kept it in our day, as
never before. Yet foolish voices clamour that Christianity is effete
and resultless ; does nothing nowadays !

Or look at prostrate and distracted Europe. What is the one and
only thing that has stood up upon its feet, and faced the storm, and
dared, where others faltered, and compromised, and bent before the
blast. Let Einstein answer : " Having always been an ardent partisan
of freedom, I turned to the universities to find there defenders
of freedom. I did not find them. I then turned to the editors of
powerful newspapers. These men were reduced to silence in a few
weeks. I then addressed myself to the authors who had posed as
the intellectual guides. They, in their turn, were dumb. " Only
the Church opposed the fight against liberty. Till then I had no
interest in the Church, but now I feel a great admiration for it,
and am greatly attracted to it. It has had the persistent courage
to fight for spiritual truth and moral freedom. I feel obliged to
recognize that I now admire what I used to consider of little value."
And this witness is true.

In Russia they gathered together all their strength to uproot
Christianity—first, by fierce persecution, then by a subtler method.
For no one under sixteen could be taught the faith, and Christ's name
was excised out of the school books—no need to hear of that complete
nonentity, who would soon be forgotten—while they were soaked

day in, day out, in the new orthodox faith.   Strange, mused Luther, that every twenty years God builds Himself up a new church out of little children.   Give us just twenty years, they said in Russia, and Christianity will be stone dead.   But the Church faced all, dared all ; clung to Christ, lived for Christ, died for Christ.   And now, it seems, that it has won.   " That Church will be free," cried Rainy, in a day when all seemed lost, " that dares to be free."

And in Germany the only being Hitler dreads is Jesus Christ. You can be a humanist, and play away with futile, feckless trivialities and soft goods like that, and welcome.   But Jesus Christ is dangerous. For where He is, men are not putty to be squeezed to any shape by any passing pair of fingers ; but men, free men, who stand up on their own feet, and think with their own minds ; who stubbornly and unalterably put Christ first, and obey God rather than men.   Look where you will in Europe, you will find the Church leading, and daring, and inspiring, at a ghastly cost, which is paid down unfalteringly.

" Say not thou, What is the reason that the former times were better than these ?   for thou dost not consider rightly concerning this."

Or think of the new acuteness of conscience about social ills these days.   They tell us the sense of sin is atrophied and dead.   And so, alas !   it very largely is about personal failings and trespasses.   But we are troubled, as rarely before, about social injustice ; and determined that this thing can't wait, must be amended now.   And much is being done which we all take for granted, but which is nothing less than the opening of a new epoch.   Our housing, for example, has been tackled as never before.   Till the war stopped the glorious crusade, the slums were melting away before our very eyes.   In a few dozen months a million people had been lifted out of them into a wholesome atmosphere, and the pace was quickening, till they were leaving slumdom at the rate of a thousand per day.   And overcrowding was being, at last, effectively challenged.   In a thousand years, said Walter Elliot, eight million houses were erected in Britain !   But, in the last twenty, four million.   And house-room was made for sixteen million of our countrymen.   The world is moving.   And God is alive.   These are great times !

Yet we have failed.   Look out across this stricken earth, more desperate than, perhaps, it ever was in all its tangled history, and judge how we have failed !   Because we imagined we were on a moving staircase, and had only to stand still, and the progress of the years would automatically lift us nearer and nearer to God's very feet.   And that dream of inevitable progress has been shattered. Because we did not believe in sin ; yet, watch what it is doing in our world and in our day. Because we thought that we could manage for ourselves and had no need of a Saviour ; and look what we have made of it ! Because we tried to heal deep-seated sores with mere external changes in our circumstances, and not by fundamental alterations in ourselves, though Dostoievsky warned us that " the form of atheism most to be dreaded, the greatest anti-religious force in Europe, is humanitarianism," —a little kindness here, and a little justice there, and that, we thought, would be enough. Because we gave our faith to the building of a new order round us, unheeding of the chaos in our characters, and the wild disorder in our hearts. And we have paid the penalty of folly. But is there not infinite hope if the very failure of our best endeavours forces us back on Jesus Christ as our one possible Redeemer ? If we have seen with Descartes " that I should always strive to conquer myself rather than fortune, and to change my own desires rather than alter the world order " ; or with Aristotle, " Men are easily induced to believe that in some wonderful manner, every one will become every-body's friend, especially when one is heard denouncing evils in the State, which are said to arise out of the possession of private property. These evils, however, are due to a very different cause, the wickedness of human nature " ; or with Bertrand Russell, found unexpectedly among the prophets, " They (i.e. the social reformers) still retain the view that the principal aim of a democratic policy ought to be to increase the wages of labour. I believe this to be too passive a con-ception of what constitutes happiness. It is true that, in the industrial world, large sections of the populace are too poor to have any possi-bility of a good life. But it is not true that a good life will come of itself with a diminution of poverty. Very few of the well-to-do classes have a good life at present " ; or with Tawney, that eager, forward-looking spirit, " No change of system can avert those causes of social illness which consist in the egoism, greed, and quarrelsomeness of human nature. What it can do is to establish a social system upon principles to which, if they please, they can live up, and not down. It can't control men's actions" ; or with Paul, that the only permanent solution of our problems is the coming of a race of men and women willing to live their lives in a new way ; not, as we all have done too long, in hot pursuit of our own selfish interests and ends, but in God's way of glorious, divine self-sacrifice.

Are you, am I, prepared to be among them, and to lead the way ?

What a tremendous day of hope and terror ; of terror and hope ! And before each of us God has set life and death.   And we must choose between them.

> "There shall always be the Church and the world,
>   And the heart of man,
>   Shivering, and fluttering between them, choosing and being chosen,
>   Valiant, ignoble, dark, and full of light,
>   Swinging between Hell Gate and Heaven Gate.
>   And the Gates of Hell shall not prevail.
>   Darkness now, then
>   Light."

But on which side are we ?

CHAPTER XV

GOD'S PATIENCE AND OUR FRETFULNESS

" And when the time was fully come."—GAL. iv. 4.

FOR even God must wait until it does. And He does wait with an awful patience, which is our one hope, yet which has something fearsome in its persistency that will not give nor break.

To us the mark of the divine is suddenness. God speaks, and it is done. He wills, and His desire grows into fact. For He is the Almighty with whom will and power are one. The sickening heave of the earthquake transforming a whole landscape in one tremendous moment, tumbling men's proudest works into a ruinous heap; the fierce, vindictive scribble of the lightning, tearing the sky open; the rattle and crash of the thunder; these are the things that make us hold our breath, feeling that God is very near, is here. And sometimes God does work through cataclysm and upheaval. But usually He does not shatter His way to an immediacy of result, but slowly, gradually, imperceptibly feels His way to His far ends. God's thoughts are long, long thoughts, puzzlingly so to our bewildered little human minds. We men are fussy, fidgety, impatient. Our little moment is so short, we clamour for immediate and large results, won't play unless our hand can plant the flag upon the enemy's fallen citadel. For ours is still the boyish dream that war is all a wild huzzaing charge, with horses at the gallop, and the enemy in full retreat. We lack that dour and obstinate tenacity of purpose that can hold a muddy trench for weeks with little to encourage one, except the hope that we are wearing down the enemy. And so we keep running on ahead of God, tug at His hand, keep crying " Hurry! Hurry! "; dare, even after Calvary, to doubt if He can be really in earnest, or why is there not far more to show! Our very prayers are often a half blasphemy—an indignant rejection of God's slow, cumbrous, hesitating plans, an eager proposal that He should substitute our own far cleverer and more effective ones! We men are hot, perspiring, desperate, premature. But God waits—till the time has fully come.

How long it is since He said " Let us make man in our own image." And, even yet, how most imperfectly that dream of His has been fulfilled! For æons, indeed, nothing seemed to happen, or even to get begun. For slowly, slowly this earth had to be fashioned ; and slowly, slowly it had to be cooled. And when life did at last appear it was at first in such crude forms. And, again it was slowly, slowly that it erected itself up and up until at long last man appeared, at first how faintly human. And even yet, how dim is the resemblance between us in our earthiness and sin, and God with His splendour of unselfishness. " If," cried Luther once in his impulsive way, " I were God, and the world had treated me as it has treated Him, I would have kicked the wretched thing to pieces long ago." But God works on with the intractable material of these impossible hearts of ours. How often, with divine ingenuity, He has contrived for us the very circumstances that gave us our chance to lift the whole world nearer to His feet, or to climb out of our own personal failings, rose to His feet, and said, " Let it be now," and looked towards us with confidence. But we never noticed, or we couldn't be bothered. And the priceless and God-given opportunity was lost ! And quietly God set to work again some other way. Ah ! cried Tertullian, irascible Tertullian, speaking about the Pharisees and Christ, " They should have known that He was God. His patience should have proved it to them."

Consider what Paul tells us here. From all eternity God had it in His heart to give us Jesus Christ. Long before time began He had thought out that " unspeakable gift " for us. Yet still He kept it back. Other mighty benefits He heaped on us—prophets, revelations, new understandings of God and life and man—glorious things showered upon us unstintedly. But that greatest of all He still held in His hand, till men had grown up enough to feel their need of it, and see the glory of the life in Christ, and thrill to the adventure to which we are called in Him. And only then, when the time had fully come, did Christ appear.

And what heartens me, is that the day of all days which He chose out as the best possible, as the appointed time for the new inrush of spiritual life and understanding which Christ brought, was an age quite curiously like our own. Then, as now, people were disillusioned, and desperate ; had found life was too difficult for them by far, and that things had broken in their hands : then as now, the foundations of life, the axioms of human conduct slowly built up out of the hard-won experience of many generations, were being impudently challenged ; then, as now, the accredited religion seemed to have completely failed, and men were casting it aside as a thing outworn and of no further use, and were eagerly trying out anything and everything that offered itself to them as a possible substitute ; and, then as now, God seemed to many markedly less real and near and effective than other older generations had found Him in their day. And it was then, in such a storm-tossed, heart-sick, desperate day that at long last Christ came.

Is that the meaning of it all ? Has God, in His great mercy been shepherding us into this narrow place so that, with our pride broken and our need of Him made clear to us, we may at last be willing to accept from Him with humble gratitude what He has all along been offering us, and we have haughtily refused ?

I know there is another view. Voices of moment, even in the Church, keep telling us that we can't expect any outstanding spiritual happenings in a world like ours. How can there be, they ask ? Put yourself in the place of millions of your fellows, with some imagination and some acuteness of sympathy. Think of the life that meets them every morning ; of their heads bent over some mechanical task-work that converts them, for hours every day, into mere living automata : or of the struggle to make ends meet ; and to provide enough for those whom God has given them. You must alter the social system—lock and stock and barrel ; you must give them some kind of chance, and then they may have time to lift their heads and see the stars, and remember the big things that matter, but which meantime are, almost of necessity, crowded out of minds harassed and anxious about many things to which they must attend. As things are, it is hopeless to expect much interest in spiritual matters.

What do you say to that reading of things ? To me it seems just rank bad history. Wesley, for example, had some of his most signal spiritual triumphs in a Bristol which was starving, as nobody need starve to-day, thanks to our social services and such like things. And, if it is bad history, it is far worse religion. I, for one, will never agree that this gallant faith of Jesus Christ is a kind of extra—like golf or bowls—something to which you turn in the evening, when the day's real work is over ; when one is washed and fed and rested, and there is nothing much to do. And so one takes to the perfectly innocent hobby of a game of bowls ; and another to the no less innocent hobby of Christianity. But no sane man would bother about either of them out in the strain and stress and struggle of real life, or until these matters of moment have first been attended to.

Ask the prophets what they think of that reading of life, and they will laugh at you ; will tell you that it is just when things are darkest and most desperate that men need God the most, and then that they watch for Him most hopefully, waiting expectantly on tiptoe and with eager hearts, certain that He is sure to come, because we need Him so. Ask Jesus Christ Himself, and He will answer that it is not even the east end with its pressing and clamant economic problems, but the west end with its enervating comforts, which is the real danger spot, where souls are likeliest to be lost. Ask many of us here, and we will tell you that it was out upon the perilous edge of things, where the winds cut and whistle cruelly, and the footing is precarious, that we have been nearest to God, and surest of His presence with us.

Is that what it all means ? The Fatherhood of God ! men's hearts used to break in, uninterestedly and even scornfully. But we don't want it, and don't need it. What would we do with it ? We are grown up, and can shift for ourselves ; are not children in leading strings, but men, as poor Heine proudly boasted long ago. But that was when this seemed an ordered universe, and life a stable, a fore-see-able and a manageable thing, before chaos broke in on us ; whereas now all security is gone, and every day the shadow, cold, and dark, and shivery, steals into some neighbour's home ; and every hour holds its grim possibilities ; and half the world, and nearly all the younger generation, are keeping life alive upon the meagre fare of hopes deferred, that might well make their hearts sick, and that often do. And now, in this strange, unfamiliar, dangerous world in which we find ourselves, it makes a mighty difference, steadies and fortifies the soul to know that we are not alone, never alone, that " there is always Someone else there more than we can see," who will never forget us, and never does forget us, nor the lads for whom our hearts are anxious even more than for ourselves ; who will spare us all that love can spare—though let us remember that He did not, and could not, and would not, spare Jesus Christ His Cross—and in the darkest hours will give us, and our loved ones, all that we need to see it through with quietness and honour—a mighty boon indeed.

All which they tell us with contempt is merely childish wishful thinking. Because life is too difficult for us, we wish there were a Father, and at last fool ourselves, poor self-deluded dupes, into imagining there is a Father, though, of course, there is really nothing there. The answer to all which is the only honest, and the only scientific one—try you it for yourself, and you will find it is no dream but solid, palpable, demonstrated fact ; that a hand, invisible but strong and watchful does steady : and a voice inaudible to the ears indeed, yet quick to speak, urgent and very wise, does guide. " If you ask me," confesses Unamuno, the Spanish philosopher, " how I believe in God, how God creates Himself in me, and reveals Himself to me, my answer may perhaps provoke your smiles or laughter, and even scandalize you. I believe in God as I believe in my friends, because I feel the breath of His affection, feel His invisible and intangible hand, drawing me, leading me, grasping me." It is as sure as that. If this is mere mirage, we can trust nothing in our experience at all. " The stupid body," wonders the scornful Psalmist, says " ' there is no God ! ' " It is indeed a very stupid body who does not come upon Him many a time in every common day.

Or, how often you have heard this offer of a Saviour. And how often has your heart remained entirely unexcited. Saviour from what ? I am content enough with what I am ; and any matters that need rectifying I myself must right, and can right. So you have felt, and said, and pushed the Gospel from you, as insulting. But to-day, looking out over a world tumbled in ruins, at all the day-dreams of a generation turned into mocking faces and to jeering voices that hoot at us, and our proud boasts of what the earth was going to see now that at last a generation had appeared with some idealism and some grit and purposefulness to arise and work it out—beaten, humbled, disillusionized, finding by bitter proof that this thing is too set and strong for our weak, human hands to wrench it into shape, are we ready now to lay help upon One mightier than ourselves by far ; ready to hail a Saviour who can save, where we ourselves have failed ? Horace, talking of the wise construction of a poem, tells us that a god should never be called in unless the case is desperate. Look at the world ! Is it not desperate indeed ? Can any one but God meet such colossal needs and sinfulness ? Are we ready, at length, to call Him in, and try His plan for us ? Has the time fully come—at last ?

Or what about yourself ? Has the time come for you ? Were it not blessed and exciting beyond words if it all happened to you here and now ; if, ever after this, you could look back, and say, " It was on such a day (this day), in such a place (this place). I don't remember who the preacher was (it had nothing to do with him), nor how it came about ; nor why it happened. I only know that, for the first time, or, in fuller measure, I found Jesus Christ ; or rather Jesus

Christ found me. How ? Why ? I do not know. I cannot tell. Except just this—that, for me, the time had fully come.

For there is this, too, to be said, with awe and bewilderment, that it is not of Christ alone, but of all of us—you and me—that it is true to say that it was when the time had fully come that God sent each of us to the appointed lot to which He had assigned us, and to the work for which He had created us. The Christian faith is staggering in its originality on many points, but in few matters more than in the almost unbelievable importance Christ gives to the individual—to any man and every man, the very stupidest and very worst among us— tailed off, by himself alone, to " every one at all who bears a human face." As Harnack says, " Jesus Christ was the first to bring the value of every human soul to light, and what He did no one can ever more undo." And MacMurray, " The modern world began with Christ's discovery of the individual." There is no doubt that that is so. And yet it is a claim that stuns the mind that Christ makes for us. Let one begin—I do not say to grasp, for our poor little human reason cannot do it—but to grow dimly conscious of the inconceivable vast- ness of the universe around us—itself, they tell us, merely one out of innumerable similar universes ;—of the unthinkable deeps of space, that the very nearest star seen from our hemisphere is forty-three billions of miles away (a million seconds is about a fortnight, but a billion seconds is some thirty thousand years) ; and that not many more than some forty are known to be within two hundred billion miles of us ; that this, our earth, which seems to us so central is nothing but a dust speck lost in an insignificant collection of the satellites of a very minor star—and then, with our minds choked with star dust, and stunned by unimaginable measurements, turn back to the Christian estimate of man, this petty insect crawling about his trivial world, so lost in the mass of his puny fellows, so commonplace, and turned out by the million, and hear again that each of us is to God unique and original and irreplaceable, that nobody in all the ages can be to Him what you can be, or do for Him what you can do—and do we not feel, as Radhakrishnan has it, that " the orthodox theo- logians seem like men talking in their sleep " ? If you or I were killed on our way home to-day, well, by to-morrow they would be discussing who would get my chair, and your appointment ; and, in a week or so, somebody else would be where we are now, and the work would go on as usual, and nothing whatsoever be arrested. " Yet," says Ecclesiasticus, " let no man say I shall never be missed in a boundless creation. For God has no need of useless souls." The fact that you are here at all is proof that God has need of you. Your work only you can do, and you were made to do it. " His enterprise was not a plot of two years or of twenty years," says Emerson about John Brown, that lover of the slaves, " but the keeping of an oath made to heaven and earth forty-seven years before. Forty-seven years at least—though I incline to accept his own account of the matter which makes the date a little older, when he said, ' This was all settled millions of years before the world was made.' " You, too, were thought out by Almighty God from all eternity as the likeliest of all possible creatures to do that work He needs from you.

Yet what, in point of fact, are we doing with our lives ? What would you like to do with yours ? Oh, you say, just the usual little things. I would wish to push on a bit in life, to have some measure of success in it, to make a home, and something over, for my dear ones, to win, if that may be, a little leisure for myself before the end.

All worthy dreams and goals ! But do you think that their fulfilment would be a sufficient explanation of your being ? Would God have created you only for that ? The poet who wrote the 119th Psalm tells us that, watching the mighty drama always being enacted before his fascinated eyes, and seeing how the seasons follow one another, and the flowers know their appointed times, and the constellations move in a majestic and orderly procession through the heavens, and all things punctually play their part—and only he was out of it, a little, fussy, independent state, he felt lonesome and lost, an alien in this universe in which everything else was helping on the plan, felt that he also must come underneath the scheme, and work out his part of it too. If we are ever to do that, we had better set about it.

> " Death closes all : but something ere the end,
> Some work of noble note may yet be done.
> The lights begin to twinkle from the rocks ;
> The long day wanes ; the slow moon climbs ; the deep
> Moans round with many voices. Come, my friends,
> 'Tis not too late to seek a newer world."

Not yet too late. But, certainly for us, the time has fully come.

And if you think that, for you, it has come, and passed, and left you still with empty hands and a heart cheated by the tremendous promises which have not worked out in your case, well, my dear teacher, Marcus Dods, was fascinated, in his closing months, by a chemical metaphor that vastly helped him. He, too, felt that with him things had moved but slowly ; and now life was ebbing, and the tide was surely lost. Yet his heart rallied and held on. " For," said he, " I have seen a scientist, with a phial in either hand, drop one drop from the one into the other fluid—and nothing happened ; a second drop—and nothing happened ; a third, a fourth, a fifth, too many drops to number—and still nothing happened ; and then one more, exactly like the others, but, in an instant, everything had changed." And, mused he, may it be that one more prayer, added to all the others that seem so futile and resultless, and one more act of faith added to all that went before and left me so unchanged, and I shall waken, satisfied, and in Christ's blessed likeness !

However that may be, the end is sure. " No one," says Paul, " who believes in Christ will ever be disappointed. No one."

> " Love, love, that once for me did agonize,
>   Shall conquer all things to itself : if late,
>   Or soon it be, I ask not nor advise,
>   But, since my God is waiting, I can wait."

Hope on, work on, believe on ! And, when the time has fully come, for you, too, it will all come true.

CHAPTER XVI

CHRIST'S APPEAL TO YOU

" Behold I stand at the door and knock. If any man hear My voice, and open the door, I will come in to him, and sup with him, and he with Me."—REV. iii. 20.

AND that, mark you, is not just a metaphor, a colourful pictorial word with nothing very definite behind it, thrown out vaguely to make things vivid to our sleepy minds. It is the simplest of facts, and the most solid of realities. To-day the Lord Christ stands at your door, and mine, and knocks, keeps knocking, and won't go away : won't take refusal.

So, of course, it is always, and everywhere.

What is that new thing in the Testament, that marvellous discovery that these people, dazed and intoxicated by their happiness, cannot keep to themselves, must share with any one and every one that they can get to listen to them ? No doubt we must be cautious what we say. For wild words are being thrown about the world these days upon this very matter ; words that, to me at least, seem almost blasphemous, and that surely forget that God has never left Himself without a witness anywhere ; and that there is a Light which lighteneth every man that comes into the world. Surely, wherever there is a needy, sinful, careless soul the whole earth over, there the wonderful Father who created each of us, whatever be our colour or our race, because there is a place in His heart that that one soul alone can fill, is there beside it, giving Himself to it, up to the full limit of the measure in which it can, or will, allow Him entrance, and ready to do more and more for it, exceeding abundantly, above all that it can ask or think. And yet, within limits, it is the bare and simple fact that the other faiths are the brave records of man's search for God. And a very gallant tale it is, that stirs the heart and shames us spiritual loafers, dawdling through life. So daringly, adventurously, audaciously, have those intrepid mountaineers climbed towards Him, through the mists and clouds and darkness, that, in amazement, we look up at some of them, standing so high, and wonder how they did it, and are very sure a hand came down to them too, steadying, drawing, uplifting them.

Ah ! but our faith is the astounding record of God's search for us ;

a long, long, patient, obstinate search, from which He will not cease nor turn away, says Christ " until He find."

Montefiore, claiming, with a proud assurance, that his own faith can parallel very much in Christianity, frankly concedes that there are certain places where it is left far behind, where Christ stands out, unchallengably, as unique, and daringly original ; and among such marked advances, he sets prominently this seeking of the lost that Jesus introduced, and Himself practised, and has taught to others. That, he says honestly, is new. We cannot match it. And the reason why this virtue, so familiar to us, yet so novel, has been practised by good Christians down the centuries is simply that, in Christ, they know that God, in His infinite mercy, missed them when they were lost ; and planned out a salvation for them costly beyond all human reckoning to Himself ; and carried it through to the uttermost, until He found them. The foolish, ragged, heartsick, shamefaced boy, and the father's eager welcome, that couldn't wait, but, seeing that abashed and hesitating figure, still a great way off, ran, and gathered him close to his heart, and blotted out the past, so far as even divine love can effect that, and made him sure he had been missed, and was still wanted, and that nobody could take his place. The sheep, wandered and lost, and those seeking eyes that wouldn't cease from searching, and those tired feet that still kept on and on, and the patient and indomitable heart that would not turn back, without the straying truant, would seek and seek, until it found, would not be satisfied till it was safely in the fold once more.

Did you know you meant, and are, as much to God as that ? That, if all the rest were safely gathered in, and only one place, your place, was left empty, there would still be a shadow on God's throne, and still an ache and longing in His heart for the one child, still lost to Him, out in the dark and cold.

Don't you hear it ? asks Isaiah—that Voice that keeps calling, calling, like a mother, seeking her lost bairn, and desperate until she find it ? That is God's voice. Aye, and it is your name that He is crying.

Do you never come on God ? asks Paul. He haunts me ; keeps following me about. And, when I peevishly push past Him, and twitch my shoulder from underneath His hand, and bury myself again in this or that, He waits ; He, the great God, stands waiting patiently, until there comes a lull in my busynesses, and, with that, He breaks in on me again with renewed offers of divine kindness.

II

Don't you realize, says Christ Himself, that God's heart is a Father's heart, and that He cannot give you up ?

Always that heart is following us, always His voice keeps calling us, always He pleads with us, who can, and do, so easily forget Him, and who are often irritated by Him, till we wish, in our childish heat, there were no God at all to bother us—pleads with us to be friends with Him, who has nothing but goodness in His mind towards us.

Behold ! I stand at the door, says Christ, and knock ; keeps knocking, and won't go away, won't take refusal.

But, as a rule, we rarely hear it—what with the bustle and the din of things—oh ! little things enough, no doubt—the clatter of dishes in the kitchen, or of typewriters in the office, the thousand and one trifles that make up our days, and to which we must attend ; the round of social functions and so on, all innocent enough, that clutter up our lives—anything, or nothing, is quite big enough to crowd God from our minds, and drown His voice to us, and make us clean forget about Him altogether, for long periods. Carlyle, once, at a levee or the like, stood watching the usual conventional doings and inanities, well-dressed women and idle men carrying through, with boredom, or vivacity, the correct well-oiled procedures of Society ; and, as he watched, went sick and cold, felt he could scream, seeing Death and Eternity and Hell glaring in at the windows— plainly there : but not one soul in all that gathering, except himself, seemed to have any notion they were there—quite near. God, too, is always there—quite near. And some happy spirits spend their whole lives, wherever they may be, whatever has been given them to do, face to face with Him, in unbroken communion, with His voice always reaching them, and counselling them, step by step. Brother Lawrence was a lamed soldier man, who, all his days, thereafter, was only a cook in a Carmelite monastery, a business to which, by nature, he had an intense repugnance. Yet there, amid the heat and smells and steam and clatter of the kitchen, with two or three different people, as he himself puts it vividly, calling for several things at the same time, he lived with God, for thirty years, in a fellowship so intimate and so unbroken that, though he went obediently to prayers, when he was told to pray, on passing back to work again, he felt no difference whatsoever, no descent from the Mount, no drop in the spiritual temperature, no sense of a thick door swung to behind him, shutting him out now from the God who, in the chapel services, had been so real and near, and evidently there ; whereas here, immersed once more in this grossly material atmosphere, he had lost Him again, so that His voice could carry to Him only faintly and remotely, if at all. Far from that, he confesses modestly and gratefully that, in that noisy place, he possessed God in as great tranquillity as when upon his knees at the blessed sacrament ; found himself even more united to God at his common tasks than in the hush and quiet of His house ; had reached a stage—won, at first, slowly, and with difficulty, and through years of effort and believing, but now grown habitual and natural to him for half a lifetime, where it would be as difficult for him not to live consciously with God, as it once had been to do it.

Hearing all which, we feel uncomfortably small, and uglily hot and flustered ; and, with it all, cheated out of the best gifts life has to offer.

Yet the thing can be done, is being done, even to-day.

I was once colleague to a man—a wonderful man, big, learned, human, humorous, eagerly interested in a score of things, in every-thing, indeed, around him ; spending himself with an unstinted and untiring generosity for his fellows ; winning the respect, the venera-tion, the affection of all sorts and conditions of men, and that uncon-sciously, without an effort, merely by passing by. Yet, with it all, this many-gifted soul, quite literally lived and moved and had his being in God, seemed never to lose contact with Him ; could pass at a step from happy hearted laughter to the spiritual deeps, and even more remarkable could take far cruder souls along with him into the Presence with perfect naturalness, so that for them, too, it was all real, and near, and wonderful. And then he went his way, and the rest of us slipped back to our accustomed level ; and the noise of the world rushed in again ; and God was gone. But he lived in perpetual communion, face to face. I don't suppose it made much difference to him when he passed over. " For thirty years," wrote Brother Lawrence, not a week before his sudden final illness, " I have lived with Him, and I hope, by His mercy, for the favour to see Him within a few days."

Yes ; but the most of us are deaf and blind indeed to the wonderful Presence that is always there. " God pity me," cried Jowett of Balliol, " I cannot keep the thought of God in my mind. I rise and say my prayers, and pass out, as I must, into the press and throng of daily duty, and waken up at night to find that, for the whole day, I have lived without God in the world." So, although Christ keeps knocking, our hearts pay small heed, and seldom ever hear.

But now that you do hear it, what is your response ? Everything turns on that. Of His fullness have all we received, so John witnessed, and grace heaped up on grace. And were it not pathetic now that that same Christ is knocking at our door, eager to bring to us no less, if we should never notice, or pay no attention, and so miss it all. Remember that the prophets, aye, and not only they, but Christ Himself, in many passages that stare at us, though we choose to ignore them, keep reminding us, gravely and awesomely, that even God's long-suffering does come to an end at last ; that we cannot insolently presume on it, willing and yet not willing ; praying, and then half taking it all back, like Augustine's " Save me—but—not yet " ; that there does come a day when God gives up the quest, knows that the die is cast, that we have made our choice, that it is no use striving with us any further. " Ephraim is joined to his idols ; let him alone." If your ideals have so dimmed that they no longer hurt and shame or sting you, have indeed—now you are grown worldly wise—been tossed away with your toys and other childish trifles ; if you have settled down to be that, that you are ; have even grown content with it ; if Christ's knock seldom reaches you these days, do you not see the terror of what is happening ? Christ is still there. But you are growing spiritually deaf, and soon you may hear nothing, may be shut into a dumb, unbroken silence, and Christ be lost to you. Your heart is hardening and ossifying, and your soul dying, inch by inch.

" And the door," says Christ, " was shut." And is there not a shuddery finality in that. " Sleep on now," He told those drowsy, blinking creatures in the Garden, who had been roused and given chance on chance, and yet had failed so wretchedly. The opportunity is gone—for ever ; all that you might have done can never be done now ; that possibility is lost and out, and will not come—ever again.

Listen ! Listen ! Can you hear nothing ? Nothing at all ! Or, if you can, open now ! Open now ! To-morrow it may be too late.

But, you object, a heart like mine can offer Christ so little—at best, so poor and pinched and niggardly a hospitality and such meagre fare ; for I have nothing, worthy of Him, to set before Him, only a kind of affection, real enough at times, but which, at others, can, and does, so easily forget ; only a will, quite unreliable, deplorably unstable ; only a faith that is the merest shadow of what His real friends mean when they speak about faith—that daring intrepidity, that unreckoning wholeheartedness, that passion that burns up life for Him—compared with that, how tepid is anything that I can give.

I know. But there was once a garret up under the roof—a poor, bare place enough. There was a table in it, and there were some benches, and a water-pot; a towel and a basin in behind the door— but not much else—a bare, unhomelike room. But the Lord Christ entered into it. And, from that moment, it became the holiest of all, where souls innumerable ever since have met the Lord God, in His glory, face to face. And, if you give Him entrance to that very ordinary heart of yours, it, too, He will transform and sanctify and touch with a splendour of glory.

But I am not the type, you say, am certainly not really spiritual, and not even churchy. I know. And Christ knows. And the fact that He is knocking at your door means that He, so knowing, will gladly enter if you let Him in. Zacchæus was no worthy or likely host for Jesus Christ, as you and I would judge. It shocked the whole populace. He has gone to be the guest of a man that is a sinner; so they bruited the incredible news abroad, dumbfoundered what to make of it, or roused to a cold anger by this unpardonable insult to their city. Yet Christ did go. Not only so, but He asked for an invitation. And, said He once, to plain people like you and me, in a tremendous promise that snatches away the breath, If you will have us, and can manage to make room for us, we will come—God and He will come—and abide with you; or, as some go the length of daring to translate it, make Our home with you.

And if He does? The Testament is crowded with a jostle of competing metaphors, thrusting each other aside, and signalling to catch our eyes, all trying to bring home to us a little of what that would mean.

The difference I make? asks Christ, and flashes before us, in a phrase or two, the picture of a tired, lean, disappointed man, with whom life has gone hardly, whose meagre portion it has been to clatter about the mucky cobbles of his half-ruinous little byre, and toil long hours out in the fields in the hot sunshine, with little leisure, and no holiday at all, and nothing to show for it all except a bare existence pruned back to the raw. And one never-to-be-forgotten day he stumbles on a buried treasure; and, in a moment, is lifted up above all that, into a life that is life, crowded with interests, with time in it for many things—his family, his mind, his soul. And I, too, give life that is life indeed, says Christ—ample, rich, exciting, satisfying.

And no fact can ever have had more witnesses to corroborate it. Millions who have tried it know and testify that this is true.

Or, as He puts it here, " If any man hear my voice, and open the door, I will come in and sup with him, and he with Me." To many of us that at once calls up the table of the Lord, and inexpressible experiences there, when He did sup with us, and we with Him. He there, so real, so near, so evident that, a very little more, and, the veil that hides Him from our senses rent and gone, we should have heard and seen Him face to face ; and, so doing, would have been no nearer Him, for our whole souls were soaked in His grace, and His presence was the most certain fact in the whole world. Yes, but the promise is an ampler and quite general one, of something that is to happen, not merely now and then, when we climb to the heights, but every day, and all the day. " I will come in and sup with you," He says. And does it startle you to hear Christ saying that to you : to be assured that you can hearten and refresh Him ? Browning was sure that even that lay in our power.

> " God, who registers the cup
>   Of mere cold water, for His sake
> To a disciple rendered up,
>   Disdains not His own thirst to slake
> At the poorest love was ever offered."

And, over and over, Christ assures us that, in a world which pours by on the other side, eager about a hundred things, but with no time or thought for Him, or any slightest interest in Him, that looks at Him with a cold, blank indifference and sees nothing in Him that it wants, it matters hugely to Him, it refreshes Him, it helps Him, that your heart is grown up enough to feel the thrill of what He offers ; and, in its saner moments, at least, chooses what He has to give, and cannot be content for long with anything but that. That Christ should deign to stoop to let us serve and be of use to Him—that is an ultimate and crowning kindness. To be allowed to help, with a child's eagerness, in a child's blundering way, not doing it well at all, but yet allowed to do it, that seems to move and win this generation more even than the mass of benefits which, on His side, He heaps on us. Ours is, indeed, a rather fussy, hot-faced, kitchen-fire kind of religion. The coolness, the calm, the spirituality of Mary—all that how far away ! Our patron saint is honest Martha, kindly, flustered, practical soul, with no time for sitting absorbed at Christ's feet, but willingly tiring herself out, and running to and fro to make things right for

Him. We are not great on prayer, and our theology is somewhat nebulous and hazy. The classical doctrines of the faith seem to be stated in a language which our minds don't use or understand. We don't so much dissent from them as never think about them one way or the other ; they are too remote from us even for that. What Bagehot set down long ago of the men of his time is true of even more in ours. " They do not deny these tenets ; but they live apart from them ; they do not misbelieve them ; they are silent when they are stated. They do not question the existence of Kamschatka, but they have no call to busy themselves with Kamschatka."

Or Denney, speaking of " the vast majority of the members of the evangelical churches," who " are loyal to Christ," and whose " attitude to Him is essentially the New Testament attitude," " but to a large extent they have lost interest in the traditional theology. It is not that they actively disapprove of it or dissent from it, but they do not think of it. It is not their own, and they have a dim or clear conviction that anything of this kind, if it is to have interest or value for them, must be their own."

We are not church-going : and devote much less time, than many former generations, to family and personal religion. But we do want to leave the world better and saner than we found it : to give our fellow-men a helping hand, and a lift out of their difficulties, and a better chance : are eager and energetic enough along such lines, some of us quite untiringly so. It sounds shallow, and trivial, and superficial, and unspiritual. But if we are allowed to run about, and wait on Christ, and work for Him on these material-looking lines, we are willing and glad to do it. And He who has warned us that the tests by which, at the day of Judgment, He is going to weigh our lives and their worth, their failure or success, are uncomfortably practical and hopelessly material, as the devout may think, may perhaps look more kindlily on this hot, fussy, busy, dusty generation than most of its critics do. I will come in, and sup with you, He says : will gladly accept your help.

But then, of course, there comes the other side—" and he with Me." Always, where Christ is, He is giving. The central word of the New Testament is grace. At His own table, He is there, as Host, a wonderful Host who comes to meet us eagerly, and draws us in, and sets us down in our own place, prepared for us with individual care, and with gifts, each with our name on it, heaped up and ready for our taking, makes it quite evident that it would not have been the same to Him at all, if we had stayed away. Always and wherever He is, Christ keeps giving and giving and still giving. And what amazing gifts ! Tell John, He said Himself, what you, with your own eyes, saw Me distributing to whoso would accept it. Tell him how you watched men born blind, who had lived all their days in a blank darkness, with a whole world of wonder and of beauty suddenly rushing in on them ; and deaf folk grown alive and responsive to a Voice that had for years and years been drowned and lost for them in the babble and roar of life ; and leprous things made clean, lifted up out of their intolerable self-disgust, granted a whole rich human life again, instead of that maimed, horrid rottenness into which they had sunk. Are you the slave of some besetting sin, slinking to heel at call ? Then Christ can make you free, done with that misery and abjectness. Is life too much for you, does it continually get you down ? Are duties, left undone and bungled, growing into a mighty avalanche that some day must begin to move, and quicken, and roar down upon you, and sweep you bodily away ? Then Christ will make you fit and able for life's calls upon you, endowing you with just that steadiness and grit you lack. Look, so He sums it up Himself, what need of pottering about with individual illustrations and examples ? And, with that, He takes a bit of common bread, and says, This is My body : all that I have : all that I am : and it is all for you. If there is anything in Me that can bring help to you, take it. The fact that it is Mine means it is yours, if you will have it. It is with gifts like that to offer, and a heart so full of grace to you, that Christ stands at your door and knocks.

Well, what do you say about it all ? Now that your soul does hear Him ? Does it break away, and to the door, crying, Wait ! Wait ! The lock is stiff : the key is hard to turn. But I am opening. Wait ! Wait ! For it is Thee I need : and Thee I want : and Thee that I must have. And nothing else will do.

CHAPTER XVII

ON THE MEANING OF INFANT BAPTISM

" And He took a child, and set him in the midst of them : and when He had taken him in His arms, He said . . ."—MARK ix. 36.

EVEN Christ never found a bonnier text than when, holding this wee man in the crook of His arm, He used him as a picture, and evidence, and proof of what He was seeking to bring home to our dull minds. And to-day another little evangelist, sent from God, is to be carried into our midst. God grant that the wonderful message that he brings us straight from Him may come home burningly to us, to whom the most amazing Scriptures have grown dim and weathered by long familiarity, so that, like worn printers' type, they no longer bite into our minds, nor leave any impression on them ; or, like hail on a roof, stot off from the blank unconcern with which, entirely unexcited, and sometimes frankly bored, we let tremendous, and, judged by human standards, incredible words slip, unarrested, through our placid inattention.

Baptism is, of course, a Sacrament—which means several things. But, to begin with, this is plain, that a sacrament is a picture of realities that lie behind it, and which it seeks to make vivid and visible to us. It is an assault upon Mansoul, as Bunyan would say, not, this time, by Ear Gate alone, where our attacks are, for the most part, pressed, but by Eye Gate as well. Intellectual giants keep assuring us—and our experience corroborates them—that, until we can see a thing, can make a picture of it in our minds, can visualize it, we can't really think of it at all.

Most of us have no brains worth reckoning as brains, but we do possess some smatterings of imagination. And, if you can make things see-able by us, we do begin to form some notion of them. If, but only if. Teach a child about something entirely outside its experience, an elephant for instance, and you may talk long enough, and only succeed in puzzling it by your descriptions of this odd monstrosity, not really conceivable, with its true tail dangling at the wrong end. But show the child a picture, let him see it, and at once he grasps, and understands. And our own brains cry out for the same visual helps—must have them, if they are to get to work at all. " The soul never thinks without an image," declared Aristotle, that master of all them who know. And Aquinas, subtlest of intellects, is equally, and even more, emphatic. " The soul understands nothing without a picture : human contemplation cannot exist without recourse to such : it is an ordinance with human nature that it should see intellectual things through the medium of pictures in the imagination." But in the Sacraments the pictures are given to us. A Sacrament, said the great church father, is a visible word—the Word of God made see-able, as well as audible. Our fathers held, and have burned into our consciousness, an august conception of these sacraments. But, none the less, true children of the Reformation as they were, always the Word comes first. In our old Scottish Confession they say with assurance " We affirm that the faithful in the right use of the Lord's Table have such conjunction with Christ Jesus as the natural man cannot comprehend." And yet, in spite of these never-to-be-forgotten experiences there, they fasten on the Word, read, but especially preached, as the Spirit of God's most effectual means of gaining and upbuilding sinful men. One of the dreariest of the early churchmen divided a Christian service into three : in prayer, man speaks to God ; in the Scripture, God speaks to man ; while in the sermon, man addresses man. Far differently have we been taught to think of and assess the majesty of preaching, in which the service mounts up to an apex and the climax, unless indeed there is a sacrament to follow.

It is a marvellous privilege that, in prayer, we, sin soiled as we are, can go boldly into the presence of the Holy God, whose eyes are purer than to behold iniquity, and speak to Him face to face, as a man to his friend. But, far, far more amazing still is it that, in the sermon, the Lord God Himself should be speaking to very us, through the stumbling tongue of His poor servant, no whit less truly than He did through the prophets long ago. And, if the man is really preaching, Christ Himself is in the midst, is there, quite near, the same wonderful Christ ; and seeing Him, hearing Him, conscious of His presence there, beside it, the soul runs to Him, clings to Him, accepts what He is offering, deals with Him face to face, and at first hand, with an intensity of worship which the rest of the service never even touched. As Miss Underhill, who herself belonged to a very different school, has put it, " The centre of all is now the constant proclamation of the Word, the vehicle of God's self-disclosure to men. The Word is, for evangelical worship, something as objective, holy, and given, as the blessed

sacrament is for Roman Catholic worship. Indeed, it is a sacrament—
the sensible garment in which the supra-sensible Presence is clothed.
Preaching of this category is to be classed as a supernatural act,
bringing all those who submit themselves to its influence into communion with God."

And in very deed, when a revival comes, when the tired, dusty,
footsore, lagging church grows young and irresistible again, it is
always because a prophet has arisen—some one who has seen God
face to face, and who must share with others what he can't keep to
himself. " What this parish needs," wrote Carlyle, in a vacancy,
" is what every parish needs—a man who knows God at more than
second hand." The priest is a useful enough functionary with a real
part to play, and to whom we owe more than we always realize. But
it is the preacher who sets men's hearts burning, and the prophet who
brings in a new day of the Lord.

Yet, even Christ found that preaching—even His own preaching—
did not appeal to every one. Unstintedly and freely He gave men His
glorious gospel. And some were not impressed ; and some were
puzzled ; and some just could not take it in. And so He broke it
down and told them stories—wonderful heart-gripping stories, like
that about the laddie who went wrong, got sick of home and its
restrictions, wanted a freer life, and got it, and landed himself in
utter wretchedness. And of the father, forgotten, yet remembering
always, wronged but how eager to forgive, and start again. So,
cunningly, unanswerably, Christ called as His witnesses against those
who doubted and objected—their own fatherly hearts ! Suppose your
boy went wrong, would you, and could you, slam the door, and close
your heart against him ; erase him from your mind, and let him reap
what he insisted upon sowing ? Could you ? Now, could you ? God,
too, has a father's heart that loves, that clings, that pities, that
cannot forget. And still they listened with that unconvinced and
puzzled look unlifted from their faces. And so, stooping, in mercy,
to our lowly level, treating us like the foolish children that we are,
He slipped into the Testament two pictures that the eye might help
us towards the truth. And one of them, of course, is the Lord's Supper,
and the other, Baptism.

But, let us remember always that it is the Word alone that gives
meaning and content and power to the Sacraments. A bit of bread !
But what is this ? A cup ! But why ? That is Christ's Body broken
for you ; and the New Testament in His blood, shed for you, for the

remission of your sins. And then how vivid grows the picture ; and how doubly sure the Word.

But a sacrament is far more than a picture ; it is also what our fathers called a seal. The Lord's Supper, for example, is not merely a commemorating of what happened for us on Calvary two thousand years ago, though it is that most surely and most movingly, was indeed designed expressly, so Christ said, to make the Cross vivid and near, that, looming up suddenly through the mists of our forgetfulness, it may lay its grip upon our hearts again, as with a gasp we half take in the unthinkable lengths to which God has gone to save our souls, to save my single, stupid, sinful soul as if there were no other. Said Mrs. Meynell, looking at a congregation at communion,

> " I saw this people like a field of flowers,
>   Each grown at such a price !
> The sum of unimaginable powers
>   Did no more than suffice.
> A thousand central daisies they,
>   A thousand of the one,
> For each, the entire monopoly of the day,
>   For each the whole of the devoted sun."

All God's all to save my soul. And it took every bit of it ! And it was gladly given.

Yes, but there is more in it even than that. Always the Central Figure in a sacrament is God—or, if you prefer so to put it, the Lord Jesus Christ. And every single time a sacrament is celebrated, God takes action, there and then—does something, not on Calvary, but in that church. And what He does is to come to each soul partaking in the Sacrament and to assure it that He stands to the best and biggest of His promises and to the fullness of His grace in Christ ; that it is still all true for it, de-universalizes the Scriptures, and individualizes them, makes them a personal promise, couched no longer in general terms, but offered to very you, and very me, as individually as if they covered no other, but referred to you and me alone. We may be cold and dead and unresponsive. None the less, something happens in the Sacrament. For God stands to His side of the Covenant, whether we stand to ours or not ; is there, making His offer, pressing it upon us, assuring us we can rely upon it absolutely.

To make it all effective, and in order that the grace that He has in His heart for us do not return unto Him void, but accomplishes that whereto He sent it, there must be response and acceptance on our side, without which all God's eager loving-kindness must be foiled. The sun, as Calvin put it, streams down in lavish generosity upon a field ; and, at its touch, green living things emerge out of the deadness of the soil, and grow to beauty and the gold of harvest. Yet, not a yard away, the same sun beats upon a rock, and warms and heats it too. But nothing happens there. So here. God's grace offers itself to every one, but not every one accepts it. It should be met by a glad Eucharist, a dazed, bewildered thanksgiving for benefits we cannot measure nor even begin to understand, and by a falling into affection for a God like this, which, leaving far behind a mere obedience, or a concussing of a still stubborn, recalcitrant will to accept grudgingly what we see to be our duty, wants to be used, and longs to give, and can't help loving One who has first so loved us.

And now apply all this to Baptism and, in particular, to Infant Baptism, and what does that mean ?

To begin at the lowest, beautiful and moving though that, in itself, is, here are a father and a mother, into whose keeping God has dared to commit a little soul, so precious to Him that Christ died for it, saying to them, " Bring up this child for Me, and I will give you your wages "—as indeed He does—wonderful wages. And they have come to dedicate this life to God ; to tell Him that, though they have great dreams for this little man, and are prepared to pinch for years that he may have his chance, out of all the possibilities life offers, what they choose for him, ask for him, pray for him, is that all his days he may belong to Jesus Christ, may live for Him, work for Him, be loyal and of service to Him. Grant us that for him, they say, and all the rest we seek to leave with Thee.

If they mean what they profess, and are prepared to stand to it, that, in itself, is certain to make an unreckonable difference in this new life. For we don't live as independent units, each by himself, in watertight compartments, but are immensely influenced and played upon, and made by others round about us. Freud goes the length of saying that our subconscious with its immeasurable potency upon our characters on to life's end is, often, largely fixed and determined in our first half-dozen years ! However that may be, the way the twig is set, the branch is apt to grow. And there is more than metaphor in God's promise that He makes His covenant not with His people only, but also with their children, and their children's children, with grace spilling over from lives loaded, as the Psalmist has it, with His benefits, into the succeeding generations. Do you remember how, when Christ was preaching once, He was unceremoniously, and indeed rudely, interrupted by a disturbance on the roof which drew all eyes, and lost Christ every one's attention, as they watched a helpless creature on a litter being lowered and steered, with a slow, hesitating care, down to Christ's feet by some ingenious and resourceful men who, blocked by the crowds in the streets, had thought out this purposeful method of winning their poor friend his chance. And how Christ, not in the least annoyed, looked up at those hot faces, peering down at Him, none too sure how He would take it, but risking it for their friend's sake, and cried to them " Your faith has saved him." Your faith up there has saved this man down here, unable to do one hand's turn for himself. And that is no uncommon thing ; far from it ! Most of us are Christians, not because, with gallant intrepidity and valour, we cut our way through intellectual problems and menacing difficulties, but simply because our father and mother, one or both, were in Christ before us, and, when we were small, turned our faces in His direction, and made Him a great fact for us, so that we could not wander from Him, and forget Him, and be satisfied—for long. For a home-sickness chased us back to our real place beside Him. In simple truth and fact, their faith has saved us. A Jewish lad was circumcised, not to make him a Jew, but because he was a Jew—though, circumcised or no, he might grow up a veritable blackguard. Still, said Paul, it is an enormous privilege to be born, not in a pagan but a Jewish atmosphere, and to be dedicated to God's service. And this baby is about to be baptized this morning—why ?

Not because we believe, as the Romanists do, that baptism is the one and only door into eternal life, and the vision of God : so that an unbaptized infant, who dies, is cast into the less terrible suburbs of hell, still hell—a grim and dreadful doctrine, which can any mother's heart really credit !

Not that anything magical takes place in the Sacrament, whereby God's attitude is changed towards the little one.

" The children of believers," says Calvin, " are not baptized in order that, though formerly aliens from the Church, they may then, for the first time, become children of God, but rather are received into the Church by a formal sign, because, in virtue of the promise, they previously belonged to the body of Christ." They, too, are born within the Covenant, and that, too, is a glorious privilege—to be brought up within a Christian atmosphere, and within sight of Jesus Christ, like the folk in the same street at Nazareth. They may never really come to know Him. But they are given a wonderful chance.

But all that is the least of the meaning of Baptism. Always, in every sacrament, God is the Central Figure, and it is what He does that is of supreme moment. So here, it is not the baby nor the parents upon whom we ought to keep our eyes, but upon the Lord God Himself, most surely in our midst—taking this little one into His arms, pledging Himself to stand—towards him—to every word of grace that He has ever spoken, erasing the general terms out of the promises, and writing in his very name instead, so that it runs, no longer, God so loved the world, but God so loved this little soul—whatever his name be, let it be boldly and with confidence inserted—that He gave His only begotten Son for very him, if he will have, and take, and use that wonderful gift. Meantime here is the personal pledge to very him, that God intends it, and has planned it all for him.

But, you say, why not wait till he has grown to years of discretion, and can immediately make the response without which even God's generosity is thwarted. Why ? Because this is the Sacrament of the Fatherhood of God—the picture of it, and the proof and declaration of it, to this individual little soul. Has God no interest in little ones ? And no concern for them until they can decide for Him ? - " Suffer the little children to come unto Me," He said Himself. Aye, you break in, but He didn't baptize them. No. But He loved them, laid His hands on them, took them up in His arms and blessed them.

And the Sacrament of infant baptism means that that is His mind and attitude towards this wee man to-day. Him too He loves ; him too He takes up in His arms ; him too He blesses. And that makes a mighty difference !

That overrated person, Goethe, blandly remarks, " If Christ were painted suffering the little children to come to Him, it would be a picture that expressed nothing, at any rate, nothing of importance ! " And yet innumerable parents have brought their little ones to be baptized. And why ? Because to them it matters immeasurably that the Lord God has an interest in, gives Himself to, pledges Himself to do all that even God can do for their child now, while he is still a child ; not only when he has grown up and given himself to Him, and become His in a yet closer and more intimate way, in Jesus Christ. And is that " nothing of importance " ? Watts has a picture of a little naked baby, with outstretched hands, and a half-frightened and half-wistful face, emerged from the seas of eternity behind him, and running up the sands of time—Whence and Whither, as the apt title says. Well, ordinarily, to a right eager welcome. When a little one is expected in a home, happy preparations are made for it and its needs. Much is thought out, and many things provided for it. And, when it arrives, they are there, all ready for it—clothes, and a cot, and so on. It does not come into a cold and unregarding world, but to where love waits for it, and surrounds it, and delights to spend itself on its behalf. And infant baptism means that far more wonderful preparations have been made for it than these ; that God's love, too, is waiting for it, and surrounds it, and will eagerly spend itself for it, from the beginning, and all through its days ; a love that welcomes it into a place in its heart which is all this baby's own, which no one else in the whole world can fill. " It is a great thing," said Rainy, " for a child to have a Father ; also it is not a little thing for a Father to have a child." This baptism to-day means it is not a little thing for God to have this child. A moment or two, and the little one will be brought in among us. And who but must be moved by the beauty and vividness and pathos of the picture held before us—the aimless, crumpled baby hands, the wailing little voice, there is the helplessness of our humanity incarnate ; and this wee soul has been set down in this dangerous world where the ways are steep and slippery, and the cross-roads intricate and puzzling, and dangers are ubiquitous and unavoidable ; and a principle of evil, old and experienced, follows it, foot by foot, with watchful and unwinking eyes ; and flying sparks of temptation blow everywhere, ready to light on its inflammable little heart. And it means much that God pledges Himself, to very it ; that He will guard it, and guide it, and surround it with an unsleeping care, and do all that a Father's heart can do, to bring it safely through. That, then, is fixed and sure and settled. This little one will never be alone, left to itself, to make such poor shift as it can, thrown on its own resources—that, and nothing further. Never. Here and now the God whose word is truth pledges Himself to that.

> " One Friend by my path shall be,
> To preserve my steps from wrong,
> Watching through the darkness long,
> Doing most, with none to see,"

said Browning. And we can say that with assurance of this child. That makes a mighty difference. No doubt, without this picture and this promise of it, the attitude of God to it was there. Yes ; but the picture, and the promise, help.

Moreover, the value and the potency of a sacrament are not confined to the moment of its celebration. God's word, said Luther, has hands and feet. It runs after a man : it seizes him. And a sacrament can chase us down the years. Every time we see another baptism, our own rises up again before us, reminding, beckoning, challenging us, insisting on response from us, for the first time, or for the hundredth time ; not to be turned aside, until we give it.

You, too, were once baptized—a long, long time ago. To you, too, at the start of life, God pledged Himself. And He has kept His word ; fulfilled His promises, full measure, shaken together, pressed down, yes, running over. Goodness and mercy have, in truth, followed you all the days of your life. " Never, never will I leave you, never, never will I forsake you ; so that we can boldly say, The Lord is my helper, whom shall I fear ? " So it was promised you in Baptism. So it has proved, in very deed. It is a wonderful story of a love that has loved on, even when we had sickened of ourselves ; and of a patience almost frightening in its set purpose to deliver us, and make us what we ought to be. And is it all to come to nothing and be foiled ? Old Samuel Johnson never could hear the wonderful Latin hymn without bursting into tears at that last line.

> " It was while seeking me Thou didst sit weary.
> It was for me that Thou didst bear the cruel pains.
> May such huge toil not be all thrown away."

CHAPTER XVIII

THE SENSE OF SIN, AND THE MAN OF TO-DAY

" Hide Thy face from my sins, and blot out all mine iniquities. Create in me a clean heart, O God : and renew a right spirit within me."—Ps. li. 9–10.

PERHAPS what strikes one first on coming within sound of this cry of anguish wrung from a tortured spirit all those centuries ago, yet still as vivid, and poignant, and moving, as if only now, and in our hearing, it was bursting from that broken, maddened, desperate heart, is—how far away it all is from the mood and feeling of the average man of our own day. That likeable and kindly soul has his faults and failings in plenty, yet he goes upon his way complacently and undisturbed. If he stumbles and slips, he picks himself up with a laugh, or a curse, brushes the dust from hands and clothes, and—thinks no more about it, simply does not credit that such failings as his can be momentous ; or that the great God is going to fuss over such passing trifles as his little self-indulgences at home, or his irritabilities and hot words down at the office, when rushed and over-driven, or rubbed raw by some junior's incompetence or stupidity ; or by such things as his own gradual slipping out of the habit of prayer, or his lack of any serious worry over a social system which secures him his own rights and comforts punctually and efficiently, though, confessedly, it does seem to leave quite a number rather out of it, and in the cold. Such little matters as his failings, he is sure, are really not worth bothering about : and, in point of fact, he is not bothering. And so this Psalm seems blown to him from another world, and to have nothing to do with him, who, thank God, has never broken down disastrously like this. If there is truth in that shrewd guess that it was written by David, that half-barbaric creature, after the worst sin of his life, that, he feels, certainly explains its heaped-up language and its horror of contrition. And these, in that case, are not by one whit overdone, for a fouler deed was never wrought. But for the faults and lapses of us decent and well-meaning folk, with our sudden spurts of temper, and our touchiness, and our chattering about our neighbours, not always too kindly, and our bickerings of party spirit and the like, this passion of self-loathing seems so wildly exaggerated that our man in the street feels that it cannot possibly refer to him, and does not fit his case at all.

No one who knows anything about the records of the past will question that, in our day, the sense of sin is abnormally atrophied and deadened, and the cutting edge of conscience turned and blunted. The age into which Christianity was born, for instance, was a time when whole masses of men, conscience stricken and immeasurably unhappy, could not get the thought that they were soiled and stained and earthy out of their minds. It haunted them, it drove them nearly crazy. Desperately they tore at this Nersus shirt that clung to them, and, burningly, ate into their flesh. Everything else had to be laid aside till this supreme and central thing had been put right. They tried this; they tried that; they would not be turned from the quest. And it was, not a little, because that atmosphere was prevalent that Christianity got its chance and swept the world. Here were men desperate to be changed and lifted up above themselves and made new creatures, done with what sickened them and maddened them, yet it was in them—a part of themselves, not to be shaken off. To people searching for salvation, it was easy to preach Christ, the Saviour. And the response was eager and immediate. They that be whole need not a physician, but they that be sick. And these folk knew that they were sick and had grave need of a physician. And so, hearing of Him, they ran to Him, clung to Him, accepted Him and what He gives, eagerly, joyfully, rapturously. But in a generation when the sense of sin is dimmed, preach the salvation that there is in Christ, and they look at you blankly, and ask coldly—Saved from what? I am an ordinary person, they will say, but I know the rules, and I have tried to play the game, and think that I have done it. Oh! a pokey kind of innings, I admit it: still I've kept up my end. And as for an occasional little outburst now and then—ah, well, no one is perfect, and one must keep some sense of proportion: and in the sizing up of things, no doubt God is not as prim as you suppose.

Yet there is this to be added that it is only on one side of his nature that the man of to-day has grown thus insensitive and callous. For, as to social wrongs, he is markedly uneasy and disquieted; and, about them, his conscience grows increasingly insistent and imperious. Nor is this odd lopsidedness of his a new fact in the world. Philo was a contemporary of our Lord, yet he remarks that, in his day, people of goodwill were apt to divide themselves into two classes—

those who lived in daily communion with the Lord God, seeking, with
diligence, to shape themselves into His character and likeness, but,
seemingly, not much affected by the troubles of the world surrounding
them ; and those who eagerly sought to alleviate their fellows' needs
and wrongs, giving, with liberality, of their means and time and lives
to that, but without any interest in personal religion. The latter,
sums up Philo, " may be called philanthropic, and the former devout.
But both are only semi-good. For perfection, one should have attained
proficiency in both these spheres." This generation is acquiring something of a reputation for philanthropy, but in devoutness it lags far
behind. Wrongs done to a whole community, injustices affecting
entire classes of society, evil on that scale, does arrest its eyes, and
does incite it to be up and doing. But to be disturbed about one's
personal shortcomings, and to toil at their amendment, seems to it
hypochondrical and small, a kind of petty invalidism to which robust
folk do not stoop.

Why has the sense of personal sin so faded out ? There have been
mid-summer seasons of full sunshine in the history of the Church
when that was overwhelmed and swept away and lost in the sheer
joy of the faith, when there was little confession at all in the Christian
services. They were aware, these folk, that they were sinners venturing
daringly into the presence of the Holy God. But they were saved
sinners. And it was that salvation they saw first, and that that held
their minds. And they drew near to God, not gravely and solemnly,
not with a sob of penitence, but dazed, bewildered, excited by new
and further proofs in their own lives of how Christ can save, does
save, had saved them from this and that, and here and here, since
they had last gathered together. " Our very penitence," said Baxter,
" is a thanksgiving."

All which was a much more likely way to spread the faith, and
to infect the world, than our own sober type of services. Outsiders
saw that these people had found something worth the sharing, and
they came hurrying to share it. Whereas we in our services
approach God with confession and keep moaning about our failures,
and so give the impression that the faith doesn't work ; we, who
have tried it, being called as witnesses to that ; nor Christ stand
to His promises. For evidently He has not made us, as it was so
confidently alleged He could, more than conquerors. Upon our own
showing, Sunday by Sunday, we are little, if any, better for Him,
still blundering and falling in the same customary ways—all which is a

sheer libel on the Master, on our part. To us, too, He has done exceeding abundantly, above all we asked or thought, or even dreamed was possible. And we ought to come into His presence with happy hearts and grateful spirits, rendering Him dazed thanksgiving and adoring praise. Newman declares that in the English Prayer Book there is " a lowering of the voice, a descent of the mind, and a humbling of the heart of the Church from the high choral tone of the missals and the breviaries and the early liturgies, till the Book of Common Prayer has become the cry of a returning prodigal, rather than an expression of the liberty and the joy of obedient children." The change of mood began far further back than that ; but it is there—a fact, and an unhappy fact. " I cannot," declared Epictetus, " give credence to a philosopher who professes to have found the secret of high living, and the power to conquer evil, if he speaks without animation, in a hang-dog fashion, with the face of a condemned man on his way to execution, and a moustache drooping in such a melancholy fashion that it seems to reach down to his knees. He does not look like a conqueror to me." There is a lesson which the Church these days might well learn and remember.

But our loss of the sense of sin does not arise because of our experiences, as a generation, of the wonders of Christ's grace, but from far lowlier sources. Partly, perhaps, because of the amazing human triumphs of the time, which have bred in us a proud and uplifted haughtiness of spirit that resents this talk of human frailty and human sin ; won't face such ugly facts, but obstinately looks the other way, and will see nothing but our glories and successes. And so, because it is unpopular to draw attention to what we all wish to ignore, we have agreed to huddle the whole thing out of sight, and say nothing about it. But that, of course, is suicidal. If you are suffering from some hideous malady, you may refuse to take advice, may keep pretending that the ailment is not there, but that in no way alters the grim facts. The thing is there. And our cheap, chirpy optimism, and our naïve chatter about the inevitability of human progress, and our complacent assumption that we were on a moving staircase which, of itself, must raise us to the very feet of God, we, doing nothing except stand still, looks silly enough in this half-ruined world, with hideous devilments we thought were dead, and left behind, and obsolete, out and about again, and, armed by modern science, more devilish by far than they have ever been.

And all that has been wrought by the same sins that we have in our hearts—which you would have it were so innocent and not worth bothering about.   Temper and selfishness and pride, such simple things as that—and out of them have come this blasted earth, and these innumerable ruined homes and broken hearts, and crowded graves, and desolation wailing eerily to desolation, and shuddering horror heaped on shrieking horror !   The Testament gave us dramatic warning of it all ;   but we knew better than that obsolete old book, and paid no heed.

Who was it that set up the Cross ?   Not fiends incarnate, but plain flesh and blood like us, quite ordinary men, decent and kindly souls enough.   Some of whom, no doubt, went to their homes that day from Calvary and took their children on their knees, and loved them very genuinely.   Only, they were a bit old-fashioned in the make-up of their minds, had grown stiff and inelastic in their thinking, inhospitable to new notions—surely a very minor sin at worst ;   and some feared for their vested interests ;   and one, poor Pilate, had lost his temper with these impossible Jews in days gone by, and had received a curt warning from Rome that there must be no further bloodshed in Jerusalem, and here was a new trouble at the very worst of times in the whole year, with fanatics in tens of thousands come up for the Feast ;   and one wanted to save the world by quick-running machinery, and so put Christ into a situation where He could no longer dilly-dally but must do something vivid, dramatic, revolutionary ;   and the people ?   No need for us to bother being there at the decision between Jesus and Barabbas.   He had the lined streets cheering for Him yesterday.   And we have relatives to see, and messages from neighbours to deliver to their kindred.   He'll be all right ;   we needn't worry to be there.   Such simple and plebian sins—minds grown a trifle out of date, a little selfishness, some temper and its consequences ;   a bit of worldly wisdom, and an indifference that did nothing at all—these brought about the shame of mankind, and the tragedy of history, and the blot upon our annals that will not rub out.   And they are all of them within your heart, and mine.

And, partly, it is owing to the fact that we have never yet really adopted the Christian standard, but still judge ourselves leniently, because against nothing more drastic than the conventions of the day, and the ways and habits of those round about us ;—do as they do ;   are what they are ;   drifting along in a lazy contentment, where the tides and currents of opinion bear us.   So long as we are decent and respectable, and keep the canons of " the world's negative holiness," we feel that we have given all that can reasonably be expected of us. "But," said Tertullian, " our Lord called Himself, not the conventions, but the truth." " The Cross," said Clement, " is our standard, and we must live right up to that boundary." Hold up your character and life against that trying background, and your complacency will wither and shrivel as in the hot blast from a furnace mouth. Come close to Jesus Christ, and you must see with shame how sorry is your record, and how real is your sinning, and how desperate your need of God's forgiveness.

And, partly, it is due to the incredible fact that we have somehow managed to caricature the God of the New Testament into the very opposite of what He there reveals Himself to be—a God who cannot bear sin in the same universe as Himself ; won't have it ; and must make an end of it ; and who is ready to go any length, and to bear any loss, and to make any sacrifice to slay it and be done with it. Yet we persist in imagining this Holy One as softly kind, and immorally good-natured, ready to pretend that we are what we are not ; to squeeze us through, and say nothing about it. And so we settle down, all the more easily because of Calvary ! When Gerontius, in the poem, reached the other side, he begged to be taken to God ; and they dissuaded him ; but he persisted, and at last they let him go. Whereat the eager spirit darted into the Presence—to fall blinded, seared, agonized by His awful Holiness ; pled to be hidden away until some time, some far-off time, these healing pains had made him at last less unworthy of the divine vision. I fear our easy-mindedness is no good sign, look at it from what angle that we may. The fact that we so easily forgive ourselves is no proof that the Lord God has forgiven us.

But this psalmist has passed all that. His whole soul shrank at the thought of himself, and cried aloud for cleansing ; begged to be made another man, quite different from what he was, would not desist from following God about, until that boon was granted him. " Our one chance against sin is that we be shocked by it," said Newman. You and I have grown so accustomed to our failings that we can settle down with them contentedly enough. But this man's soul was shocked, was horrified. " A gentleman is one who finds something scalding in the touch of evil," replied Confucius, very grandly, to a questioner. And this man—sin or no sin—was gentleman enough for that, which many a one is not.

Moreover, he makes no excuses for himself, that second line of defence on which we ourselves fall back so truculently, throwing the blame for anything amiss in us on our heredity, or our environment, or our education, or our glands—anything, everything except ourselves, poor injured innocents.

There is nothing wrong with us, so we protest, and, if we had been given a half-decent chance, we should have risen to it. But, set down, as we were, in this impossible world, and handicapped so mercilessly, and under the grotesque provisions God has made for us, what wonder if things have gone less than perfectly. This man is done with such bleatings and whimperings : is facing the whole ugly truth with steady eyes. When a Buddhist appears before the Judgment Seat of Yama, he is forced back and back by searching questions, until he confesses humbly that it was not his parentage, nor his environment, nor anything external to himself, but his own choice and will that have brought him to this sorry pass. And, in the Roman service, there is a cry of penitence, which lays the whole facts, hiding nothing, humbly at the feet of God, with a stabbing iteration of abashed and personal confession. " My sin, my own sin, my own most grievous sin." When a soul deals with God as honestly as that, there is an infinite hope for it ; and anything may happen ; and the best is the likeliest.

So here. For the glory of this psalm is that this desperate fellow-mortal of ours still believes that by God's infinite mercy his soul can be cleansed, and his whole nature radically changed, wholly rebuilt on a new plan. Let us come boldly to the throne of grace, advises the writer to the Hebrews, himself among the most audacious of minds, " that we may obtain mercy, and find grace to help in time of need." And here, in very deed, is a soul coming with a boldness that bewilders, pushing in determinedly, and not to be held back, with a sheer daring of intrepidity that would have stormed Christ's heart. Frankly and repeatedly, the man admits that he has no beginning of a case, founds his whole plea on the nature of God, feeling somehow that, just because God is so holy, He will not turn away from one so sinful with a shudder of loathing, an ungovernable repulsion, but will have pity upon a poor wretch so desperately needing help. And so he keeps piling up the case against himself. It was no accident, no unaccountable thing into which I somehow stumbled. It was characteristic, it was typical, it was the real me. For I was shapen in iniquity : and am not merely touched by the pollution, but am stained with it, through and through. A holy God cannot permit a soul so foul, so tired of being foul, live on in its pollution.

Wash me and I shall be whiter than snow. Create in me a clean heart. Make me a new man, quite different from this I am, with new likes, new dislikes, new possibilities, new powers, and another nature altogether, fashioned in Thine own likeness.

There is a lesson we would all do well to learn and practise. Found, not upon anything in yourself, but upon everything in God—not on your faith, which is a fickle thing, but on His faithfulness which is most sure and certain : not on your love to Him, which flows— and ebbs, but on His love to you which is from everlasting to ever- lasting : not on your crumbling efforts after something better, but upon His eternal purposes of mercy towards you, which have gone the length of Calvary—for you.

How this man came to learn all that, we do not know. But we ourselves have Christ to help us. And He does help. Do you re- member that poor wreck, scarcely perhaps recognizable as human, from whose approach clean people started back with shuddering, and turned away their eyes from the half-eaten face, aye, and their noses from the smell of the disease, and kept with care out of the winds blowing from his direction—a mere pollution and infection and disgust ; a living misery, a pitiful death in life, who, standing afar off, cried, " Lord, if Thou wilt, Thou canst make me clean." And his impossible hope came true, and his preposterous faith was justified. And if you will but try Him, Christ can cleanse you too. " Be of sin the double cure, cleanse me from its guilt and power." How many have cried that cry out of a great agony of soul to Jesus Christ ! And He has heard them, and has done it, and has been it ; has given them back their self-respect, so long and sadly lost, and put the peace of God into hearts redeemed and recreated ; and enabled them to look their conscience in the eyes again, as a man should. And all that lies within your reach, if you will take it from Christ's hand.

But do you really mean that, guarantee that—really ? you ask. I do. But have you yourself tried it ? Yes, I have. And did it work ? It did. Do you assert that there are sins that used to have dominion over you, and, through Christ's help to you, their reign is over, and their sovereignty broken ? Yes : I do. This Christ does save : does cleanse : does give a new and cleaner heart to whoso will accept it from Him ; and can do it for you.

But this wise singer, experienced in life's dangers as he is, promises us more and better even than that ; far more, and vastly better.

" The first step," said Ovid, " is half the journey." True. For it is difficult to get our lethargic, or day-dreamy, or procrastinating souls really to rise and set to it, and get begun. Yet many an one, who starts, turns back. He had no staying power : or was cowed by the difficulties : or was laughed out of it : or he fell into step with others, and yielded to the pressure of the crowd ;—any way he slipped out of the adventure, and crept home. The desert can reclaim its own. So that where, through long, hard toil, there were a clearing, and happy human homes, and cultivated fields, and living greenness, there can be, once more, only the tangle of the jungle, and the lairs of evil beasts. And this is a perilous world ; and we are frail, and wayward, and unstable. When Buddha made his resolution to seek and seek till he had found something that would ease and save the world, Mara, the evil spirit, laughed aloud. From henceforth, so he promised grimly, I will follow you, step by step, watching you with unwinking eyes, and waiting for the time that must some day come, when, for a moment, you are off your guard, and in that second I will leap at you, and drag you down, and foil you. " Sin that steals back upon a soul half saved," says Browning, summing up many a page of arduous human effort, suddenly torn across and ended : and of real glory that went out.

What we need is, not cleanness only, but steadfastness, else we shall quickly lose again what we had won, we so frail and fickle and undependable, and with two jarring natures at hot clash within us. The dam, built with such toil, may burst ; and hideous ruin, worse than ever, roar across our lives. And that, too, thinks this audacious psalmist confidently, God can do for us ; is sure that out of the wretched material we have made of ourselves, out of the mess into which our possibilities have melted, out of our wills grown so limp and flaccid, out of our soiled and desecrated characters, He can build up another person ; strong, where we have been so lamentably weak, and pure, where we are so dusty and earth-stained—the man that God intended we should be; and that we threw away; and that Christ can restore to us.

CHAPTER XIX

SOME SAFE DEDUCTIONS FROM A KNOWLEDGE OF LIFE

" Surely goodness and mercy shall follow me all the days of my life ; and I will dwell in the house of the Lord for ever."—Ps. xxiii. 6.

HERE is a man who, having reached the summit of a ridge in life, turns to look back along the way by which he has come, winding up through the years from babyhood to where he stands, and then out, and on ahead, till the track quickly loses itself in the mists and the uncertainties of the unknown future ; and so looking, feels a deep peace settling down upon his heart, almost as if the dove of God's own Holy Spirit were alighting on it ; and a firm conviction forming itself in his mind that there is, and can be, nothing in time or in eternity of which he need be afraid ; and that, for his part, he is done with fear ; means to live henceforth in that quietness of heart and that happy confidence, which are the only reasonable moods for one whose own experience has proved to him how safe he is in the unsleeping care of God.

And when you look back at your past, what do you learn from it ; and to what conclusions have you come ?

Any life story, however tame and flat and almost dreadfully without episode it may appear to others, seen from inside it, is a strange and moving tale—the unexpected, unpredictable happenings that burst in on the placid and monotonous routine ; the calls on faith and courage, some of them sudden, and perhaps soon over, some of them wearing and lifelong ; the cross-roads where we hesitated for a moment, or, perhaps, never realizing that it could have any manner of importance, turned, without thinking, right or left, and all the difference that made ; the chance meetings, and the little nothings that proved to be the big and formative events ; the doors that opened, where there was no door ; or shut fast in our faces, leaving us outside ; the hopes, that all but became facts, and then went out, leaving us wondering why they were sent at all, if this was to be their wounding and tantalizing end ; the joys that blossomed all along our path, scattered there by God's own liberal hand ; the sorrows that tore our very hearts ; the helps that came to us, when there seemed no help—how much goes to the fashioning of the most ordinary soul, and to the making of even the dullest life !

But, as you turn the pages of the records of your own, and read, here and there, where your eyes light and are arrested, is not the central fact that keeps obtruding everywhere—the obviousness of God in it all ; that you have never been alone ; that always there has been a watchfulness beside you, caring and providing for you, guarding you in dangers and in difficulties, many of them made by yourself, patiently heading you back from each of these wayward breaks-away to which we foolish, dim-eyed, easily scared creatures are so prone, panicing, often for no reason, or simply because others are panicing ; and running, as if for our very lives, because others are running, no one of us knows why. All my days, says this man, the Lord has been shepherding me, surrounding me with grace and kindness, spending Himself on my behalf.

As a bewildered poet of last generation put it,

> " Had God in Heaven no work to do
> But miracles of love for me ? "

And, indeed, it is an amazing thought that all this care and watchfulness He lavishes upon us is not something unique ; but that He gives Himself in like unstinted measure to every one of His innumerable creatures. But then, as a wise church father tells us, it is a divine property not only to be everywhere, but to be wholly everywhere. So He can spend Himself upon each of us, as if there were no other claimant for His grace, giving the whole of it to each. A shepherd worthy of the name, said Christ, gives himself to, and for, the sheep, all the day long, and every day, devoting the whole of his own bigger life to the safeguarding of these lesser ones ; ready unhesitatingly to lay it down for them, if that be needful for their safety. And this I know, He adds, for I am the Good Shepherd, and I, Myself, have gone, and am always prepared to go, that full length for you.

So this man, looking back upon the past, founding on his own experience, and on what he has learned of God from his own dealings with Him, says, with a quiet confidence, " Surely goodness and mercy will follow me all the days of my life." And, knowing what I know, worry and fretfulness and care are not for me, surrounded by a love so watchful, so sufficient, and so wise.

It is the goodness of God that strikes him first, as he looks back— the amazing bountifulness with which He heaps gift upon gift upon us.

That is by no means the mood of the day. Rather, masses of men are snarling angrily because the provision made for them is so grossly and insultingly inadequate. If, they protest indignantly, they were to be at all, a far fuller and more satisfying life ought to have been assigned to them than this meagre and stunted lot they know.

And it is true that human greed, and our crude methods of distribution, have so ordered things that some of us do have too much, and many others of us far too little—though that is being corrected year by year before our very eyes. But God's sunshine, and God's rain are free to all; and the earth's generous harvests provide more than sufficient for the whole of us, if only God's lavish plans were given a chance to work themselves out.

And, even as things are, a thin bare life, as it looks to others, is thronged with crowded benefactions—wonderful things, not one of which was earned, but all of which are given us as free gifts. Think the thing out a little way. From all eternity God loved you with an everlasting love, and patiently, for æons upon æons, worked His way towards fashioning you; until, at long last He could summon you out of the blank of nothingness into this mystery of being. He made you a great creature, high in the scale, able to look before, and after, and up towards Him; and think His vast thoughts dimly afar off after Him, and hold communion with Himself. He gave you how wonderful a heritage—the senses, each of them another avenue leading out into another world of mystery and of beauty, which, but for them, would have been absolutely lost to us; and memory, " giving us roses in December "; and reason, with its spacious and lordly domain; and conscience, with its strange authority, and its arrest, and its appeal; He set you in a home, where you were surrounded by unselfish love and kindness, and where they turned your face towards God, making Him a great fact for you, so that you know that you are His, that He is yours. More, He permitted you to live for years with those who are now among the blessed saints in light, under the influence of their life and faith and character; He thought out Jesus Christ for you—the wonderful Christ, in whose face you have seen God's face, in whose life you have learned what yours should be, at whose hands you have received grace that has helped in how many a time of need; and in Him He has called you, redeemed you, forgiven you, ennobled you, granting you an ever-widening experience of His sufficiency, and the greatness of His power to us wards who believe even a little. He has set before you great and precious promises, and assured you that they are not mere dreams that will go out, but real and true, and will be so for you, if you will have it so.

What wonder that Paul, looking at this glorious inheritance of yours, thinks that the pains and the troubles and the sorrows that life is sure to bring you are trivial against that background, and not worthy to be compared with what you have already, and will have.

Stevenson used to confess that he couldn't use the prayer of petition, that the words stuck in his throat and wouldn't utter ; for, having received so much already, freely given, how could he ask for more ; felt that, as often as he came into God's presence, it must be to praise and bless and magnify His holy name for all that He had heaped on him, so thoughtless and so undeserving.

Yet many, these days, bleat and whimper, hungrily itching after more and more and more. " Enough," so Canon Green reminds us shrewdly, " has been defined as a little more than you have." Or Plato, " deeming poverty to consist in the increase of one's desires, rather than the lessening of one's possessions." " We believe," says Barth, " in a civilization of things : Christ believed in a civilization of persons." A civilization of things ! That is, indeed, our axiom and our panacea. The more things one possesses, the richer by that is the life. And Christ flatly denies it : " A man's life consisteth not of the abundance of the things that he possesseth." Yet, as a generation, we are truculently dissatisfied with what we have : and boast of it as our crowning virtue, are set on gaining ever more. And that will never bring you peace and satisfaction, declared Christ, is not the road to it. You are drinking salt water, and that can only make you thirstier and thirstier. Try you, so He advised, the moderating of your own hot hearts, and your greedy desires.

As Carlyle put it vividly—in the vulgar fraction of life, the top figure represents our possessions, and the lower one our wishes. Four over two equals two, by much too small, we say, and strain to increase our possessions. Eight over two is four. Ah ! that is vastly better. Yet, says Carlyle, you would get identically the same answer if you would lessen your desires. Four over one is also four, as truly as the other.

And in these days of rationing and taxes and limitations of our wonted freedom of all kinds, are we not finding that the extras can be taken from us, and it makes no vital difference at all. For life, real life, the life that counts, consists, not of these trivialities, but of the major things we still possess, and which God still heaps upon us as lavishly as ever.

Were it not well for us to escape from this peevishness and discontent that has engulfed us, to learn that spirit of amazed thanksgiving which is the only language in the heavenly places. For, otherwise, if we ever attain to them, we must be dumb; or, at the best, be foreigners, slowly and stumblingly translating into what ought to be our native tongue.

The goodness of God! As this man looks back over his life, that is what strikes him first. And yet, hardly has he set that down than he catches his breath, and caps it with another fact in it, every whit as obvious, and yet more amazing—God's patient, and persistent, and unbreakable mercy: His willingness to bear with souls that are just flatly impudent towards Him, with crawling little creatures such as we, who keep on defying Him, sure that their petty brains are wiser than His divine mind, determined that His blessed will for them must give way to their own foolish wishes; incorrigible, unteachable, who wont take in what is so plain to Him, and who insist on choosing what He knows must be their ruin.

As George Herbert summed it all up in his wonderful little poem:

> " Lord, with what care hast Thou begirt us round!
> Parents first season us: then schoolmasters
> Deliver us to laws; they send us bound
> To rules of reason, holy messengers,
> Pulpits and Sundays, sorrow dogging sin,
> Afflictions sorted, anguish of all sizes,
> Fine nets and stratagems to catch us in,
> Bibles laid open, millions of surprises,
> Blessings beforehand, ties of gratefulness,
> The sound of glory ringing in our ears:
> Without our shame; within our consciences';
> Angels and grace, eternal hopes and fears,
> Yet all these fences and their whole array
> One cunning bosom sin blows quite away; "

breaking through His devices for our help, and turning His gifts to us to our hurt and doom. And yet, with His goodness met by so poor and disappointing and infamous a return, God's answer is to add to it a daily and hourly mercy towards those who, judged by our human standards, are just unforgivable, and past excuse or bearing.

Looked at from that angle, any life, even the tamest, becomes an audacious legend wildly improbable and remote from fact. And yet it is fact.

How is it possible : how, indeed, is it believable ? God being what He is, we being what we are ? In all literature is there a more dramatic, a more convincing, a more satisfying answer than that wonderful passage in Ecclesiasticus, which book might well have been included in the Canon of Scripture, when the author, watching, with an awed, hushed heart, the orderly procession of the mighty, far off constellations, lost in the immeasurable deeps of space, and stunned by the inconceivable immensities of this unthinkable universe, is, none the less, not dwarfed into an utter insignificance before the God who fashioned and who rules all that, rather takes heart of grace from it, for he ends with a sudden unexpected stabbing phrase that catches at the heart. "As is God's power"—and there, crowding in upon us, is the evidence of how vast that is—" as is God's power, so also—is— His mercy." It too, is on that same tremendous scale. And even that is putting it too low, by far. For power is God's attribute. But He Himself is Love : and " His delight is in Mercy "—a mercy to be measured on that scale, and more.

Once, reading Paul's great hymn on love in the Corinthians, a sudden light flashed on the page, and showed me deeps in it I had not grasped before. For God is Love. And all these heaped-up phrases are a description of His nature. So that, legitimately, we might substitute God for Love, whenever that occurs. " God suffereth long, and is kind " : how long, how kind our own experience has proved ; God envieth not. No, said Plato, there is nothing of the dog in the manger about God, but His joy is to share. God vaunteth not Himself. As Avicenna put it, When you meet some one humbler than you ever saw, and more unselfish than you thought was possible, down on your face, man ! down on your face ! That is God ! And so, through the glorious summary—on to the end—God beareth all things, God believeth all things, God hopeth all things, God endureth all things. Think how He has believed in us, who have so often failed Him : and hoped for us, when we ourselves had quite lost heart ; and endured shameless things at our hands. But God's love never faileth. We can quite safely venture to the throne of grace. Often though we have come, we can still come : and many a time although we have broken the vows we made, though really meaning them when we swore them, God's goodness holds and His forgiveness is still sure : and even yet, we can obtain mercy, and find grace to help in time of

need. I know it, says this man with confidence, for I have learned
what God is like : and He will not change now. Or, as they say in
the New Testament, " Jesus Christ is the same yesterday, and to-
day, and for ever."

For ever! And you note this old poet also fastens upon that, and
makes his audacious deduction.

In those days, even among the Hebrews, they had a grim conception of the beyond—a bleak world, dark, and thick in dust, silent
and soundless, with good and evil herded indiscriminatingly together.
And God never looked that way : and had no interest whatever in
such shadowy beings, only half beings at the best.

But certain daring spirits had begun to doubt that, and deny it.
And always their argument and proof and evidence is the same.
Always they found, not on the greatness of human nature, or the
like, but on the hugeness of God's affection. This, they said, does
not look like a mere passing fancy : seems, to us, more like an everlasting love. Goodness and mercy will surely follow me on to life's
very end. But, that is little. For, throughout all eternity, I shall
dwell securely in my Father's house, a happy child surrounded by a
care and kindness that will never end.

And we Christians reached belief in our own immortality in precisely that same fashion. The love of Christ seemed too big to be
meant only for seventy years : seemed planned upon an infinitely
vaster scale than that : can never be exhausted, must run on and
on, for ever.

And, indeed, all we know of the beyond, unto this day, is that God
is there, and that Christ is waiting for us. And that seems to us
enough. Given these facts, we have all the essentials, all that matters;
and don't need, or even want much, to know more.

That is a moving moment at the docks when a liner casts off, and
the gangways are hauled in, and the great boat begins to move ; and,
slowly, surely, inexorably, cruelly, that little ribbon of separating water
widens and widens between her and us, till she is off, and our dear
one only a speck among the other specks, until at last we turn away,
with a lonesomeness in the heart. For who knows what is awaiting
him, or may befall him, in that strange and unknown life into which
he has gone ? But when death separates us from our own, the heart,
God knows, is sore enough. But we have never a fear for them. They
are with Christ. And where He is, nothing but good and kindness can
befall them. What a tremendous tribute to the Master it is that, as a

13

matter of course, we leave our loved ones in His keeping, with entirely quiet hearts !

John Watson, that consummate preacher, used to tell us that, sometimes, when one of his flock was dying, and seemed gone, he would kneel down and whisper into the quickly dulling ears, " In My Father's house are many mansions." And, with that, the soul, three-quarters through the river, turned, and came back to listen (and you could see the soundless lips making the motions of echoing the familiar " Father's house," " many mansions "), and waited till there came the words of invitation and of welcome, " I go to prepare a place for you. And, if I go and prepare a place for you, I will come again, and receive you unto Myself ; that where I am, there ye may be also." And at that, with a contented little sigh, it was gone, entirely unafraid.

CHAPTER XX

THEN COMETH THE END

" And I saw a great white throne and Him that sat on it, from whose face the
earth and the heaven fled away ; and there was no place found for them. And I saw
the dead, small and great, stand before God ; and the books were opened ; and another
book was opened, which is the book of life. And the dead were judged out of those
things which were written in the books, according to their works."—REV. xx. 11, 12.

IN the days of the French Revolution when the aristocrats had
been penned into the prisons and were waiting their inevitable
doom, they sought to carry on their lives and their social relationships
as usual—so far as that was possible—unbroken, and still cheerful and
debonair. Morning by morning a door was flung open, and a list of
names read out. Whereat those cited, with a gay gesture of farewell,
were gone—to face the guillotine. For their turn had come. And the
rest, meantime left behind ? Once the door had sullenly clanged-to
again, the momentary silence that had fallen broke into the usual
animated hum, and life went on. In all which there was something not
merely frivolous, but big-hearted and wise—saving their sanity and
reason.

And to-day we men and women seem to have adopted the same
practice and procedure. We know our lives are but a handsbreadth
at the most, that grim and ghastly possibilities lie crouched, ready to
leap on us ; that some of them must, in a little, fall upon us—a hideous
pain perhaps, a crippling disappointment, a shattering sorrow that
leaves life only an interlude between a memory and a hope ; that our
own death, on soft and silent feet, steals ever nearer—all that we realize.
And yet, with avidity, we fling ourselves into the life around us, and
the little nothings that make up our days. And that, too, surely is
not merely giddiness, but brave and wise. The constant brooding on
mortality common in other days, the grinning skulls upon their monuments, the breath as from a charnel house, blighting and withering
clean and simple pleasures, that blows from not a few of the religious
books of former times seems to me morbid and unhealthy and, on
occasion, odious.

Once on a day men's hearts, if they were serious at all, looked
forward very solemnly to that tremendous moment, surely waiting for

us all, when for us life will be over ; and, the dear faces round us fading
from our dimming eyes, we must rise up, and go our lonely way,
leaving this homely earth with its familiar ways, adventuring forth
into that vast unknown, where all we thought and did and were is
waiting for us, like a lovely maiden or a repulsive hag, so Zoroaster
thought, to lead us to our natural destiny.

> " Ah ! little at best can all our hopes avail us
>   To lift this sorrow, or cheer us when in the dark,
>   Unwilling, alone we embark,
>   And the things we have seen, and have known, and have heard of, fail us."

Or, if it is not as bad as that for a Christian—why should it
be ? How can it be ?—at least all life, thought Plato, ought to be,
and for a wise soul is, a long and careful preparation for that epoch-
making hour. But there has come reaction. The centre of gravity
has shifted notably from death to life. " There is nothing," says
Spinoza, " on which a free man lets his thoughts dwell less than on
death, for true wisdom is a meditation, not on death, but on life."

The modern mind applauds that loudly. It was Hort, that sanest
of theologians, who declared that " secularism is preferable to a consistent adoption of the view that this present life is to be disparaged
and made a mere antecedent to the future." And, indeed, timid souls
were wont to let themselves become not a little fussy and fidgety and
unhealthily self-centred in this matter. Goethe, for his part, remarking
that ever-recurring reminder on innumerable gravestones, *Memento
mori*, thought it over-grim, and psychologically unsound and pernicious.
Rather be you sure you are really alive, he counselled. Not unwisely,
surely. For, because the evening is certain to fall, why should we not
use the hours of generous sunshine now ? Death must soon knock
upon our door. But meantime here is this rich life God has planned
for us, let us use it eagerly and heartily and thoroughly ; and here
this world of men and women round us whom we can befriend and help,
let us be up and at it then ; and so when, for us, the end here comes,
pass over to the other side, eager for what God's loving-kindness has
ready and waiting for us there. " Death doesn't count," wrote Nettle-
ship. By which I take it that he meant : here is this chapter of our
life, and by and by there will result another out of it. And who bothers
about the little space of blank white paper between the two ? And that
is all death is. It is the story that matters. Let us get on with it,
and make it a brave tale.

" No," said Rainy to me once. " I don't think much about dying.
Are we not here to do whatever God may ask of us, as each new duty
comes ? To-day I have to work at a sermon ; to-morrow to preside
at several committees ; and one day it will be to die. Let us seek to
do each of them, as each comes, with all our heart, and unto Him."
That seems to me a sane and a gallant religion.

Yes ; but Meredith warns us that the progress of mankind is
never a steady advance down the centre of the road, but rather a
drunken and precarious tottering from one extreme into the other ;
a tipsy stumble almost into the hedge on the one side, from which we
hardly save ourselves by an uncertain plunge almost into the ditch
upon the other. So, from extreme into extreme, and back again, man
reels upon his perilous way. And to-day, in our recoil from other-
worldliness, surely we have grown too earthbound, too parochial,
stupidly Ptolemaic, living as if these seventy brief years were all our
all, forgetful of the vast eternities reaching out endlessly, and waiting
for each one of us, only a little way ahead ; of the time which is so
surely drawing ever nearer, when, you on one sure fixed day, and I
upon another, we must pass forth into the great adventure.

To forget all that, obstinately to push it out of mind, and to avert
our eyes from the palpable facts, is to dwarf immortal creatures into
mere ephemerids, which we are not ; is to use standards of measure-
ment and scales of value and petty yardsticks nothing less than
ridiculous for our affairs ; is to cramp the architecture of a life, that
should be built with splendour to endure for ever and for ever, into
the rough fashioning of a rude hut, run up to last a few brief years.

" He parted at the turning of the tide ; for after I saw him fumble
with the sheets, and play with flowers, I knew there was but one way.
For his nose was as sharp as a pen, and he babbled of green fields.
' How now, Sir John ! ' quoth I. ' What man, be of good cheer.'
So he cried, ' God ! God ! God ! ' three or four times. Now I, to
comfort him, bade him he should not think of God. I hoped there
was no need to trouble himself with any such thoughts yet. So he
bade me lay more clothes on his feet. I felt them, and they were as
cold as any stone."

How many do not trouble themselves with any such thoughts
yet ! And life glides on and on ; till, suddenly, it is over ; and, for
them too, one by one, the Judgment Day, that seemed so shadowy
and nebulous, is the only reality, and all else faded clean away.

Were it not well to catch this vision of the great white Throne before whose awful purity—that symbol of the Holiness of God—earth and sky, like guilty, hunted, desperate things fly hither and thither, seeking for some hiding-place, and can find none ; and the dead, small and great, none missing, waiting in tense, strained silence —you and I among them—and every eye fixed in that breathless hush upon the opening books—life over, our life over, and the judgment on it come.

What will they show, these books, when they are opened ? Nothing, it seems, ever dies. There is no blotting out in life. What we have written, we have written ; and the record stands. This life of ours slips past, soundlessly for the most part. We sleep and rise ; and our days glide away full of the little incidents of which their web is woven. And always our character is forming, has been forming all these passing years. More and more naturally our feet turn of themselves into the customary paths : firmer and firmer the shackles of our habits tighten on our wrists. For every word that we have spoken, every thought that we have harboured, every deed, mean or magnanimous, that we have done, have been depositing themselves under the surface of our personality, and there building up the character, which, out of the infinite possibilities within our reach, we chose to be. And one day it will be matured and finished; and we be ready for the destiny which is inevitable for that into which we have made ourselves.

> " Fool ! all that is at all,
>   Lasts ever, past recall ;
> Earth changes, but thy soul and God stand sure,
>   What entered into thee,
>   *That* was, is, and shall be."

That, and the destiny for which alone it is fitted, and in which automatically it must end.

And, in our case, what will be the verdict on it all ? Turn the pages of memory, prejudiced in our favour though it be, and are we not confronted by a soiled and sorry record ? Here and here we sinned with a cold deliberation, so that Christ cannot pray for us " Father, forgive them, for they know not what they do " : for we did know, and sinned against the clearest light. And, here and here, poor fools, we blundered into other sins, not realizing they were sins. And yet once granted entrance, some of them became an inherent portion of our personality, as much a part of us as our right hand or eye ; a characteristic of us, rising up before people's minds when we are mentioned ; or, if hidden away and unsuspected by those around us, hatefully familiar to ourselves at least. And so, as we look back over the story of how we gradually grew to be this that we are, it is the awful inevitability of it all that grips one. " Sow an act, and you reap a habit ; sow a habit, and you reap a character ; sow a character, and you reap—a destiny," is an inexorable law of life. " What strikes me more and more," wrote Dale of Birmingham, " is the permanence of one's early life—the identity between youth and mature manhood. I do not mean that God has not lifted me out of many unsatisfactory things which surrounded and entangled me in youth, but that very habit—good and evil—of those early years seems to have permanently affected my whole life. The battle is largely lost or won before it seems to begin. The temptation in the wilderness determines, or largely determines, our fate."

And is it not a daunting thing to note how often the momentous seed slips from our hand without our noticing that we have sown it ? A child runs through the meadow, never pausing to think out its route. Yet from that moment, where the grass is slightly trodden down, other feet will tend to follow ever more automatically, till a path is beaten, bare, and hard, and broad. So, some petty nothing, unnoticed at the time, and long forgotten, and buried in the far past —some trivial incident, or some chance meeting, or some haphazard choice, made thoughtlessly, on the spur of the moment, has proved to be a determining factor in our life, like that rock at the Great Divide, against which the waters break, and separate for ever, farther and farther, till they are hundreds of miles apart. So that forgotten nothing, as it seemed, turned us towards heaven, or towards hell.

> " In ancient shadows and twilights
>   Where childhood had strayed,
> The world's great sorrows were born,
>   And its heroes were made.
> In the lost boyhood of Judas,
>   Christ was betrayed."

One day, like any other day, something blew into the mind of a fine lad in Kerioth which, left unchecked in the man he grew to be, a man of noble spiritual possibilities and real lovableness, else Christ had not chosen him as one of His best friends, or called him as one of the likeliest to help His mission—with a heart to respond to it, and a soul to dare for it—spoiled everything, and led him to his fearsome place in history.

Still, unaccountable or inevitable, there is our record written with our own hands, and chosen by our own wills. Muhammad has it that each man appears for judgment with his life story, written by himself, hung round his neck, and is bidden to take his book and read it, and be his own judge. It is all there. It is all settled. It is registration more than judgment, the separating of types already fixed into their natural habitat and element. Sheep and swine, said John Watson, feed together in one field. But when the evening comes, the one turn of themselves into the fold ; the other, squealing joyously, make greedily for their sty. " One fears," he adds in an appalling phrase, " some will inherit hell, and be content."

And in our case what will the books reveal, when they are opened ? Surely some little kindliness, please God, " that best part of a good man's life—his little, nameless, unremembered acts of goodness and of love " ; and, here and there, a touch of courage, where our sore hearts were hammered into a kind of grit and hardihood and faith and patience and understanding tenderness towards our tried fellow-men ; some deepening as life went on, some breadth and hospitality of mind, some growing up, and some escape from childishness, and putting away of childish things—like selfishness and temper and irascibility. And, for the rest, only some broken purposes that came to very little, some dreams that dazzled and went out, some high intentions that kept breaking in, and haunting us, and calling to us ; and we wished to follow, and did rise up to follow, agreed that this and this must certainly be done, is going to be done—almost immediately ; at times leapt to our feet to set about it there and then ; but our mood cooled, or something else broke in on our attention, like that poor fool from Porlock, a bill collector or the like, who, when Coleridge, his strange eerie magical genius in full flood, had started " Kubla Khan," broke in on him, and the checked inspiration never flowed again. So, often our goodly intentions have been edged out and silenced. Until, after a whole lifetime of opportunity, we can bring back to our Father only a bairn's foolish little offering, its bunch of wild flowers, say, rather of weeds, held withering in its hot little hand. And this is all there is in us to show for Calvary, and all God's patient grace !

Far worse than that. For all that we have done amiss, and all the opportunities we have let slip, when we should have been Christlike, and were only lazy, or selfish, or somehow characteristically just ourselves, will flout and mock us at the Judgment Seat, before God

and men, like poor, aimless, procrastinating Peer Gynt, beset and
maddened by the voices, whispering endlessly, " We are the thoughts
you should have thought ; we are the songs you could have sung ;
we are the deeds that you were meant to do," till the man was near
crazy. Ours, too, is but a sorry record. " If Thou, O Lord, shouldest
mark iniquity, O Lord, who shall stand ? " And if the dead " are to
be judged by the things written in the books, according to what they
have done," what end is to be looked for, except to be tossed aside,
as a dream of God that came to very little, as a possibility that has
gone out ?

No doubt, if we assess ourselves merely against the conventions
of the times, and the accepted ways of people round about us, it is
not difficult for certain temperaments, in certain favourable circumstances, to reach that standard. But, in its heart of hearts, mankind
is well aware that it is built on bigger lines, for loftier ends, than that.
So, for example, Eliot turns upon some of the belauded prophets of
the day with a hot scorn of their insulting reading of humanity, " The
kind of philosophy which Mr. Wells had to offer no doubt seemed
to him to be satisfactory for all, because it was satisfying to himself.
If you are so fortunate (from the point of view of this world) as to
have no immortal longings, and are, furthermore, gifted with such
fluency in writing as to be kept perpetually interested by your own
talents, you can be easily satisfied." But, thank God, the mass of
men are not as small as that. One of the oldest writings extant in the
world is the Book of the Dead, a venerable classic in Egypt long before
Abraham was born ; and its tremendous, awe-inspiring Judgment
Scene leaves trivialities like mere respectability and common decency
far, far behind, as a beginning barely worth the counting. For, first,
the soul, taking its stand in turn before each of the forty-two gods,
must be able to claim, looking into the very eyes of the guardian of
that particular virtue and the abhorrer of that particular sin, " I have
not been unchaste, I have not been niggardly, I have not exacted more
work from the labourer than was just, I have not spoken falsely," and
so on to each of all the gods deciding the case. And, if that negative
test is safely passed, if the life is admitted to have been, not a polluting
and infectious thing contaminating others round about it, there is
still the positive proof required, and evidence demanded, not of innocence
only, but of a life eagerly spent for others. And only if the soul can
say with truth, " I have given bread to the hungry, and water to the
thirsty, and clothing to the naked, and a boat to the shipwrecked—I

am pure ; I am pure ; I am pure," may it pass in to the final and decisive test, and be laid in the balances, and weighed against truth and righteousness—as if to say that we are judged not by our standards but by God's ; and stand or fall as we do, or do not, satisfy, not our own complacent easy-mindedness, but what He meant that we should do and be. And, face to face with that test, what hope can there be for us ?

Ah ! but there is more, far more, in the pages of the books that are headed by your name, or mine, than what we have so far mentioned. An epoch may be called after some dull, crass, wicked king, or after some unusually stupid woman—the times, we say, of George III, of James II, of Victoria. Yet the outstanding figure of them, the real power and glory of the period is *not* that thing at all, but a Chatham, or a Pitt, or a Nelson, or the like. So, I am not the central figure in my life, although it is called mine. There is Another, and far greater, who does all the things in it that matter. Leave Him out of the story, and the whole grows lustreless and, indeed, incomprehensible. For, rightly viewed, your life, my life, is only another chapter in the life of Jesus Christ ; and an astonishing one, at that, even for Him. Look for yourselves and see ! How, here and here and here and everywhere, it is His acts, not mine, that really count and tell. It was His voice that called me. That all-important fact, in my life though it be, and colouring how much of it, was not my deed, but His. " I thank Thee," prayed Lancelot Andrews, " for my call, for my recall, for my many calls beside." And here and here, where all seemed lost, I had despaired. And it was Christ, not I, who shielded the poor cold ashes— out, we would have said ; and stamped on them—He, and not I, who breathed them into a newness of warmth, and coaxed them patiently to flame and fire again. These are the big facts of my life. But it was Christ who did each one of them.

In heaven the redeemed keep ringing out, in a dazed thanksgiving, the wonders of their lives. And it is never what they did, but always what Christ did in them, that is the theme of their eternity of praise. He loved us ; He washed us from our sins ; He made us kings and priests unto God and His Father. But if that is the test, and such things are acceptable evidence, we also can produce it, masses of it. For us too He has cleansed, and us too He has redeemed from shameful bondages, and us too He has made new creatures, who can live in a new way ; done with things that, for years and years, had baffled and foiled and beaten us to the earth time after time. If we must stand or fall by what we did, we have no case. But if account is taken of what Christ has done in us, then we have facts in plenty, facts of our lives, each one of them there in the records, and indisputable.

And then, there is that other book laid open—the Book of Life. And what does it signify ? In the Egyptian Judgment Scene, at the very climax of the tremendous moral claims it makes upon us as a minimum, suddenly, unexpectedly, raising new hope, there slips in this wonderful touch—that when the soul is being weighed in the balances, the god Thoth lays his little finger on its scale, and presses somewhat, knowing that men's hearts are frail. Long, long ago these men, with their exalting estimate of what a human life should be, and who so ruthlessly refuse us any compromise or any concession whatsoever, had found that there is more than a strict justice at the back of things, had learned out of their own experience that God, Guardian of Holiness although He be, is merciful and gracious, and willeth not the death of any sinner. So they had found as a plain fact of their own lives, and honestly set it down, although it seems to clash with their whole picture.

Or, surely one of the most unexpected facts in the whole history of human thought is this—that, whereas Buddhism, as it emerged from its creator's mind, was built up on a tremendous, an unfaltering realization and insistence that this is a moral world, governed by laws, not merely good advice which one can take or leave, but laws with dreadful sanctions and penalties attached ; that every single thought and word and deed comes to fruition ; that what a man sows, that he reaps ; that there are no exceptions, no favouritism, no forgiveness, no bending aside of the shape of things so that, squeezing through, some may evade the inevitable consequences of what they have done and been ; no gaining of a destiny which is not the natural outcome of one's past—while the whole system is built up on that, on a keen and exacting conscience that faces the grim facts, and does not falter, does not even want things to be altered, and knows they can't be altered, is content to be assured there is an even-handed justice in the stuff and the make-up of things : none the less, as the centuries rolled past, some sects of Buddhists felt, and found, and said, that there is more in the essence and constitution and governance of the world than justice. That is there. But also something else—not a Personal God, not a Loving Father, not a Redeeming Son, or a Patient Holy Spirit, yet something that helps, that hurries to help ; that gives, for no discoverable reason except eagerness to give, something like what the Scriptures call grace, that gives to those who merit nothing, and forgives even the most undeserving.

So, even in this terrifying statement of how inexorably a man's destiny depends on his own character, that indeed Heaven and Hell themselves are characters, not places—characters, as Christ tells us in His Judgment parable, built up, from day to day, out of such homely practical plain things as—were you kindly to distressed folk round about you ? Were you touched by their needs ? Unable to shut yourself off in your own cosy comforts, and compelled to spend yourself for those who had no claim upon you, as we say ? The answers to these simple questions, says Christ, Yes or No, makes the whole yawning void, the great gulf fixed between Heaven and Hell. Yet, even here, there breaks in the inevitable characteristic New Testament note of grace ; of things, not earned, but given for nothing, accepted as a gift, not won.

Aye, and why not ? For one of the most fundamental laws of life is this—that we are not isolated units, dependent wholly on ourselves, and gaining what we need only through our own hard-breathing efforts. Life teaches us the very opposite—the facts of our interdependence ; of vicarious toil, and of vicarious suffering ; that one bears, and another, who was not in the thing at all, receives the benefit. We are born, only through another's pain : we are free, only because numbers have died, and are still dying, for us. All that we value comes to us as a free gift from others, who lost everything that we might have ; or who laboured, and we have entered into their labours. Are not innumerable all-important things done for us every day which we could not do for ourselves ? And the big things can be received only on the same humbling terms. We can't win heaven by our own righteousness : we can only take it of pure grace. We can't gain our salvation by our own worthiness. If it is ever to be ours at all, we must accept it from a Saviour.

And there is a Saviour, and a Book of Life. Whether your name or mine is entered in it, it is for Christ to say. Why should it be ? how can it be ? conscience asks derisively. Well ! there is this to give us hope—that Christ's eyes can see, and often do see, what others never saw, and won't believe is there.

Every one was unanimous about Zacchaeus. There was not one dissentient in the whole outraged city. And all the sordid facts of years and years flocked, hurrying to add to the huge weight of evidence against him. Every one had the same damning opinion—every one—

except Jesus Christ. Not all the facts, He said, not all the possibilities. And in the Book of Life, openly, daringly, confidently, He wrote down that outcast's name. " This day is salvation come to this house."

There was a woman whose life had broken down in open and unblushing infamy, from the contamination of whose pollution decent folk shrank back ; whose whole being and character were summed up in one comprehensive blasting phrase. For, when any one thought of her, or named her, the one thing that rose up in people's minds was —that she was a sinner. But Christ did not shrink back. There is more here than sin, He said, far more ; and put her in the Book of Life.

And once a wild passionate career was ending in unendurable agony, in open infamy and shame, and in a horror of gross darkness. Yet when the poor throbbing head managed to turn in Christ's direction, and the parched lips to whisper, " Lord, when Thou comest in Thy kingdom, remember me ! " then, when life was over, when there could be no rubbing out, no emendation, " To-day," said Christ, " shalt thou be with Me in Paradise ! " So that name, too, stands, plainly written by our Lord's own hand, in the decisive Book of Life.

Where Christ is, there is infinite hope. And, for my part, I mean to trust Him even on the great White Throne. I have no plea except just this—that He said, " Him that cometh to Me, I will in nowise, for no conceivable reason, for no statable case, cast out." And here is a poor failure coming to give in his account. As Christ decides, so may it be. So it will be. But where Christ is, there is a wild, a wonderful, an infinite hope. And Christ is still Christ even on the Judgment Seat. And those who saw Him face to face for years have set down this as one of His most certain characteristics—that, having loved His own that were in the world, He loved them unto the end. And to us also He clings in that same unbelievably loyal way ; loves on whatever we may do, will not be turned from it. And when at last we reach the other side, and stand there, muddy and ashamed, and very conscious how unlike we are to all these clean and shining spirits round us, eagerly He will come to us, with outstretched hands and happy face, and let us see how much it means to Him that we are there. I know it, because I have proved it ; because He has done that very thing to me, time and again, and yet again. And He is the same yesterday, and to-day, and forever. " I know," says Paul, " in whom I have believed, and am persuaded that He is able to keep that which I have committed unto Him against that day." And so do I. And so am I.

> " And so, beside the silent sea,
>   I wait the muffled oar.
> No harm from Him can come to me
>   On ocean or on shore.
> I know not where His islands lift
>   Their fronded palms in air.
> I only know I cannot drift
>   Beyond His love and care."

No. For the grace of our Lord and Saviour Jesus Christ, and the love of God our Father, and the fellowship of the Holy Spirit have been given to us, and are ours, now—and for ever. Amen.